the compleat MEADMAKER

HOME PRODUCTION OF HONEY WINE FROM YOUR FIRST BATCH TO AWARD-WINNING FRUIT AND HERB VARIATIONS

KEN SCHRAMM

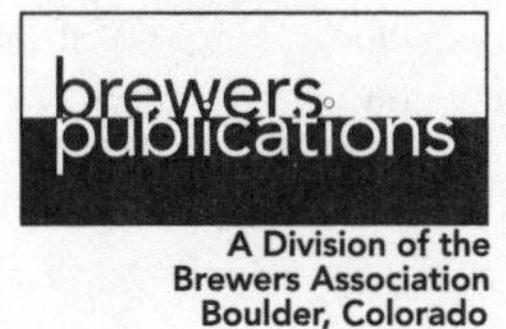

A Division of the
Brewers Association
Boulder, Colorado

Brewers Publications
A Division of the Brewers Association
PO Box 1679, Boulder, CO 80306-1679
Telephone: (303) 447-0816 Fax: (303) 447-2825
BrewersAssociation.org

Printed in the United States of America.

10 9 8

ISBN-13: 978-0-937381-80-9
ISBN-10: 0-937381-80-2

Library of Congress Cataloging-in-Publication Data

Schramm, Ken, 1959-
The compleat meadmaker : home production of honey wine from your first batch to award-winning fruit and herb variations / by Ken Schramm.
p. cm.
Includes bibliographical references and index.
ISBN: 0-937381-80-2 (alk. paper)
1. Mead. I. Title.

TP588.M4S35 2003
641.8'72–dc21

2003009083

Technical Editor: Dick Dunn
Project Editor: Stan Hieronymus
Copy Editor/Indexing: Daria Labinsky

Special thanks to Redstone Meadery for contributing the meads shown on the front cover.
Cover photo by Rick Souders, Souders Studios
Interior photos by Jim Johnston and the National Honey Board
Cover and Interior Design by Julie Korowotny

table of contents

dedication

This book is dedicated to the memories of four great meadmakers.

To Dr. Robert Kime, Best-of-Show winner of the first Mazer Cup Mead Competition, whose work with honey and with ultrafiltration helped spur renewed interest in commercial meadmaking.

To Dr. Roger Morse, pioneer in modern meadmaking, beekeeper, scientist, author, and great contributor to the body of scientific knowledge about mead, and a man who lived with a deep dedication to this earth and the bounties that it gives us.

To Susanne Price, fierce and dedicated advocate of meadmaking, who bore the mantle of President of the American Mead Association until her untimely death in 1996.

And, most personally, to Dr. Bill Pfeiffer, 1987 American Homebrewers Association Mead Maker of the Year, who helped put knowledge of meadmaking into my soul, and who encouraged and taught me in the most profound and productive ways.

May they all be sharing a mazer in Valhalla.

acknowledgements

More than anyone else, I need to thank my wife, Jean, and daughters Sarah and Alyson for putting up with the commitment it has taken to prepare this book. Their patience and forbearance have given me the latitude needed to complete this work, at the expense of their Internet access, the freedom to do their homework at their leisure, and worst of all, their playtime on the computer.

Dan McConnell showed me the finer points of meadmaking, and together we embarked on many crazed adventures concocted to learn more about mead. His knowledge of yeast varieties and fermentation has been integral to my understanding of that aspect of mead. Dan, Mike O'Brien, Hal Buttermore, and I hatched a scheme many years ago to found the Mazer Cup Mead Competition. It has proven most instructive to all of us.

Larry Yates and the members of the Southeast Michigan Beekeepers Association have taught me much about honey, bees, and beekeeping. They have also taught me that the gentle, patient ways of beekeepers are to be admired and emulated.

Dr. Landis Donor and Dr. Jonathan White have generously shared their knowledge of honey and their materials with me. Theodore Grootendorst of Southmeadow Fruit Gardens taught me to graft, and instilled in me a deep thirst for knowledge of and experience tasting the many varieties of fruits (apples, especially) that can be grown in Michigan. Dr. Amy Iezonni of Michigan State University introduced me firsthand to the spectacular gamut of tart cherry varieties. Through conversation and the many transcripts he provided, Morten Meilgaard has helped me understand flavor and our perception of it.

Ray Daniels, Dick Dunn, Stan Hieronymus, and Daria Labinsky worked hard to make this a book that an intelligent human would not resent reading. It is a much better work for their efforts.

Last, but not least, I have to thank my father, Jim Schramm, who taught me that Dortmunder Union was way better than American beer; my grandfather, Harold

Schramm, without whose counsel my attempts at orchardry would have suffered greatly; and my brother Mike, who bought me a beermaking kit for Christmas in 1987 and started me down a path that led here.

foreword

Mankind's record on taking care of its treasures leaves much to be desired. We have a habit of moving on to the next great fad, and forgetting everything worthwhile that has happened prior to fifteen minutes ago. We blindly allow our pace of life to be hastened beyond the pace at which life can be enjoyed, and fail even to take the time to ask ourselves what it is that life and our world offer us that give us pleasure and make it gratifying to await the change of the seasons. The cellular phones, answering machines, and Email meant to bring us freedom simply expand the amount of time we are accountable to our superiors and available to overcommit ourselves further. We abide by the rules and norms set before us by rulemakers, governments, and corporations, by advertising agencies, public opinion consultants, and management, and never stop to see if they make any sense or have any real value when viewed as part of the glorious web of life in which we spend our days.

Mead provides but one of a host of examples of this thoughtless rush into the future. Once the noblest of beverages in the northern European countries, it declined not due to its lack of worth, but rather as a casualty of it, as honey and its cherished product mead became affordable only to the extreme nobility and to the beekeeper. It was brushed aside in a maddening new rush of choices, novelty, and a love of convenience at all costs. The same can be said for cider, perry, and connoisseur fruits. Mead, once considered far superior to both wine and beer, fell into obscurity as honey became scarce and expensive, and was never reclaimed from the nobility's vault in which it was laid. Through the work of many people, and by virtue of the quality of the beverage itself, mead is making a comeback. This book endeavors to push that comeback along.

The goal of this book is to bring the resources available to meadmakers nearer to the breadth of scientific knowledge and diversity of technique that are applied to amateur brewing and winemaking. I hope that these chapters provide a resource of new and valuable information about the various aspects of meadmaking that you can use to improve your mead. If you are totally new to meadmaking, you'll soon be capable of making meads that compare with the best being made anywhere. If you have been making mead for several years, I hope *The Compleat Meadmaker* provides the type of information you have been seeking but have been unable to find compiled in one book elsewhere.

part one
BACKGROUND

chapter one
From the Beginning to a Modern Revival

Mead has a rich tradition in every corner of the world—longest, perhaps, away from its much-heralded northern European heritage. A comprehensive look at the documentation of the uses and distribution of mead around the globe and throughout history would easily fill an entire book. That, however, is not my sole goal, so I will focus on some of the less well-explored aspects of the history of this storied and fascinating drink.

The Great Debate

When it comes to the title of "The Oldest Fermented Beverage on Earth," each of the fermented beverage factions seeks to make the claim, and certainly the historical documentation of beer- and winemaking are substantial. In terms of written or pictorial evidence to bolster their argument, the beermakers currently have the upper hand, with pictorial records of beermaking that date back to Mesopotamia in about 4000 BC In the pictorial archaeological records of brewing and winemaking (about 3000 BC), each craft is depicted unmistakably and in a form that intimates that the activity had developed to a plateau wherein the process had become standardized. Wine- and beermaking had been undertaken for a sufficient period to become sources of employment and trade by the time these records were made.

The winemakers counter with evidence from Soviet Georgia dating back to 5000 to 7000 BC: grape pips in sufficient quantities to document viticulture (the raising of grapes), evidence that has been extrapolated to support winemaking with some logical but debatable extensions of the evidentiary record. Even older grape pips from Turkey, Syria, and Jordan have been (again debatably) dated to 8000 BC. Certainly, winemaking was a central catalyst for grape cultivation.

But the beer faction rebuts those arguments with more widely accepted evidence that barley and other cereal grains appear to have been cultivated very early on, with evidence ranging from 9500 BC to 8000 BC. The case is made by many historians that the cause of this coincidental historical chronology of horticulture and viticulture is the end of the Ice Age; that climatic conditions prior to that era made any horticultural activity difficult if not impossible. Both courts have legitimate claims to the first fermented beverage crown, and each claim can be convincingly refuted. It is held in both cases that grapes and grain were sought first as food and later became the recognized source of fermentable sugar. Both groups make the assumption that storage of their foodstuff resulted in fermentation through some very logical and easily accepted sequence of events.

Grains can, in fact, become malt without human intervention (partially germinate, and then, under the right conditions, have their growth cycle arrested), and Neolithic farmers or gatherers would have found the malted grain sweeter and more nutritious. To be eaten easily, the malted grains would have been made into some sort of gruel, which would have fermented naturally during storage. Grapes collected in the wild and stored in any earthenware vessel would have become active in a few days under almost any circumstances. The absence of any real fermentation equipment, or of residues or pictorial evidence, leaves these assumptions only reasonable conjecture about the "discovery" of fermentation and the precursors of developed wine- and beermaking practices.

The true genesis of fermentation itself will remain forever shrouded in mystery, but the folklore surrounding these events is colorful and amusing, at least. While the debate has raged on between the two main camps, the meadmakers have similarly laid some claims to the crown, but without the body of substantive evidence of the other claimants. This is due in large part to the lack of a well-funded (read: "rich") commercial patron such as the major vintners who fund the wine research, or brewers—like Fritz Maytag of Anchor Brewing Company—who have supported the beer archaeological research front. But what the meadmakers lack in support of their argument for greatest possible antiquity, they make up for in the logic of honey as the first fermentable, and in the earliest true pictorial evidence.

Honey as Paleolithic Food

For those anthropologists and historians who view humans from a "species" perspective, this conclusion is eminently logical and reasonable. Humans, as with any other land-based species that foraged for its food, would have sought out the most calorically rich food sources available at any given time in the annual cycle of plant growth and animal behavior. Present-day so-called "primitive" tribal cultures still engage in structured and regular honey gathering from hives in and around their foraging territory. Similarly, bears, another omnivorous, mammalian, foraging species, actively seek out hives and raid them for their delightfully sweet honey and protein-rich brood combs. In all likelihood, man has been eating honey since, and probably before, his evolutionary separation from other primate species.

The records of honey use and gathering predate those of winemaking, beer brewing, or any recognized agricultural or horticultural practices. Cave paintings and rock drawings of prehistoric honey hunters abound throughout Europe, Asia, and, most especially, Africa. Rock drawings from near Valencia, Spain, dated as far back as 15000 BC indicate that humans may have been raiding beehives for honey in Paleolithic times. Other more conservative datings place the age of these drawings between 8400 BC and 6000 BC. Eva Crane, in *The Archaeology of Beekeeping,* dates the La Arana shelter drawing, "discovered" in 1924, closer to that most recent date. But she and many archaeologists familiar with Paleolithic and Neolithic humans cite repeated and reasonably conclusive instances of honey hunters at their craft from long before any accepted pictorial or written evidence of beer- or winemaking. This in and of itself would lend credence to the contention that mead is the oldest of all alcoholic beverages.

The Earliest Fermentation

Humans, it seems, have pressed virtually every grown or gathered foodstuff into the production of intoxicants in one form or another. Somewhere in the world, we make wine, beer, or liquor from just about every source of sugar or convertible starch we can find: fruits, vegetables, grains, and grasses. We humans have a glorious habit of fermenting pretty much everything we can get our hands on. No other foodstuff available to early civilization could surpass honey—could provide a higher percentage of fermentable sugar with so little processing or care. It was available year-round in tropical climes, and even some temperate ones, and could be gathered by both nomadic and settlement-building cultures. The "logical extension" progression of "gathering-storage-resulting fermentation" assumptions—made to support the notion of beer or wine being the earliest fermented beverage—must either be discarded or become compelling arguments for mead having been discovered first.

A reasoned assessment of all of the early fermentation hypotheses shows a number of similarities and begs one particular question. All of the posited scenarios include the gathering of a quantity of a source of fermentable sugar, attempts at its short-term storage, "spoilage" of a sort—actually fermentation, and then the consumption of the now-transformed elixir. Each involves chance, and each involves the gathering of naturally occurring foodstuffs, all of which were probably being systematically collected by humans by around 10000 BC. Central to all of these scenarios is storage in some sort of watertight vessel, which facilitates fermentation. So the lowest common denominator is not which foodstuff was being collected and consumed; in all likelihood, the determinant factor in which tribe or group "discovered" fermentation first is not the food crop, but the development of a watertight container. First watertight vessel = first fermented beverage. So . . . who had the first vessel?

My inclination was to pursue the earliest records of pottery and earthenware vessels. They are repeatedly mentioned in the myths and folklore surrounding the first wines and beers. But a discussion with William Peck, Egyptologist at the Detroit Institute of Arts, set me straight. The first watertight "vessels" were not pottery, but skins and animal organs used by Neolithic and possibly Paleolithic humans to collect water and other materials. Pottery came much later. The first pottery vessels were baskets that were lined with clay. Eventually they were fired to burn away the basket. The potter's wheel was invented in about 6000 BC in what is now Turkey, and most archaeologists and historians hold that wine and beer had long since been established in Sumeria by then. Prior to pottery vessels, gourds also would have been used for food gathering; Crane documents both leather and gourd containers being used by African honey hunters.

Consider, then, this possible scenario for the advent of fermentation. A group of Paleolithic hunters (European, Mesopotamian, Indian, or African, take your pick) prepares to embark on a hunting expedition of unknown but presumably significant duration. They fill their water skins and set out. Early on in their hunt, the dominant male comes across a hive of bees, and, not wanting to pass up a food source, drains off some of his water and fills the skin with the honey from the hive. In the interest of preserving the honey for the rest of the tribe (or in the interest of keeping it all for himself), the honey water is carried for the rest of the hunt, and he drinks a lower-ranking male's water. Another possibility is that the honey is parceled out to the rest of the hunting party, each of whom adds it to his water supply. In either case, spontaneous fermentation ensues, and by the time the hunting party returns from the hunt, a magical transformation has taken place. The honey water is mood elevating, and makes the female members of the tribe more receptive to sexual advance. A similar possible sequence of events would have the honey being collected by other members of the tribe while the alpha male and others are out hunting. After a few days, the hunting party returns to a skin of honey water with a whole new twist.

In either case, the transformation of the honey into mead causes great amazement. During fermentation the skin would have swollen of its own volition and required venting, although this might not have been apparent had the skin been drunk from on a regular basis during fermentation. In all likelihood, the skin would have been attributed with magical properties causing this metamorphosis and would have been revered for this capacity. Attempts would have been made to repeat the phenomenon, which would have been successful. The reuse of the skin would result in the establishment of a resident yeast culture (this should sound familiar to lambic beer aficionados), and the subsequent addition of honey and water to the skin would have resulted in a self-perpetuating fermentation.

The nature of this process and the presumed reaction has led a friend of mine to dub this conjecture "the Magic Bag Theory." If this had been the case, though, the bag in question would probably have been pressed into service testing other foodstuffs. Or, equally plausibly, the fermentable jammed into the sack could have been apples, grapes, grains, dates, or figs, or any combination of the above, and the "first" fermented beverage could have been any number of different concoctions. Interestingly, the advent of fermentation could easily be pushed back by millennia or even as much as hundreds of thousands of years. Researcher Dan McFeeley has suggested that knowledge of fermentation could have been passed down but could also have been gained and lost countless times.

In fact, many Paleolithic and Neolithic historians have concluded that mead was the first fermented beverage. For some reason, the idea of rainfall collecting in a hive in the crook of a tree or other bowl-shaped crevice—with the ensuing fermentation having been discovered by a passing human—has gained currency. It is curious to me, as I have never seen a modern record of any such discovery. The dilution required to overcome honey's self-preserving properties would have been substantial. While I would guess it is possible, and I have in fact posited this scenario in the past, it now seems to me improbable in comparison with the "Magic Bag Theory."

The production of mead would not have been limited by any geographical constraints, because honey is produced in areas that support neither wild grape production nor wild grain. The consensus date among anthropologists and food historians for earliest mead production is around 8000 BC. Wine and beer may not have been far behind, but mead may well have been around for quite some time before that, as far as I can tell.

Honey: The First Fermentable?

The most numerous of the rock paintings and drawings that bear testament to honey hunters are in Africa. Crane notes that while they are the most common, few have been accurately dated. The African paintings and drawings depict a number of honey-related activities, including the use of smoke and fire to aid in the collection of honey.

Further attention to the written record backs up the history of honey being used in fermentation at the earliest written accounts of both brewing and winemaking. The ancient Egyptians were using honey as a household sweetener as early as the fortieth century BC, but it is not clear that bees were domesticated as such until later. Beekeeping procedures are documented in the Neussere temple, dating to the Fifth Dynasty (ca. 2500 BC) of the Old Kingdom. These earliest beekeepers built clay hives for their colonies, and developed some rudimentary tools for collecting and extracting honey. Honey is mentioned in funerary rights, in recipes, and bee farms and honey are mentioned in Eighteenth and Twenty-fifth Dynasty tombs. Two jars from the tomb of Tutankhamen were labeled "honey of good quality."

Beekeeping and honey were obviously of significance to the ancient Egyptians. Honey is mentioned as a fermentable by name in the *Hymn to Ninkasi,* the poem or song from the nineteenth century BC that has been interpreted as both an ode to the goddess of fermentation and as a beer recipe. The reference is disputed to be either to honey or a date nectar, but is clearly mentioned as a brewing ingredient. Honey was a traded agricultural commodity by this time. This use of honey in alcoholic beverages also may be mirrored in other cultures outside of the Egypt. In India the soma wine, conjectured by some historians to be a mead or meadlike substance, is the focus of an entire chapter of the *Rig Veda* from roughly this time period (1500 to 1200 BC). It is likely that mead, like agriculture, was developed concurrently by several different cultures, working without knowledge of their counterparts in other areas of the globe. It was, however, the Greeks who coined the terms "ambrosia" and "nectar of the gods."

Mead and Honey in Mediterranean Culture

As in Egypt, Greek culture also developed a hive system to replace honey hunting as the sole source of honey. Their hives looked more like flower pots and permitted the honey to be collected without destroying the colony. One form of hive in use in ancient Greece is known as the top bar hive. A predecessor to the modern box-type hives, top bar hives have removable bars onto which vertical combs are constructed by the bees. These hives are easy to maintain and make collection of honey possible without disruption of the brood. Top bar hives are in regular use in many parts of the world even today. They are a valuable option for apiculture in regions where the cost of Langstroth frame hives is prohibitive.

Mead, and in particular metheglin, were considered high beverages among the Greeks. The gods and the wealthy sipped on mead. The writings of ancient Greece use honey and sweetness as superlative descriptions of wines. Honey could be used to make meads with high residual sweetness (sweetness and a buzz in one package—nectar of the gods, indeed), and also could be used to sweeten drier or underaged wines. The Greeks did a great deal to develop the use of herbs in Mediterranean cuisine and were fond of spicing wines and meads.

The Romans also were given to the sweet. Their *mulsum* was traditional grape wine, heavily sweetened with honey. Mulsum was the predecessor of the modern pyment. It, too, was often spiced with any of several floral Mediterranean herbs. The Welsh and Irish combined the Latin *medicus* (medical or medicine) with the Old Irish *llyn* (liquor) to get *meddyglln,* which became, in time, our modern "metheglin." *Meddyglln* remains the Welsh word for medicine. Pre-Christian European metheglins contained the classic woodland herbs of Europe north of the Alps: thyme, woodruff, chamomile. Medicinal herbs would have been served in two ways by their infusion into mead: the alcohol would have been a better extractant for their medicinal compounds, and the mead would have masked unpleasant flavors from some medicinal plants. As trade stretched the domain of tropical spices into northern Europe, they quickly made their way into mead.

Through what would appear to be a combination of expropriation and genuine innovation, Roman beekeepers seem to have availed themselves of many developments in apiculture. Crane notes that nine types of Roman hives have been documented, made of clay, wicker, cork, wood, and other substances. Many were cylindrical, and were positioned horizontally with a bee opening at one end. Many of their hive systems permitted the honey to be harvested without any detrimental trauma to the hive. Removable closures at one end made it possible to remove honeycomb without disturbing brood. The Romans could stack these horizontally aligned hives into large catacomblike assemblages, which meant that individual beekeepers could produce quite substantial quantities of honey.

The Roman taste for mead is overshadowed in modern history by the Italian taste for wine. Another distressing but perhaps predictable predilection among Mediterranean wine and beverage historians reveals a bit of elitism: Mead appears to have been held in very high favor by Romans in the centuries immediately before and after Christ. The superlative references to meads or wines of this period are to "deliciously sweet meads" or to "wines as sweet as honey." Modern wine purists are given to granting esteem only to grape wines, and in some cases only dry French or Italian wines. They find references to the excellence of meads or sweet wines (especially those sweetened with honey) repugnant. Their acknowledgment of these references is usually framed in terms of "unrefined palates" and "coarser tastes." It does seem logical that with sweets in such short supply, sweet wines and meads would be novel attractions, but at the same time such condescension can make one question the line between purist and snob.

From the Paleolithic era until well into the Roman Empire, honey was the only sweetener available throughout Europe and the Middle East. Cane sugar did not make its way from its origin among Indian cultures into the Western world until the time of Pliny. Even then, cane sugar was regarded as something of an oddity and did not make its way into common usage in Europe for several centuries. Honey, therefore, held a very high place in the hierarchy of Middle Eastern cultures and early European clans.

Mead Across Europe

The role of mead in Europe from pre-Roman times through the Renaissance has been very well documented. The Eurocentric take on the preeminence of Nordic and Anglo-Saxon mead has come by its roots honestly. Nordic and Germanic references, both archaeological and literary, are myriad. Artifacts such as cauldrons with residues of possible mead beverages from Germany and the British Isles date back as far as 1000 BC. A burial site at Ashgrove in Fife, Scotland, dated to 1000 BC, yielded a beaker and other evidence suggesting a spiced mead. Other finds from pre-Christian times push the chronology of alcoholic beverage use in northern Europe back further than previously believed, and force a reexamination of prevailing theories on both Bronze Age knowledge of fermentation and the overall state of societal advancement of supposedly barbaric tribespeople. Brewing also had become commonplace, it seems. Evidence of brewing from several hundred years before Christ has been found near the modern Kulmbach, in Bavaria, and in Trier, now in southeastern Germany, one of the earliest settled cities of central Europe. However, mead, as the beverage of choice, apparently maintained its position of status among the upper classes.

The status and widespread distribution of mead among the Nordic cultures in post-Roman Europe is borne out in *Beowulf,* the epic poem from the 700s. This tome is the written record of an oral legend—the battle between the hero Beowulf and the evil creature Grendel. As such, the tale was probably in existence and in a constant state of metamorphosis and transformation for decades or even more than a hundred years prior to being captured in print. Mead is strewn liberally throughout the saga. It is first mentioned in the fourth line of the work, and virtually every few pages thereafter; sessions of celebration and diplomacy are inevitably held in the "mead hall." Each of the major occasions—victory in battle, a new alliance, a betrothal, even death—is consecrated with copious quantities of mead. While the work itself is meandering and can be difficult to decipher, it is clear evidence of the role of mead both before and during the period when this tale was transcribed from its oral tradition and committed to written record.

During the period between the dominance of Rome and the Renaissance, mead was at the confluence of two rivers of magic: honey and fermentation. The chemistry, botany, and mechanics of how bees make honey were not well understood until the Industrial Revolution, and the magic of honey and beekeeping were ethereal in the minds of even the most scientifically literate. Bees were believed to have procured their honey from heaven. The link between collection of nectar, enzymatic activity, and curing of honey in the hive has only been isolated quite recently.

The transition from honey hunting to beekeeping across northern Europe did not happen rapidly. The archaeological record as noted in Crane's *The Archaeology of Beekeeping* shows that the development of beekeeping was patchy and advanced far more rapidly in some parts of Europe than in others. In forested areas, the change often included a period during which bee trees were located and managed, even becoming part of the acknowledged riches of a given property. Eventually hives were literally cut out of their trees and moved whole to the homes and fields of those who had managed them, and beekeeping began in earnest.

Honey, Wax, and Mead: A Powerful Trio

Those who kept or dealt with bees were very highly esteemed. From both written and physical evidence, it is apparent that much of the crop of honey from early beekeeping was destined for meadmaking. Bees provided another highly coveted substance: beeswax. Beeswax was a means of making candles, and it, too, was in great demand by royalty and the church. The other method—using tallow, or animal fat—produced foul-smelling, faster-burning candles. Bees, therefore, were directly tied to the finest, most controllable form of manmade illumination available. Both honey and beeswax were used as key items of trade and were regularly in demand as taxation by royalty or as tithing to the church. Beekeepers were generally kept close to royalty and to the church, and their powers and abilities were akin to those of alchemists, seers, and magicians.

While clay hives were, and in some places still are, the main form of hive throughout the Mediterranean, skep hives became the norm for many centuries throughout Europe and North America. A skep is a hive made of woven material; it is, at its most fundamental evaluation, simply a basket inverted onto its open end. The earliest skep hives appear to have originated in what is now Germany sometime between 0 AD and 200 AD. The archaeological artifacts were made of wicker and mud; others may have been made by weaving together the branches emanating from the trunk of a small tree with cross hatches, then covering them with mud or clay. Straw skep hives, which are far more weatherproof and sturdy, were the primary form of hive for northern European and New World beekeepers from around 1200 AD to the mid- to late nineteenth century. A well-made skep hive can provide more than a hundred years of service. The cone shape of skep hives continues to be used as the symbol of beekeepers and their wares.

Skeps played a huge role in increasing the availability of both honey and mead in northern Europe. Modern straw skeps could be huge affairs, filled with massive combs of both brood and honey. They were constructed of uniformly sized, coiled bundles of straw supported with interlaced strips of wicker or briar. It is a difficult task to extract honey from a skep, and because brood and honey are together in the lone chamber, skep hives initially required the beekeeper to kill off the colony with smoke (heresy to modern beekeepers) before the combs could be removed and their honey extracted. Later, beekeepers devised a process to transfer the colony to a new hive before removing the honeycombs. The process can only be successfully executed in the fall, when the colony is not aggressively defending brood. If the skep is inverted, and an empty skep placed over the open bottom (now top) of the hive, the colony will crawl into the new hive.

The advantage of a hive system like skeps is that they can be moved to a nectar source early in the season before the hive is heavy with honeycombs. They can be suspended in trees if bears or other animals become a problem. Skeps also were routinely kept in catacomblike enclosures in walls and gardens. These partial shelters, 15 to 20 inches deep and tall enough for a skep hive, are known as bee boles, and can be found in ruins and ancient structures throughout Europe. Using bee boles, hives could be kept close to cottages, close to abbeys, close to castles. In short, honey could be close at hand for the meadmakers. Bee boles were common in the British Isles and to some extent on the continent, in France and Greece, from the twelfth century to the nineteenth century. Some bee boles in structures from those times have been in use with skep hives even in postwar Europe.

High-quality wax, honey, and eventually mead were the products of these skeps, and those products were most often destined for the local bishop or duke. Without the benefit of modern extraction equipment, the process was destructive, to say the least. After the combs were removed from the hive, they were cracked to allow the honey to flow and emptied. The remaining honey would be extracted from the comb by placing the crushed comb in a pot of hot water, and heating the lot to melt the wax. The wax was skimmed, and the must would be fermented by the beekeeper to provide his household with a table-grade mead.

Those seeking more information on the place of mead in European civilization will enjoy *Brewing Mead: Wassail! In Mazers of Mead*, a collaborative effort first published in 1948 by Robert Gayre with recipes and updating contributed later by Charlie

Papazian. It is filled with many references to the history of mead in Europe and elsewhere. Gayre is a mead enthusiast of the highest order, and may have let his enthusiasm cloud his objectivity. Some of his theories require substantial leaps of faith. Some of the work's propositions have been pretty conclusively refuted. Archaeological and literary evidence now proves the widespread availability of both wine and beer during periods and in locations Gayre suggests supported only mead production.

On the other hand, the depth and breadth of Gayre's research into literary references to and about mead in Europe between the fall of the Roman Empire and the late eighteenth century is most rewarding. Clearly, Gayre went to great lengths to make as complete a record of the documentation of mead use throughout Europe in that time period as he possibly could. His tireless work on the subject is unlikely to be matched.

Honey and Mead Beyond Europe

Explorers and colonists brought European honeybees to the New World in the 1600s, but the native population was not unacquainted with honey when Columbus arrived in the 1400s. The Americas have smaller native honey-gathering bees of the genera *Trigona* and *Melipona*. They are stingless bees, native to a band of Central and South America extending roughly from Cuba and north-central Mexico as far south as Brazil. *Melipona* species are also the only honey-producing bees native to Australia. These bees do not produce honey crops of nearly the size that a colony of European bees can put up in a season; average yields of 2 kilograms per hive are the norm, although some hives have produced crops of up to 45 kilos under spectacular conditions. In Crane's compilation *Honey: A Comprehensive Survey*, Morse and Steinkraus note that both honey cultivation and the production of fermented beverages were recorded when the Spaniards began New World conquests.

In Africa, honey hunters and cultivators had to contend with aggressive bees, but that did not seem to deter their efforts. In some areas of Africa, honey hunting is still a regular part of the food-gathering activities of tribal peoples. Fermented honey beverages have been and still are produced in Central Africa from coast to coast. It is very interesting to note that the concentric regions of native *Apis mellifera* and *Melipona* species on the African continent represent the areas richest in Australopithecine and other pre-hominid fossil remains, and also reflect the areas wherein mead, Tej, or some other fermented honey-based beverages are still produced. It goes beyond presumptuous to make the correlation between the availability of honey and the development of successful early man, but the development of such a species in an area with an abundance of calorically rich foodstuffs does not seem farfetched in the least.

There are three other species of true honeybees: *Apis cerana, Apis florea, and Apis dorsata. A. dorsata* and *A. florea,* which both produce only one comb, are native to the Indian subcontinent and Asia through Thailand, Cambodia, and on into the South China Sea. *A. dorsata* is known as the giant honeybee. *A. florea* is smaller, as is its honey yield. *A. cerana* covers much of the same geographical range, but the northern end of its range extends well into China and on up to Japan. These bees are not domesticated for the most part; their honey is gathered by honey hunters. Their presence in Asia accounts for the production of fermented beverages from honey in India and the Pacific Rim.

The Decline of Mead

Outside of Africa and Poland, mead has slipped from the mainstream over the course of the last few hundred years. The reason for this "decline" has been the cause for much conjecture. Gayre accounts for the decline as the result of a dramatic rise in the cost of honey during a "shortage" that he writes occurred in Europe in the Tudor era (late fourteenth to early seventeenth century). Gayre does not actually so much document a decline in production to prove his shortage as he documents an increase in the price of honey. While many of Gayre's points are sound, his thesis is highly "Britain-centric," meaning many of his arguments are made in the context of mead's decline in Great Britain but may not explain the decline throughout northern Europe. Mead's transition from prominence to scarcity occurs slowly, from about the eleventh century to the late eighteenth century. Over that time period, mead fell prey to the force that has brought so many products and technologies to their knees: competition. Competitive pressure brought to bear on both mead and honey led to a slow decline into obscurity.

Since mead did not see as dramatic a decline in production throughout Africa, Poland, and European Russia, we must look more for the causes of its decline among the western European countries. Probably the most influential event in terms of its effect on the culture of mainland Europe and the British Isles during the heyday of mead was the Norman Conquest. In one short week in 1066, the armies of Harold, the reigning king of England, defeated and slew the invading Harold, king of Norway. Harold, in turn, was killed, and his armies defeated, by the invading Earl William, the first of the Norman rulers of the British Empire.

William was then crowned king of England on Christmas of 1066, beginning a reign over England by the Normans that would last for four generations. This French invasion of British soil was to bring systemic change to the aristocracy of the British Isles, influencing their dress, their tastes, and the development of British commerce and industry. The Normans brought to the British Isles their affinity for both wines and for hard ciders and perry. Mead now faced competition for market share in Great Britain from both a high-quality beverage, French wine, and from inexpensive, low-alcohol fruit beverages. The defeat left Norway—another stronghold of mead consumption—leaderless, as well, with its army in disarray and its culture weakened to outside influence.

The Norman Conquest also began an era of vastly increased trade among the countries of Europe, both north and south. In addition to the trade of highly profitable, less bulky commodities such as spices and silk, trade in less gainly items, such as wine, grain, and sugar, became both feasible and profitable. By the thirteenth century, refined sugar (albeit not white and granulated) and finer French and Mediterranean wines were being freely traded across northern Europe.

By the fifteenth century, sugar was ubiquitous throughout Europe on both sides of the Alps. French, Spanish, German, and Italian wines also were improving in their quality. The French were refining the regional differences in their vintages, while the Austrians and Germans were experimenting with *trockenbeerenauslesen* and other vinting techniques that dramatically increased the complexity and dynamism of the wine's flavor profile. Mead-lovers though we may be, it is difficult to argue that fine wines would not have provided very welcome, novel diversions from the traditional meads and beers of very inconsistent quality available.

Another historical advent in alcoholic beverage production also would have proven influential in the declining stature of mead among the alcohol-consuming public. In the 1400s, brewers across Europe began accepting hops as the preservative herb to be used in beer. Although it may sound inconsequential, the advent of hops was a turning point in the history of beer; hops made beer a far more consistent and stable product. Beer could now be produced with a dramatically reduced risk of contamination and could be stored for much longer periods of time. While I can't be unequivocating in making statements regarding hopped beer's taste compared to beers brewed with other spices, in all likelihood, hopped beer probably did taste better. The Czechs make the claim that hops were being cultivated there as early as the ninth century, but it took until the fifteenth and sixteenth century for hops to be universally incorporated into standard brewing practice throughout the mead strongholds of the British Isles and Scandinavia.

This meant that beer could become a serious competitor for the hearts and minds of the proletariat. Beer was refreshing and did the same magic trick as mead, but could be consumed over a far longer period with the same effect and at a much lower cost. Now mead had lost a sizable portion of the top end of its market to imported wines and would lose a chunk of the bottom end of its market to higher-quality beer. Monastic brewing played a large role in both the acceptance of hops among brewers and in the overall improvement in the quality of beer being produced. Monks were intelligent, proud, and could devote a great deal of effort to upgrading the overall quality and consistency of their beer. Monasteries were the buttresses of their villages and neighborhoods. Beer became available at the local abbey, frequently in a publike setting that provided camaraderie as well as nutrition and satisfying inebriation.

The last serious competitor for the hearts and tongues (and coin) of the alcohol consuming public was a big gun: *Uisga Beathe.* The Water of Life. Whisky. And *eau de vie,* and vodka, and brandy and eventually, rum. Distillation is believed to have originated in Asia sometime in the early ninth century, and by the eleventh century, knowledge of distillation technique had been disseminated throughout the developed world. Distilled wines (brandies) and distilled beers (whiskies) were regional adaptations of this knowledge, and showed the inventiveness of the newly informed public, as did the advent of vodka and gin from more neutral fermented bases.

We can be haughty about it, but the truth is that we would be completely deluding ourselves if we denied one basic fact: All arguments about connoisseurism and high culture aside, it's all about the buzz here, folks.The history of human affinity for alteration of our mental state is beyond debate. Mead did the magic trick and so did beer and wine. But as well as they did the trick, they couldn't hold a candle to a distilled spirit. By about 1400, the Scots had whiskymaking down to an art that remains largely unchanged among the finest single malt distilleries today. And, by golly, they sure make some fine, fine whisky. So, too, the French learned to make deeply complex and delicious *eau de vie* and Cognac; the rest of the world followed suit with their own high-quality regional specialties. Each of these provided an option to the regular mead consumer, and appealing options they were, indeed. The impact of distilled beverages on our welfare has been anything but gleaming, but here to stay they were. There were issues of taxation and regulation to be ironed out, but by the early 1700s, trade in distilled beverages was essentially global, market niches had been carved out, and the alcohol market reached a demographic stability that has changed little right up to the present.

The Survival of Mead

How did mead survive this fragmentation of its theater of prior dominance? Probably the most critical contributors to its longevity are the beekeepers, who have been making some form of fermented beverage from honey since the Egyptians. Beekeepers in Europe and the United States have passed along their knowledge of meadmaking through clubs and social gatherings and share their wares at local and regional beekeepers' meetings. Mead has never ceased to be in production in this at-times loose and at-times very tightly knit network of mutually interested individuals.

Medieval historians also have played a role in keeping mead alive.The Society for Creative Anachronism is a very active group of historical enthusiasts with a strong bent for accuracy and re-creation of pre-Renaissance culture and life. Its members take great pride in utilizing authentic period techniques and ingredients and have produced high-quality meads from period recipes for many years. Quite independently from the homebrewing and amateur winemaking organizations, the SCA has been a dedicated group of guardians of mead.

Another standard-bearer for mead was the monastic community, and Brother Adam in particular. Brother Adam was the monk in charge of mead production and beekeeping at Buckfast Abbey in England. His meads were, and in fact still are, renowned. His production techniques were traditional in the utmost. He believed in the use of good honey, a short boil, and long barrel aging, and his pride in mead was unbridled and genuine. His work is referenced in the texts of both beekeepers and mead enthusiasts, so deep was his dedication to these two compatible dispositions.

Mead has never really ceased to be in production in Europe and Africa. If you look at the geographic distribution of cultures in which mead remains one of the primary sources of alcoholic libation, they have not, for the most part, been subject to the influences above. Trade and the availability of refined sugar and distilled beverages have not been defining cultural advances throughout central Africa and have been of less influence throughout countries like Poland and the former Soviet republics in Eastern Europe. Those cultures all have options in their choices of alcoholic beverage, but still rely heavily on mead or honey-based beverages as the source of their alcohol.

Perhaps most important in mead having stood the test of time is its longstanding reputation as a powerful aphrodisiac. Any food or drink professed of such properties will not likely be soon forgotten. If mead is truly the oldest fermented beverage, then its reputation for loosening the inhibitions of its imbibers may be the oldest and most reasonable of any substance so proclaimed.

Aphrodisia

Mead has been ascribed with the properties of aphrodisiac from ancient times right up to the present. Throughout the Western world, it has ushered in orgies and has been held responsible for the successful consummation of marriages. A recent urban myth holds that the term "honeymoon" is derived from the practice of providing the blessed couple with a month's supply of mead (one cycle of the moon). The custom was said to improve the couple's chances for successfully starting a family. This practice is said to have originated in the Middle East and spread across central and northern Europe. The story is an interesting one, but its veracity in etymological circles has never been confirmed. Inebriation at weddings and a prolonged period of privacy for the lucky couple thereafter, though, remain widely practiced ritual behaviors in many cultures. In modern times, party-crazed homebrewers I have met have told me they have dubbed mead "panty-remover."

We live in times of extreme skepticism, triple blind studies, molecular analysis, and literal interpretation of cause and effect on everything in our lives. Our view of the thousand- or even hundred-year-old claims of aphrodisiac effects of various foods, herbs, and spices deems them comical or, at a minimum, dubious and primitive. While we are given to believing that an aphrodisiac is only truly effective if it can produce a clinically proven biochemical response that increases blood flow to the genitals or generates frenetic demand for copulation (or some other such response), authorities on sex are in general agreement that the largest part of sexual desire and response are rooted most firmly in the minds of the partners. The chemistry of sexual response based on activity in the brain is at the center of current research on drugs to treat sexual malfunction in humans. Putting one's self and one's partner in a sensual frame of mind are critically important to engaging in and being truly satisfied by a sexual experience. And that is where honey, and many other aphrodisiacs of old, have claimed their fame.

To those living in northern Europe prior to the advent of extensive and affordable trade in sweets and spices, the sheer novelty of these now-common goods was cause for

APHRODISIA *CONTINUED*

anticipation and heightened awareness during their use or consumption. This focused attention on the senses is absolutely in keeping with the desired mental effect of these so-called aphrodisiacs. Getting a partner concentrating on sights, smells, textures, and tastes—his or her sensual response—is the perfect prelude to a welcomed sexual advance (dinner and a movie, anyone?). Now add to this the effects of mead used in moderation, and the stage is set for romance. In reviewing the accounts and descriptions of the desire-inducing properties of various aphrodisiacs and love potions, many call for such a series of rituals or procedures, that, one suspects, they could hardly yield any other results. The Kama Sutra, Arabian Nights, and the Anunga Runga, among others, call for anointing the genitals, or inducing intoxication with various narcotics and psychotropic substances, in the course of securing the effectiveness of the aphrodisiacs mentioned therein. One can hardly imagine such precursor activities finishing up any other way.

Aphrodisiac recipes from pre-Christian times through the nineteenth century are most often based on the theory of "like-makes-like" (oysters, etc.), or on sensuous, spice-laden concoctions. Nutmeg, cinnamon, allspice, cloves, and honey are all routinely mentioned in these potions. Honey is included in potion formulas across many different cultures, but most notably the Middle Eastern cultures and in India. Through it all, the mind's the thing. The success of mead as an aphrodisiac in modern or ancient times is dependent on the attitude of the parties involved. The tender loving care in its preparation, and the intent of drinkers of mead, will be the determinants of its effectiveness.

THE RESURGENCE OF MEAD

Having survived the onslaught of competitive pressures, mead now finds itself firmly planted in the midst of a revival. In the United States, a significant part of the genesis of the resurgence of interest in mead came from Charlie Papazian's *The Complete Joy of Homebrewing.* One of its appendices sang the praises of mead in superlatives, and included a quirky recipe for "Barkshack Ginger Mead." That recipe served as the entry point for thousands of homebrewers into the pleasures of mead. In 1986 Pamela Spence founded the American Mead Association. Her leadership role was eventually passed on to Susanne Price, who labored on behalf of the beverage until her untimely and tragic death in 1996.

The number of commercial meaderies around the world continues to grow, and commercial offerings are finding their way onto the shelves of more and more wine shops. Meads are now routinely offered to patrons at brewpubs. In 2002 Ray Daniels held the first U.S.-based international festival and competition for commercial meadmakers in Chicago. Twenty-one meaderies submitted entries. At the time of this book's publishing, www.gotmead.com listed nearly 70 U.S. meaderies, and more than a dozen others around the world.

Mead faces the same commercial competition that it has for the last six hundred years. Beer offerings are better made and more diverse than ever before. The distilled beverage component is at the same time broad in scope and distinctive in its styles, and its marketing efforts are well financed. Mead faces a wine industry that has defined itself well and has built a common understanding of the varieties and their respective roles in complementing various foods. Mead needs to establish a vocabulary of its own, and a place in the culinary repertoire of restaurateurs and publicans. Mead needs a level of understanding among its consumers that creates a niche—a specific set of foods and occasions with which it becomes associated.

As occured with the rebirth of interest in high-quality beer, much of that awareness will come from beverage hobbyists—the amateur meadmakers of the world. From you. You will educate your own palate, and develop a set of tastes for quality meads that you will pass along to your friends, family, and acquaintances. You will help to stretch the limits and boundaries of the beverage and its styles, limits and boundaries that are as fictitious and contrived as the borders we draw around our countries. Some of you will become so enamored of mead and its allure that you will be compelled to pursue meadmaking as a profession. It is a fine thought indeed, that one among you reading this book will one day be the "Brother Adam" of another mead book, much like this one, being written in another place and time. Thus the future becomes the past, and the past the future. Today is tomorrow, and a new chapter of meadmaking history is begun.

chapter two

Defining the Styles

Mead knows many different naming conventions around the world. Even in the English-speaking world, mead is referred to differently by people seeking to make use of the terminology of cultures or historical periods they find important or romantic. It is a testament to the wonder and influence of the powerful and ever-changing symbolism of language. The terms used to describe mead are most frequently differentiated by the ingredients used in its preparation:

Traditional mead generally describes mead made only with honey as its fermentable sugar and flavor source. Some meadmakers hold that traditional mead can contain only honey, yeast, and water. Others contend that traditional (primarily Anglo-Saxon post-Renaissance) meads were made with any number of adjunct flavorings in small amounts.

For the purposes of competition, the Mazer Cup used a distinction made in some European mead competitions, and designated the *"Show"* mead category as one in which no additional flavorings could be used.

Sack mead, or simply *sack,* is a strong, sweet mead.

Melomel is a mead fermented or flavored with fruit.

Cyser is a melomel made from apples, apple juice, or cider.

Pyment is a melomel made with grapes or grape juice, and also can refer to a wine that has been fermented with or sweetened with honey.

Hippocras is a pyment to which spices have been added.

Metheglin is a mead that has been fermented or flavored with herbs or spices.

Braggot, bragot, or *bracket* is mead made with malted grain, usually malted barley.

There are many other terms for fermented honey beverages that have been culled from historical references. The Celts had their hefty *zythus* and less potent *corma,* the Aryans *soma* and *amrita*. Some historians claim the Greek *ambrosia* is mead, others that it is a sweet food made with honey. *Nectar* is more likely the Greek term for mead. *Rhodomel* is a Roman term used historically to describe a honey drink flavored and scented with rose petals. *Morat* was used for a melomel made with mulberries. *Hydromel* has been described alternately as a French term for mead and as the name given to weaker or watered-down meads. It is difficult to discern from Gayre and other historians whether or not some or all of these admixtures were actually fermented or consumed as sweet drinks.

Some mead enthusiasts have adapted, created, and applied a whole host of names to meads created with different ingredients. They can be interesting, in some cases even amusing (*capsicumel* or *capsimel*, for a mead made with hot peppers). That, however, could go on without end (*molassocassioconiferamel:* a mead made with molasses, cassia [cinnamon], and pine-bough shoots!). At some point, the meaningfulness of a term is determined by the sphere of its usage, and although it gives me little pleasure to admit it, the number of people making hot pepper meads is not all that large. Yet.

Nomenclature has never been anything other than arbitrary in any discipline. Which of these names you choose to adopt is a matter of your own inclination.

part two

PROCESS

chapter three
Changing Honey into Wine

It goes by the name of "mead" or "honey wine." Some call it "ambrosia," others "nectar of the gods." By whatever name, no beverage serves as the focus for more myth and folklore—and no beverage is less understood by the public—than this romantic and resplendent elixir. Thanks to the global distribution of bees and, therefore, honey, you'll find meadlike drinks in virtually every corner of the world. No wonder historians recognize it as one of humankind's oldest fermented beverages.

Perhaps you've already tasted mead, either one made by a friend or one of the growing number of commercial examples. What you had piqued your interest, and now you want to learn more. Be assured that meadmaking is quite simple, and within the next few pages, this book will teach you everything you need to make your first batch. At the same time, it takes a lot to justify the title of "complete," no matter how you spell it. While many wonderful meads consist of little more than honey and water, others incorporate fruit, spices, herbs, and even the malt sugars familiar to brewers. Thus, thorough coverage of meadmaking must explore not only the broad subject of honey, but a number of other fields as well. Fear not: You can explore as few or as many as you desire, at your own pace and in your own time.

A resurgent interest in mead and meadmaking in recent years has created a boundless frontier for experimentation and research into the possibilities of fermented honey beverages. Winemakers, homebrewers, and history enthusiasts, particularly those with an interest in the Middle Ages, have taken up the quest for perfection in meadmaking. As they learn and experiment, they stretch the limits of mead tradition. The results have been truly inspiring and have given rise to a rebirth of this noble drink on both the amateur and commercial levels.

While I value tradition and history more than many, this book strives to move beyond traditional accounts and bring meadmakers a broader, more scientific knowledge of their craft. Anyone familiar with amateur brewing and winemaking has seen a similar trend in the past decade or so. As these hobbies expanded, so did the amount and quality of information available to amateur practitioners.As a result, people make better product and enjoy it more—and that makes everyone happy.

Few compliments warm the heart more than genuine and sincere praise of your handcrafted mead, wine, or beer from a true friend. The advantages of good knowledge and the use of sound technique help make brewers and winemakers proud to serve the fruits of their labors to their friends and relatives. This text strives to bring the same advantages to meadmakers around the globe.

Of all the home beverage fermentation pastimes, meadmaking is by far the easiest and most foolproof. It is forgiving of the forgetful, the busy, and the careless. It can be very inexpensive and indeed requires quite a bit of effort to become pricey. Above all, meadmaking is fun. It can be dirt simple or as complex and involved as you would choose to make it.

Finally, perhaps the finest characteristic of mead is that it seems to improve with age almost indefinitely. Mead "lost" in the cellar for many years is not a "loss," but rather a real "find" when it emerges. Such is the joy of having a case of mead tucked safely away in your storage space. So what do you say we get started on creating your own mead cellar, eh?

A Little Shopping Before We Start

To make your first mead, you'll need some basic equipment and a few simple ingredients. In this section, I'll tell you what you'll need and how to go about getting it. In the next, we'll actually make the mead and start the fermentation. Finally, I'll detail the process of bottling your mead so it will be ready to share with others.

In this chapter, I'm going to give the simplest, easiest method for making a medium-sweet mead. Some meadmakers follow other procedures—usually because they think it improves the finished product—and I'll teach you about those later on. For now, I'll keep it simple so you can learn the basics and get on with making your first mead. If you are an experienced beer or winemaker with an urge to skip this part, feel free to skim through this chapter and start reading again at Chapter 4, "Beyond the Basics."

The 5-gallon batch size has been a standard among homebrewers for some time, and it is common to a certain extent with winemakers as well. As a result, much of the readily available equipment is designed for hobbyists making 5 gallons at a time. Rather than buck that trend, I am going to give you directions and commentary designed for making 5 gallons of mead. If bottled like wine, that'll give you 25 750-ml bottles; if packaged like beer, it produces a little more than two cases of 12-ounce bottles (53 bottles, to be precise, if the carboy is full and nothing is lost to sediment).

If 5 gallons sounds like a lot to you, just remember that mead gets better with age, so you'll be able to enjoy this first batch for many years. Of course, if for some reason you really can't make that much product and want to cut it down to a smaller size, you can—just reduce all the measurements proportionally. In some cases, equipment can be smaller, too.

Where to Shop

Before you make a mead, you'll need to have two types of things on hand: ingredients and equipment. Many of the items you need will be found at a home winemaking or homebrewing store in your community. Check your Yellow Pages for suitable listings and give them a call to see if they carry the items you want, or just stop by for a visit once you have your complete shopping list.

If your area doesn't support a store for beverage hobbyists, check the World Wide Web for mail order suppliers that have what you need.

The one thing that you may not find at a homebrewing or home winemaking shop is the most important ingredient for mead, namely the honey. For that, you may want to start at your local farm market, where beekeepers often market their wares. The Yellow Pages often have listings under "Honey"—with the added benefit of buying directly from the producer. There are many good suppliers on the Web for those with the lead time (see the National Honey Board's www.honeylocator.com). Another option is your gourmet grocer. The honey there is often of very high quality, but may be sold in small 1-pound jars, which can get a bit "spendy." Warehouse and grocery stores may offer bulk packaged honey, although not always great varieties. Honey packaged for grocers is often heated repeatedly so that it can easily pass through heavy filtration. Both of these processes degrade its quality for meadmaking.

To compile your shopping list, the first thing you need is a recipe. For this first recipe, I looked for something not too sweet, not too dry. In addition, I wanted you to be able to make a mead that will bring out the appealing notes of a characteristically aromatic and flavorful honey without any edgy or angular elements. I'm recommending orange blossom honey, as it has a singular profile that carries through delightfully to the finished mead. Finally, I picked a mead that contains all of the ingredients that will normally be included in any mead you make. Here is the recipe:

Medium Sweet Orange Blossom Mead

Recipe for 5 gallons

15 lbs. (5 qts.) (6.82 kg) orange blossom honey
4 gals. water (15.14 L) (3 gals. chilled to refrigerator temperature)
2 tsp. (9.9 mL) yeast nutrient
1 tsp. (4.9 mL) yeast energizer
2 packets (10 g) Lalvin 71b-1122 yeast or suitable alternative

Note: 5 grams of Lalvin Fermaid can be used in place of nutrient and energizer

Throughout this book, I'll remind you that raw ingredient quality has a big impact on the flavor of the finished product. Thus when you purchase honey, you want to get a good-quality product that will make a nice mead. The best way to determine the quality of the honey is to smell and taste it. Make sure the honey doesn't display any offensive characteristics such as musty or barnyard aromas; also notice if it is tart or too strong in flavor, or if the color is unattractive. Try to pick a honey that you really like. If orange blossom honey is not available, try to find a high-quality alternative from your region. Tupelo and sourwood are wonderful honeys from the Southeast. Mesquite honey is available in the Southwest. Raspberry blossom is a wonderful honey from the Northeast and Northwest. Five quarts are what you will need for a medium-bodied, mildly sweet but not too sweet mead.

You will also need some yeast nutrient and yeast energizer to get your fermentation off to a good start. Yeast nutrient provides nitrogen. Yeast energizer provides vitamins and compounds your yeast will employ as it prepares for a massive amount of reproduction followed by vigorous fermentation. An alternative to yeast energizer is Lalvin Fermaid K, which will provide both the nitrogen and the other micronutrients at the correct dosage rate. Lalvin recommends adding 5 grams to a 5-gallon batch, which weighs out to about 1.75 teaspoons, along with a dose of nitrogen.

Yeast nutrient, yeast energizer, and/or Fermaid K should be available at your homebrewing or winemaking store. The terms "energizer" and "nutrient" are used quite loosely by beverage hobby suppliers. They are also confusing in their own right, as yeast needs more than one "nutrient." A knowledgeable vendor can be a great asset here. You need a source of nitrogen and a source of micronutrients.

When it comes to water, you'll want some you find pleasant to drink—something with no apparent flavors from chlorine or other sources. Also, for the simple technique I'm going to describe for this first batch, you'll need a way to get 3 gallons of the water chilled to refrigerator temperature. For most folks, the easiest way to do that is to buy three 1-gallon jugs of distilled water and put them in the fridge the night before you make mead. If you're just as happy using tap water, just find a way to get it chilled to refrigerator temperature. The fourth gallon of water called for in the recipe can be room temperature when you start the meadmaking. Use either bottled or tap water, depending on your preference.

Finally, you will need a nice wine yeast. While some shops may steer you toward liquid yeasts, you are better off starting with dry yeast packets. The dry yeasts are convenient and very easy to use. They come in foil pouches, pretty much like the stuff you use to make bread. For this first batch, I'm recommending Lalvin 71b-1122, which is available at many winemaking and brewing supply stores. If you don't find it, ask your merchant for a wine yeast that will leave some residual sugar, such as Epernay 2. The dry yeasts usually come in packets that weigh 5 grams. I recommend that you buy at least 10 grams of yeast, or two packets.

Once you have all these ingredients, you have what you need to create your first "must"—that's what you call mead before it is fermented. Now let's see what equipment you'll need to actually make that must.

Basic Equipment for Meadmaking

The basic equipment needed for meadmaking isn't very expensive, and it generally lasts for a long time. Most homebrewing and home winemaking shops will

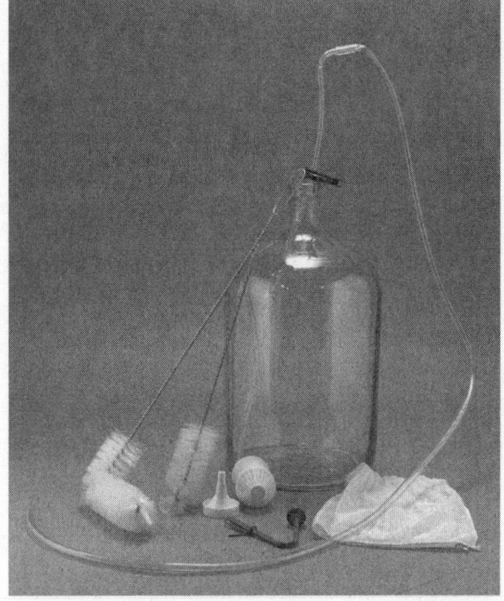
Basic equipment, from left: carboy brush, large bottle brush, plastic siphon starter, jet bottle washer, 5 gallon glass carboy with racking cane, hose and cane/hose clip, and nylon hop strainer bag.

have all of these items and may offer them as part of a "starter" kit. As with anything, there are some "nice to have" and advanced equipment items that I'm not going to list here but will include in "Beyond the Basics." Depending on your budget and level of excitement about meadmaking, you might want to read through that list as well before you do your shopping. Here's the list of items I recommend you have in order to make your first batch of mead.

Stainless steel stockpot
Thermometer
Hydrometer
Plastic fermenter
Glass carboy
Fermentation lock and stopper
Racking cane and tubing
Bleach or sanitizer

Note: Later on you will need bottling equipment, so if it is a big chore to get to the store, you may want to read that section and get those supplies as well during your first trip.

Here are some additional details on each item to help you know what you are looking for.

Stainless steel stockpot. For the first batch, I'll have you heat a honey-water mixture, and the best way to do that is in a stainless steel stockpot. You will need a pot large enough to hold more than a gallon of honey and another gallon or more of water with room to spare for stirring and so you can pour from the pot without risk of spillage. You will also want one with large, sturdy handles that can be firmly gripped, even when wearing kitchen mitts or using hot pads. The handles should be solidly attached to the pot walls: That is very important.

If you don't already have a pot that will do the trick, you might be able to borrow one for a day, or you may be ready to purchase one. If you decide to buy one, you'll want to get one with a capacity of 16 to 20 quarts (15 to 19 L). Usually you can find one at any department store or warehouse outlet at a reasonable cost (especially if you watch for sales).

Thermometer. Dairy or kitchen thermometers will perform the task equally well. Glass dairy thermometers float upright in your must, making them easy to read. The drawback is their fragility. More than one batch has been lost to a broken dairy thermometer. Metal probe thermometers, with dial read-outs, are a bit more expensive and a little more difficult to read but don't present any risk of breakage. As you get more involved with meadmaking, you may want to have two or more thermometers. For this first batch, the most important thing is that the thermometer read in increments of 10° F or less across the range from 50° F to about 200° F (15 to 95° C).

Hydrometer. This device looks a bit like a floating glass dairy thermometer, but rather than reading temperature, it tells how much sugar is dissolved in a solution. The most common scale of numbers on a hydrometer is known as specific gravity. Pure water at a temperature of 68° F (20° C) has a specific gravity of 1.000. Adding sugar makes the density of the solution—and therefore the specific gravity—rise. When this occurs, the hydrometer floats higher in the solution, changing where its scale will be read.

Once the must is prepared, we read its specific gravity before adding the yeast and starting fermentation. The gravity of your must before it ferments is called the original gravity, or O.G. or sometimes "starting gravity." Typical mead original gravities range from about 1.060 to 1.120, with some going beyond these norms.

There are other scales of dissolved sugar concentration, such as Balling, Brix, and Plato. These scales reflect the exact same properties with different numerical values.

Plastic fermenter. To use the procedure I recommend for your first mead and other early recipes, you will need a plastic fermentation bucket. Plastic fermenters come in sizes from 5 to 8 gallons (19 to 30.5 L), and come with lids fitted to create an airtight seal. Buy a large one, and you'll have room for fruit (I know you'll be making a mead with fruit soon enough). There is a hole on the top for a fermentation lock as discussed below.

Because the plastic fermenter is a cylinder with a large round lid you can remove, it is both easy and safe to work with. Plastic fermenters won't break (or melt) when filled with hot liquid. They are also very handy to have around at bottling time; they will serve as ideal vessels into which you can decant your fermented mead before bottling. Plastic fermenters also make great receptacles for sanitizing such peripherals as the racking cane, hoses, fermentation locks, and rubber stoppers.

The downside of plastic bucket-style fermenters are 1) the potential for bacterial growth in their scratched interiors, and 2) their geometry. The large surface area of the mead that is exposed to air creates a higher risk of oxidation under some circumstances. Despite these limitations, they are great for the vigorous primary fermentation using the technique I'll be describing.

Glass carboy. Carboys are the large 5- to 10-gallon glass bottles once familiar to everyone as bottled water bottles. These days, plastic is replacing glass in the water cooler business, but the old glass carboys are perfect for making beer, wine, and mead.

The shape and volume of 5-gallon glass carboys are ideal for 5-gallon batches. When filled, they leave a very small surface area of must or mead open to the air, thus reducing the risk of oxidation. They do not scratch easily and so with a little care, will last forever.

Remember to be careful with your carboy. A dropped carboy can propel shards and chunks of broken glass toward arms and legs at great speed and with tremendous force. Use plastic crates or other handling aids to reduce the risk of dropped or broken carboys. Rubber-coated carboy handles are cheap and convenient, too. Just remember to use two hands when handling a full carboy. Also, avoid handling one with wet hands, and wear a sturdy pair of shoes, just in case.

Fermentation locks. Fermentation locks provide the barrier that prevents contaminating bacteria or wild yeast from entering your fermenter and your mead. They are simple mechanical devices that allow the carbon dioxide to escape from your actively fermenting mead while sealing out the external environs.

Fermentation locks take a variety of shapes and sizes, but all perform the same function. They use a liquid, like water or—as I prefer—cheap 80 proof vodka, as a seal. The carbon dioxide produced by the fermentation builds up pressure below the barrier, and eventually the pressure forces the gas to bubble through the fermentation lock. The vodka keeps everything sanitary, but needs refilling more often than water, as alcohol will evaporate more quickly. Don't use 190 proof spirits; they will damage the plastic.

Fermentation locks do not need to be expensive or pretty to do the job; the cheapest plastic fermentation lock will work just as well as its blown glass counterpart. You can create your own fermentation lock by inserting a hose into the rubber stopper in your fermentation vessel and placing the other end into a sanitized jar filled with fluid. This method is even preferable to commercial locks when you are making a large batch or have a particularly vigorous fermentation. Your locks just need to be clean and full of sanitary liquid, and they will do the job.

Drilled rubber stoppers. A drilled rubber stopper is needed to join your fermenter with the fermentation lock. The stopper goes in the fermenter and the fermentation lock into the hole in the stopper. Buy two stoppers, one for your plastic fermenter and one for the carboy. Stoppers No. 6 through 7 will work with 5-gallon carboys; consult the shop where you buy your plastic fermenter about the proper size for that vessel.

Siphon hose. Siphon hoses are simply sections of clear, food-grade vinyl tubing. They can be obtained from brewing and winemaking supply stores, but also may be obtained (and sometimes at better prices) from hardware and home supply stores. The most common diameters used in mead and winemaking are 5⁄16 inch and 3⁄8 inch inner diameter (ID). You will need sections about 6 feet long, and should plan on replacing your hoses regularly, probably every six months or so.

Racking cane. Siphoning without a racking cane is possible, but difficult. A racking cane is a piece of clear, hard plastic food-grade tubing, straight or bent at an angle near one end. Your siphon hose fits snugly over the end, and the cane is lowered into the mead being racked, to provide you control over siphoning. This allows you to avoid the sediment pack or fruit residue, which will keep the hoses free of blockage and maximize the clarity of the siphoned mead. Most racking canes come with a formed plastic cap on the bottom to keep the opening off of the sediment at the bottom of your fermenter. You may or may not find the cap helpful.

Bleach or sanitizer. To sanitize your meadmaking equipment before you start, you'll need some kind of sanitizer. Ordinary household bleach (unscented) that you get at the grocery store will work fine. Otherwise, your home wine or brew shop will most likely offer several alternatives for sanitizing equipment, and you can select and use one of those.

OK, that's about it for the shopping list. Get these items and ingredients procured and you'll be ready to actually make your mead. In the meantime, you can read ahead to start thinking about what comes next.

Musting About

Once you have assembled all the ingredients and supplies discussed in the previous chapter, you are ready to make mead. More accurately, you are ready to prepare your must—the honey-infused liquid that the yeast will feed on to produce the alcoholic beverage that you want as a finished product. The recipe and procedures here will make a medium-sweet, still mead that will highlight the floral character of the honey. For review and easy reference, here's the recipe for the must we'll be preparing:

Medium Sweet Orange Blossom Mead

Recipe for 5 gallons

15	**lbs. (5 qts.) (6.82 kg) orange blossom honey**
4	**gals. water (15.14 L) (3 gals. chilled to refrigerator temperature)**
2	**tsp. (9.9 mL) yeast nutrient**
1	**tsp. (4.9 mL) yeast energizer**
2	**packets (10 g) Lalvin 71b-1122 yeast or suitable alternative**

Note: 5 grams of Lalvin Fermaid can be used in place of nutrient and energizer

The equipment you've acquired will be used to prepare the must by gently heating it. We do this to sanitize it, knocking out the many organisms that occur naturally in all food products. By doing this, we can rest assured that our winemaking yeast will have the must to itself during fermentation—and that makes for good-tasting mead.

Generally, meadmaking is pretty quick, but for this first effort, give yourself a whole morning, afternoon, or evening to get everything done. Overall, you'll complete six basic steps to begin a mead:

1) Sanitize your equipment
2) Heat the must
3) Chill the must
4) Rehydrate the yeast
5) Pitch the yeast in the must
6) Oxygenate the must

Please read all of these six steps before you get started. Some steps, like one of those trick tests you got hit with in school, can send you back to the beginning to try to redo or undo steps you would have known about if you had read all of the directions first. Trust me. Read it all. Then get started.

1) Sanitize your equipment

Before you get started, make sure all of your meadmaking gear is clean. Even if it is brand new, a quick wash with dish soap followed by a good rinsing is a good idea.

Next, you'll need to sanitize all of the utensils and items that will come in contact with your must. That includes your fermenter, a large and small spoon, thermometer, fermentation locks, stoppers, ladle, and a small 1- to 2-cup dish for your yeast.

If you are using bleach, fill your plastic fermenter with hot tap water and add about 2 fluid ounces of bleach, and then soak all the equipment in this sanitizer bath for at least 20 minutes. When you remove things from this bath, you can rinse them once with cold tap water or simply lay them on clean paper towels to dry until they are needed.

If you have selected a different sanitizer, follow the directions provided on the package.

2) Heat the must

If your honey is crystallized, immerse it in a sink of warm-to-hot water to liquefy it enough to get it out of the container. Now put the unchilled gallon of water in your stock pot and bring it to a vigorous boil for 10 minutes. Take the pot off the heat (you don't want to scorch your honey), add the yeast nutrient and energizer, and pour in the honey. The honey will sink to the bottom; don't stir it quite yet. Wearing a kitchen mitt or other protective hand gear, grab your honey containers, and ladle some of the hot water into them until they are about one-third full. Put the lids back on and shake them to dissolve the honey still clinging to the sides and bottom. Be careful to open the jars upright, and use caution to open the lids slowly: The now-heated air in the jar will have expanded. Carefully add that liquid to the pot. Repeat that until you have recovered as much of the honey as you can, and then stir the pot carefully until the honey and water mix into a uniform solution.

Using your thermometer, get a temperature reading on your must. It should be around 160° F (71° C). It may be a little above or below that. As long as it is above 150° F (66° C), you're fine. You want to keep it there for about 10 minutes before we proceed to the cooling procedure. If your mixture is between 130° F and 150° F (54° C to 66° C), which may occur at higher altitudes, let it sit at least 20 to 25 minutes.

Please be very careful when you move this pot of hot honey water around. Again, I speak from experience. This stuff will burn fingers, arms, and feet both efficiently and effectively. It doesn't cool down quickly or come off easily at all. And it will make an astounding mess out of your kitchen or laundry room if dropped.

3) Chill the must

While the hot must is sitting, empty the sanitizer from your plastic fermenter, rinse it thoroughly and get it positioned to receive your must. With this done, you are ready to add the three gallons of cold water from the refrigerator to the fermenter. You'll also want to make sure you have your clean, sanitized large spoon nearby, and your fermentation locks and vodka at hand.

After the hot must has finished its 10-minute sanitizing period, you are ready to carefully pour it into the fermenter that is now about half-full of cold water. Once you do this, stir the mixture with your sanitized spoon. Now, you'll want to monitor the temperature of the must, so that you know when to add the yeast mixture. Place your floating thermometer in the mix or take a temperature reading, so you know where you stand.

4) Rehydrate the yeast

To prepare the yeast for its work, it is best to rehydrate it before use. It has been dormant in a dry package for a while, and you want to get it used to being wet again before you put it to work on the sugar in your mead.

To do this, fill your sanitized little dish with the recommended amount of water at around 100° F (38° C). Manufacturers' recommendations run from 95° F to 109° F (35° C to 43° C). Add the yeast and let it sit for 15 minutes to become acclimated to its new environs. Then, using your small sanitized spoon, stir it thoroughly to suspend the yeast.

5) Pitch the yeast

Once the yeast is ready, you'll want to make sure that the must has cooled sufficiently before adding it. You'll want the must below 80° F (27° C) before the yeast is added.

Give the yeast a quick stir with the small spoon to make sure it is well mixed, and then pour it right into the center of the must in the fermenter.

6) Oxygenate the must

The yeast in your must needs oxygen to reproduce quickly and get a healthy start. To accomplish this, you'll stir your must vigorously with the big spoon for five minutes. There are other ways to do this—you can use an electric beater if properly cleaned and sanitized first, and I have gone so far as to run a portion of my must through a blender. The main point is that if air gets into the must, it's a winner.

Before you seal the fermenter, you'll want to determine the original specific gravity. Grab your hydrometer, and carefully set it into your must. Spin it to make sure that it is floating freely in the must. With your eye as close to surface level as you can get, read the gravity markings on the side of the hydrometer right at the surface of the liquid, and record the reading. It should be between 1.112 and 1.128. Remove the hydrometer and wash it well before storage.

With the stirring done, you can attach the lid to the fermenter. Be sure to snap it down all around so that there won't be any leaks. Now, before you attach the fermentation lock, you'll want to move the fermenter to a good location for fermentation. Ideally this will be someplace out of the way where the mead can reside for several weeks while fermentation runs its course. The temperature should be cool for the indoors, but not too cool—temperatures in the range from 60° F to 75° F (16° C to 24° C) would be great. The basement is a popular choice, if you have one. A nice closet on the cool side of your abode will work just as well. A spare bedroom or a corner of the dining room can serve just as well if that works best for you.

Now, once the must-filled fermenter has found a home, you are ready to affix your fermentation lock and fill it with liquid. One trick on rubber stoppers: A dab of water or glycerin will make the insertion of your fermentation lock into the stopper easier.

Don't use anything in your fermentation lock that you are worried about having in your mead; as the temperature stabilizes between the liquid and air in the fermenter and the room, or if you lift a full plastic fermenter fitted with an airlock, a small amount of the liquid in your lock may be sucked back into your must. Don't be too alarmed about that, but be sure to keep enough liquid in the fermentation lock to provide a proper barrier—many of the devices have a line on them to indicate the proper fill level.

OK, once you have done this, everything is done except for cleanup of your equipment and your meadmaking area. Get that done, and relax for a bit before reading the next part, which will tell you all about fermentation and racking before getting into the final step of bottling.

Fermentation, Racking, and Bottling

When you add the yeast to your fermenter, wonderful things begin to happen inside. The yeast gobble up all the oxygen you stirred in, grab a bunch of the nutrients you added to the must and then reproduce until their numbers are approximately five times what you originally put in the fermenter. Then, assuming all goes well, they begin a robust fermentation of all that sugar that the honey provides.

During fermentation, yeast convert sugar into carbon dioxide and alcohol. When this is happening, you'll see bubbles of carbon dioxide escaping through the fermentation lock. In most cases, you should see this starting to occur about 24 hours after you add the yeast. If it doesn't happen that quickly, don't worry, it will most likely kick in after a few days, and everything will be fine.

About two weeks after you first notice the bubbling in your fermentation lock, it will begin to slow down pretty substantially. At this point, your yeast will have done the yeoman's share of its work, and it will be time to rack your mead into a new vessel for additional aging.

Racking

Racking is the process of transferring mead from one fermenter or carboy to another. We rack to get the mead off of the spent yeast, to separate mead from fruits or other adjuncts, and to aid in clarification.

Before racking, you'll need to sanitize your empty carboy and its stopper plus your siphon hose and racking cane with sanitizing solution. Next you'll need to position both the fermenter and the carboy to let gravity do the work of moving your mead. To do this, you'll need to have the full fermenter of mead above the empty carboy. That means putting the carboy on the floor with the fermenter on a chair or a couple of milk crates or some similarly sturdy platform. When you are ready to go, place a small pan or bucket right next to the empty carboy. Put your hydrometer flask or tube next to the pan. Now remove the lid from your full fermenter.

If you haven't already done so, attach the hose to the racking cane, and fill the siphon hose/cane completely with tap water. You'll want to coil the hose to ensure that it does not come into contact with unsanitized surfaces. With the water running to keep the hose and cane full, lift both ends to the same height, pull them away from the faucet, and fold over the hose end to crimp it. Keeping the hose firmly crimped, put the cane into the full fermenter. Use a clothespin or racking cane clamp to hold the bottom of the cane off the bottom of the fermenter and clear of the yeast cake. Lower/uncoil the hose down to the pan. Release the end and let the fluid flow until the water is flushed out, and you see mead starting to flow into the pan. Quickly fill your hydrometer tube before you start to fill the carboy. Crimp the hose, then move the end into the empty carboy. From here gravity will do the work of moving the mead from the fermenter to the carboy. During racking, you will want to keep an eye on the bottom of the racking cane to keep it from siphoning the yeast and sediment from the bottom of your full fermenter. Make sure that the hose end is below the surface of the liquid in the carboy, to avoid splashing and aerating the liquid. Cease racking when the mead in the cane and hose begin to become cloudy.

Measure the specific gravity with your hydrometer. At this point, your must should have fallen to about 1.030 or less. If you had a very vigorous fermentation, it may be as low as 1.010. If it is above that range, though, there is no real need for concern. Patience, yes. Concern, no.

Place a fermentation lock on your new fermenter, and return your mead to its cool dry place. Be sure to clean the now-empty fermenter and all the gear you used, so they'll be ready to use the next time you need them.

Bottling

When your mead has cleared in the carboy, and you have not seen signs of fermentation for two weeks, you are ready to bottle. I am generally not too impatient about bottling, because mead will take at least six to nine months of aging before it hits peak drinkability.

Bottling is the most satisfying of all of the steps in meadmaking. It will take you about two hours, assuming you have clean bottles to start with, don't have small children present, don't get phone calls, and generally keep the process moving along.

One of the decisions you will make about every batch of mead is whether to make it sparkling (carbonated) or still (non-carbonated). Commercial meads tend to be still, but one of the beauties of making your own is that you can decide what you want the finished product to be. For this first batch, I recommend that you make a still mead, but in the future if you decide to make sparkling mead, you'll add some carefully measured additional sugar before bottling. For details on this, see "Beyond the Basics."

Bottling essentials: Phil's Philler, crown caps, double-lever capper, small bottle brush. Long necked bottles are sturdy vessels, and clear bottles make color and clarity apparent.

Bottling Equipment

Several of the items you already have will be used again for bottling, but you'll need some new stuff as well. Here's what you'll want to make sure to have:

Bottle filler
Bottle capper
Bottle caps
Bottle washing brush or jet bottle washer
Bottles

Bottle filler. You can fill bottles without a filler, too, but you will want one eventually. You could just use a pair of hemostats to clamp off your siphon hose, but that will get old quickly. You can fold it like a kid with a garden hose, but you'll end up dripping mead all over. If you buy a bottle filler early, you will be happier, believe me. Fillers stop the flow of mead into your bottles as you fill them. They use a valve to cut off the flow, closed either by spring or gravity. The metal, gravity-driven systems, like Phil's Philler, are reliable and easier on your mead. They have a lower flow rate and dispense from the bottom and not the sides; in so doing, they don't splash the mead around as much, and that reduces the risk of oxidation.

Bottle capper. The easiest and most economical closures for bottling are crown caps. They come uncrimped and require a bottle capper to crimp them onto the top of the bottle. Cappers cost more than most other meadmaking equipment, and there are several different models to chose from, so let's take a minute to understand the features and tradeoffs.

The two styles of cappers are bench cappers and lever cappers, also known as two-handled cappers. Bench cappers sit on a bench, table, or floor, and press the cap down onto the bottle using a single handle. Lever cappers press the cap onto the bottle by grasping the larger rim (about ¾ inch below the lip of the bottle) with two or three claws and squeezing the cap down. Both models get the job done, and lever cappers are less expensive. Bench cappers are easier to use in general, but only when the bottles you are using are uniform in size. If your bottles are a melange, a lever capper can be quicker. Lever cappers can be a bit testy when using bottles with larger diameter necks. You need to use care when exerting any amount of force with a glass bottle—breakage wastes mead and can be hazardous.

Bottle brush or high-pressure (jet) bottle washer. Unless you are buying new bottles from the home winemaking or brewing store, you'll probably need some help cleaning out the bottles you use. One approach is a suitably sized brush. Another is the so-called "jet" washer. These gizmos attach to your wash basin spigot and channel the flow into a small-diameter copper pipe with a valve. A bottle is placed upside down over the pipe and pressed down to open the valve. A jet of water blasts into the bottle, cleaning or rinsing the bottle quickly and efficiently. Irreplaceable.

Do not substitute a bottle washer for elbow grease when attacking a case of really dirty bottles, though. No amount of jet pressure will remove the truly grungy stuff from a bottle that was never rinsed and has been sitting, uncared for, for the last seven months. For that job, you will want a bottle brush.

Bottles. A 5-gallon batch of mead will fill about 53 12-ounce bottles. Alternately, it will fill about 25 American Champagne-style wine bottles (they hold 750 ml or a little more than 25 ounces). You can purchase new bottles at the homebrew or home winemaking store, or you can collect empty bottles from a variety of sources for free. If you collect bottles, you'll need to pay attention to a few issues. When it comes to beer bottles, not just any bottle will do. You'll want strong bottles that are intended for re-use, not thin bottles that were never intended to be refilled. Personally, I like to use longneck beer bottles that do not have twistoff cap threads. True longnecks are sturdy bottles. Most twistoff bottles will stand refilling and mild abuse, but they may not be strong enough to stand the pressure of carbonation levels that can build up in a sparkling mead.

Good American sparkling wine bottles are terrific for meads; they will accept a crown cap and can easily withstand the pressures that build up in a sparkling mead. When it comes to sparkling wine bottles, you need to be aware that European bottles require different-sized crowns from those used on American bottles. Since you'll be working with American crowns, you have to make sure you get American bottles. Cases of good sparkling wine bottles can frequently be procured at restaurants and banquet halls. If you phone ahead and ask politely, large numbers of bottles may be available—in their boxes, no less, especially after weekends or big holidays. Rinse them thoroughly when you get them home.

You can collect beer bottles yourself, if you drink beer. Make life easy for yourself: Rinse each of the bottles two or three times after drinking the beer, and they will be ready to sanitize and use when your mead is ready to bottle. Or make life hard: Leave that little bit of beer in the bottle, and end up having to scrub out 55 nasty, hard, black, furry growths until the wee hours of the morning when you go to bottle. Go ahead. We have all done it. It'll be good for you. On the other hand, I always say, "A smart person learns from his mistakes, but a truly wise person learns from the mistakes of others."

Bottling Procedures

OK, once you have all the desired equipment and a suitable set of clean bottles, you are ready for a bottling session. Start by sanitizing all of your bottles in a utility basin or bathtub, using recommended amounts of sanitizer and the warmest water you can tolerate. Rinse the bottles very thoroughly, and drip dry them as completely as is practical. If you are using wine bottles, you might want to have one smaller bottle on hand for the last bit of mead.

You'll also need to sanitize your racking cane and siphon hose, your bottle filler, caps, and a large container from which to bottle—a plastic fermenter will work beautifully for this purpose. You'll also need that small pan or bucket you used to help start your siphon while racking.

If you are bottling on the floor or a workbench, put down a clean, large, old towel over which to work. This will be much appreciated at cleanup time. Arrange all of your bottles there, along with your caps and capper. Move your full fermenter of mead to a position from which to siphon. To keep the lifting of full fermenters to a minimum, I put the full one on my washing machine, the empty one on a chair or milk crate below, and the bottles on the floor. Lift a full fermenter once, and let gravity do the rest. Siphon your mead into your plastic fermenter (or other racking container) as with racking. Along the way, collect a sample of the mead so you can test the specific gravity—and also taste the stuff to see how it is turning out. Don't be discouraged if the mead doesn't taste like you had hoped at this point. Unless you are possessed of some meadmaking magic, it shouldn't. It will improve dramatically with aging.

Now place your bottle filler on the end of your siphon hose (the other end from the racking cane) and again fill it with water by placing the end of the racking cane under the faucet and holding the filler open. Once more, begin your siphon by putting the bottle filler in the pan to flush the water from your hose, and then begin filling the bottles. Some in the brewing and meadmaking community say you should place caps loosely on the bottles as they are filled, so that the carbon dioxide being released from the mead will fill the airspace and prevent oxidation. The merit of that practice is debatable, but if it suits you, try it.

When the bottles are filled, use the capper to crimp the caps on tightly. In addition, you'll want to label your work. Remember that mead keeps for many years, so you'll want some system that will help you identify bottles well into the future. At a minimum, I would recommend labeling the cases or six-packs of bottles with some information as to their content. Better yet, label each individual bottle on the cap. Small round stick-on labels from an office-supply store work nicely on the caps. If you use a code of some sort, make sure that it isn't so abbreviated that you can't decipher what is in these bottles if they stick around for five or six years. Batch numbers that correlate with a brewing journal are effective (more on this in the next chapter), and I also recommend putting the bottling date on each bottle.

chapter four
BEYOND THE BASICS

If you are a beginning meadmaker and have made your first batch, congratulations. You could go on making delicious mead that way for the rest of your days. On the other hand, if you are like most hobbyists, you will soon begin to look for ways to improve your efforts. If you are an experienced brewer or meadmaker, I'm sure you know what I mean. Some folks get compulsive, while others are content to tinker at the edges with equipment and techniques that yield maximum results for minimum efforts.

This chapter will cover techniques, equipment, and additives that should help you make better-quality mead easily and consistently. Some will allow you to explore new territory—working with fruit or spices. But let's start with two practices that you will be well served to nurture: recordkeeping and sanitation.

YOUR JOURNAL

It is a good idea to document your meadmaking exploits. Keeping a journal as a reference will help tremendously in your efforts to improve and tinker with your mead. A three-ring binder or spiral notebook is fine, but may get a bit dog-eared after a few years. Computers work well but don't take too kindly to being used with hands sticky with honey solution or dyed crimson with fruit. Pick what works best for you, but stick with it. My memory doesn't work well enough to remember nuances of spicing or acid balance when re-creating a mead five years hence. If yours does, more power to you. But I like a paper backup.

SANITIZERS AND SANITATION

If you are going to make great mead (and that *is* the goal of this book), cleanliness is next to godliness. Your mead needs every chance to get off to a good start without competition with bacteria or wild yeast. There are lots of things that can mess up a batch of mead. Being too clean is not one of them. For those who have just made their first batch, especially, you will now need to become vigilant about cleanliness. Your brand-new meadmaking equipment was free of any of the sugary residues that can harbor bacteria. Now that it has been exposed to the sweet must, you will need to make every effort to ensure that it is as free of contaminants as you can get it.

In a larger sense, your sanitation concerns occur on two fronts: eliminating contaminants from all of your meadmaking equipment, and eliminating contaminants from your must. The means of sanitizing anything come down to two central methodologies: killing contaminants through the use of 1) chemical sanitizers or 2) heat. Sanitizers kill bacteria and wild yeast cells in solutions or on surfaces through exposure to toxins: chlorine, iodine, and sulfur compounds. Both have their advantages and disadvantages. First off, let's get our gear clean.

Sanitizing Your Meadmaking Equipment

The first step is to remove the visible, physical dirt and other deposits from your gear. Clean everything that will come in contact with your unfermented mead, and clean it thoroughly. That means fermenters, fermentation locks, stoppers, hoses . . . everything. Spare no sweat here. Use soft cloths, the hottest water you can stand, a good strong dish soap, and a hot rinse. Now you are ready to sanitize.

The most commonly used liquid equipment sanitizers in homebrewing, mead-, and winemaking are bleach and iodophor.

Bleach is a solution of sodium hypochlorite (NaOCl) and water. It is available in concentrations of 5.25% ("regular" bleach) and 6% ("ultra" or "concentrated" bleach). To be effective, the concentration of available chlorine in your sanitizing solution should be 100 to 200 parts per million. The regular stuff will work fine. One tablespoon per gallon (5 tbsp./5 gal.) will yield 200 ppm of available chlorine. The standard recipe of ¼ cup (4 tbsp.) in 5 gallons will sanitize very adequately. Wash everything thoroughly with dish soap and water first, rinse well and expose to the bleach solution for 15 minutes or longer. Rinse with warm-to-hot water until no scent of bleach can be detected. Remember that sodium hypochlorite is corrosive to metals, so don't leave spoons or other metal objects in a bleach bath for longer than 15 minutes.

Of the two, though, iodophor gets my nod for sanitizing equipment for a few good reasons. It is a powerful surfactant and requires very minimal amounts to be effective. Iodophor at a concentration of 12.5 to 25 ppm will be effective against microbes and can be used on meadmaking equipment without rinsing. Use it at the dilutions directed on the container. Iodophor will not corrode metal. Lastly, and perhaps most importantly, it introduces no additional chlorine to our freshwater ecosystems.

There are also a number of commercially produced sanitizing compounds, like Five Star Chemical's STAR SAN, which will sanitize adequately. STAR SAN is an acid-based sanitizer that kills microorganisms with a blend of phosphoric acid and dodecylbenzenesulfonic acid. When used at a concentration of 200 ppm of dodecylbenzenesulfonic acid (1 ounce in 5 gallons), STAR SAN will sanitize in about two minutes without need of rinsing. Five Star also produces a number of acid and alkaline cleaning products that will be of service to advanced or commercial meadmakers. Clean in Place (CIP) products sanitize large pieces of equipment that cannot be moved easily, such as converted stainless steel kegs used as fermenters. CIP products are a godsend to those who have stepped up the scale of their meadmaking exploits.

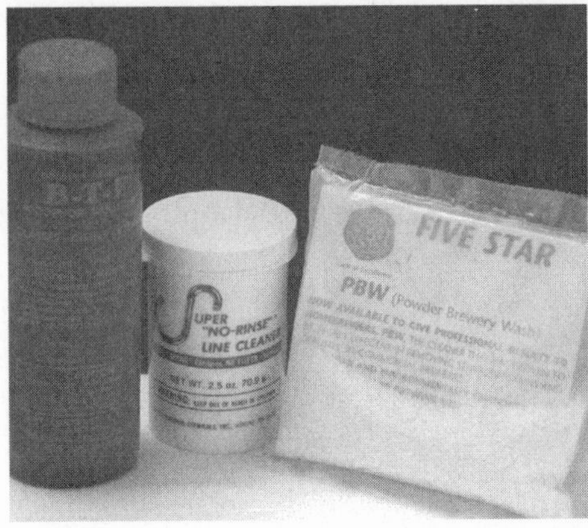

Sanitation aids: Iodophor for vessels and implements, line cleaner to clean stubborn racking canes and tubing, and PBW for difficult cleaning tasks.

Iodophor and the other cleaning agents can be purchased at any brewing or winemaking supply shop and through several mail order and on-line outlets.

Sinks, washtubs, large bowls, plastic fermenters, and 5-gallon plastic buckets are all fine places for soaking equipment in sanitizer. Make sure they are clean and free from any residues.

Remember, though, no matter which contact sanitizer you choose, you still have to get all of your meadmaking equipment fundamentally clean before sanitizing. No amount of sanitizer can overcome basic breaches of cleanliness. Sanitizer does not replace elbow grease.

Now that we've beaten every germ on our equipment into submission, let's have a look at our options for sanitizing our must.

Heat

The preponderance of meadmaking recipes dating from before the Renaissance right up to the present call for some heating of the must. Most call for boiling the honey with either part or all of the water in the recipe, with the added step of skimming off the foam that will accumulate at the surface of the mixture. Much of that would have been unwanted components of the hive: honeycomb and cappings, dead bees and bee parts, even straw or propolis from the hive (see "History"). Our honey today is not subject to such crudities. To top it off, they attained their desired gravity levels by adding honey "until an egge swim on it." Heaven knows what levels and types of infection awaited therein.

Heating will, in fact, kill off the organisms that might compromise your mead. The main threat to your must is wild yeast, which can have unpredictable effects on the quality of your finished mead. Dr. Jonathan White of the United States Department of Agriculture (retired) did a tremendous amount of research on honey and concluded that the amount of heat exposure needed to kill off the wild yeast in honey is as little as five minutes at 150° F (66° C), or about 22 minutes at 140° F (60° C). I recommend the lower and slower approach. The aromatic compounds in honey become more volatile at higher temperatures. Those aromatics will account for much of the appeal of your mead, and you want to preserve them as much as possible. Another reason not to boil is that I am also not much for removing the foam. The foam is composed largely of protein compounds, and they contain nitrogen that your mead will need to ferment strongly.

The upside of heating is that it is quick and easy and doesn't require any additional chemicals. If you chill the must, you can pitch yeast immediately and get the fermentation under way quickly. The downside is handling heated liquid and the possible loss of precious aroma and flavor compounds.

Sulfite

The most popular chemical compound for must sanitation in use today is potassium metabisulfite ($K_2S_2O_5$), shortened alternately to Meta or Sulfite. Potassium metabisulfite is the active compound in Campden tablets. Sulfites are used regularly to treat the must in both commercial and home winemaking. They are used at the point at which the grapes are crushed or juiced at a rate of about 50 parts per million (one Campden tablet per gallon) in red wines and 100 ppm (two tablets/gal.) in white wines. The crushed grapes or juice are allowed to set for 24 hours before yeast is pitched. In the most comprehensive regime, sulfites are dosed again at the first racking, at 50 ppm, and yet again at bottling at the lower rate of 25-30 ppm.

The same procedure is used by many meadmakers when the must of honey and water is mixed. Traditional meads should be sulfited at about 50 parts per million (one Campden tablet per gallon). If you have concerns about fruit or other ingredients in your must, sulfiting at the higher rate of 100 ppm will not adversely affect your mead. The need for the successive sulfiting steps is debatable. Some contend that late-stage sulfiting serves as a remediation or prophylaxis against problems that could have been prevented with stringent control of sanitation.

In their favor, sulfiting procedures virtually ensure that the mead will have tremendous stability against biological spoilage hazards, even over prolonged aging times. Sulfiting requires no ungainly handling of hot must, and eliminates the use of one more piece of equipment, which cuts down on cleanup. On the other hand, sulfites can bleach the color out of some fruits and berries. Finally, to those who prefer a totally natural approach, sulfites are a chemical additive that is not absolutely necessary. A growing body of winemaking literature questions the entire sulfiting practice, both in the interest of purity and because sulfites can cause reactions in asthmatics.

All that said, I have to come clean (nyuk, nyuk) on my own must sanitation procedures. I have not heated or boiled my must for several years now, nor do I use sulfites in my musts. In all that time, I have not produced one batch that I would categorize as infected or otherwise adversely affected. I religiously sanitize anything that will come in contact with the must and the fermented mead. It just makes sense to me that the complex blend of compounds that make fresh honey so alluring are compromised by the abusive practices of boiling or heating.

I also believe that the natural antibiotic qualities of honey prevent bacterial infection (see "Honey"), and that most of the wild yeast strains that are present in honey cannot take root in a must with the specific gravities that meadmaking dictates. Lastly, pitching a large population of healthy, thriving, and active yeast cells will overwhelm the possibility of any infection getting off the ground, *given that good sanitation procedures are adhered to stringently* for all implements, instruments, and vessels.

The No-Heat Method

Here, then, is the procedure I have been using to prepare a batch of must. I have completed preparing a batch of must in an hour and fifteen minutes using this method, sanitation and cleanup included. The recipe and sanitation processes remain unchanged. Do not misinterpret the relatively laissez-faire approach of this method as condoning inadequate cleanliness with respect to your equipment.

You can use the same recipe as we used for our previous batch. The basic steps in the no-heat method are:

1) Sanitize your equipment.
2) Mix the honey and water.
3) Rehydrate the yeast.
4) Pitch the yeast.
5) Oxygenate the must.

Start with Step 1, and sanitize a fermenter (glass or plastic), thermometer, a large spoon, and a 16-ounce measuring cup for rehydrating the yeast. A sanitized spatula with a long handle can help get all of the honey out of its container(s).

Next, you will need to mix up your must. Put about 3 gallons of tap water at room temperature into your fermenter. Dissolve the yeast energizer and nutrient in the water. Add your honey to the water, and mix and splash thoroughly. Add hot or cold water to make sure your mixture is within 5 degrees of ambient room temperature.

Rehydrate your yeast by adding the two packets of yeast to half a cup of water at 104° F to 109° F (40° C to 42° C) and allow it to stand 15 minutes (and no longer). Stir it thoroughly, and pitch it into your prepared must.

Now, oxygenate your must to the best of your abilities. Stir it, splash it, beat it, blend it, swirl in the carboy. Add whatever additional water is needed to bring your batch size up to 5 gallons. Fit the fermenter with an airlock, and place it in a cool, dark place.

Making a Sparkling Mead

Sparkling meads are a real treat. The combination of effervescence, honey aroma, flavor, and a light sweetness can make for a heady experience. And it is not all that hard.

Typical pressure levels in beers run about two atmospheres (twice the level of pressure in the airspace of the bottle than normal pressure at room temperature). Champagnes and other sparkling wines are carbonated to pressures as high as four atmospheres. That requires a very solid bottle, a reliable closure, and another trick or two to present a drinkable product to the consumer.

The most basic process of carbonating a mead is through the addition of a small amount of sugar—"priming" sugar—to the batch just before bottling. One-half cup of honey, or ¾ cup of corn sugar, dissolved in 16 ounces of boiling water, will deliver about two atmospheres of carbonated pressure. The sugar must be stirred into the mead just before bottling, and the bottles should be capped as indicated in "Getting Started." The small amount of yeast remaining in the mead will consume the sugar, produce a small amount of carbon dioxide and alcohol, and yield a mead with a decided sparkle.

Your mead will take at least a week, and generally more like a month, to become carbonated. If you have aged your mead for a prolonged period—more than six months—it is a good idea to add a small amount of fresh yeast to ensure that you will have strong cells to complete the carbonation. I have used half a package of yeast, rehydrated according to package instructions. Use the same strain used to ferment the mead. If you use a different strain with a higher alcohol tolerance, you run the risk of overcarbonating, and that can mean exploding bottles. Sparkling mead can be served easily and attractively (chilled), by decanting carefully off the sediment of spent yeast cells in one smooth pour, stopping when the sediment moves toward the neck of the bottle.

You can produce higher carbonation levels by using more priming sugar, but that will present another problem. More sugar will create more yeast sediment. The CO_2 at higher pressure levels will vent quickly when the bottle is opened, as with Champagne or soda. The turbulence will rouse that sediment from the bottom of the bottle into your mead, which will not be picturesque when it is served.

The technique called *Methode Champenoise* is used in the production of bottle-carbonated sparkling wines in France. When used elsewhere, the technique is called *Methode Traditionelle.* It involves inverting the bottles and repeatedly turning them (riddling) to create a yeast plug in the neck of the bottle. The plug is then frozen and then the bottle is quickly opened, the plug removed, some dissolved sugar added, and the bottle resealed. It takes two people to perform correctly. It is not a task to be taken lightly, and will take some practice (read: you'll mess up a few bottles) to master. If you are genuinely interested, get a good set of instructions before giving this a shot. The process is very well explained in Philip Wagner's *Grapes Into Wine.*

Equipment

All right already, enough about technique. I'm a paraphernaliac. Let's talk about gear.

Immersion or Counterflow Wort Chiller

The term "wort" means unfermented beer. Wort chillers are used primarily in brewing, but meadmakers using heat pasteurization require the function they perform, as well. You can reduce the temperature of your hot must by: a) immersing a coil of copper tubing in the hot must and running cold water through it (immersion), or, b) running the hot must through a copper coil jacketed with a hose, through which cold water flows in the opposite direction (counterflow). There are some other beautiful counterflow designs out there, using cylinders or baffled hose jackets. All accomplish the same thing. I prefer immersion chillers for the traditional heat-it-up-in-a-pot meadmaking process. They are easier to use and keep clean. Easier is good.

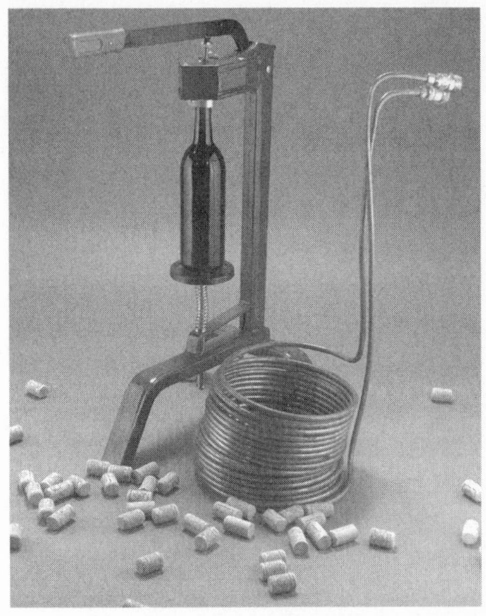

Advanced meadmaking equipment: Copper immersion chiller and corker.

You don't need a chiller right away, and they can cost fifty dollars or more, but they are very useful for a variety of meadmaking practices. You can make an immersion chiller easily, cheaply, and quickly by yourself. You'll need a 50- or 75-foot length of ⅜-inch or ½-inch copper tubing, available at most appliance repair and larger hardware stores. You'll also need a coffee can or other cylinder 6 to 10 inches in diameter, a short garden hose, and two 1-inch hose clamps.

Beginning about 24 inches from the end, carefully wrap the copper tubing in a tightly spaced coil around the coffee can. Be gentle, wrap closely and carefully, and do not crush the tubing. Leave a slightly longer straight section at the other end, as well. Bend the ends upright (perpendicular to the coils) by using a smaller diameter cylinder (smaller can, large coffee mug), and bend them off again at right angles to the vertical about 3 inches from the top.

Cut a small-diameter, 25-foot garden hose in half. Don't carelessly use a razor knife and a lot of brute force and cut the webbing of your thumb deeply and have to go to the clinic for stitches on a holiday and be late for dinner. Not that I ever did that. Just don't do it. You can use a shorter hose, but the extra length will give you some flexibility—you won't have to be right next to your water spigot.

Attach the severed hose ends to the ends of the copper tubing (again, please sever ONLY the garden hose), using the two hose clamps. If you are using smaller diameter copper, you may want to put a 1½-inch sleeve of vinyl tubing over the copper hose first, and then the hose and hose clamp. Tighten the clamps firmly, add water. You are in business.

Funnel

A large food-grade funnel will be necessary to transfer the must from the pot into a carboy, if that will be your primary fermentation vessel. If you do choose to pour through a funnel, chill your mead to ambient temperatures first (the last thing you want is a shattered carboy), and be sure to enlist the assistance of your spouse or other nearby helper, since a spill of diluted honey must will prove to be a very unfortunate circumstance (trust me again here, I speak from experience). Find the largest funnel you can, and make sure the small end will fit down into the neck of the carboy. One-gallon sizes are available from some cooking stores. A large funnel, especially one with a handle on it, will pay for itself the first time you use it.

Muslin Bag, Hop Bag, or Empty Tea Bag

Muslin or nylon bags are very useful when making a melomel. Hop bags are mesh bags used to infuse hops into beer. When you are making mead, the bag can be placed in the fermenter or Cornelius keg, filled with fruit, tied off with string or heavy thread, and left right there for the desired length of time. They make cleanup much easier.

Tea bags can be filled with spices or spice blends and tied off with thread, as well. Spice and tea stores sell small, cloth drawstring bags for this purpose. They make additions more precise, and can similarly be removed when the desired balance is achieved.

Brushes for Carboys and Bottles

A carboy brush is a cylindrical brush with a long handle used to clean carboys. Carboy brushes make the task easier and more thorough than any other method. A right angle bend in the brush makes cleaning the bottom a snap. They are cheap, readily available at brewing or winemaking supply stores, and positively necessary. Get one. Bottle brushes are similar beasts, with smaller diameters and shorter handles. There are smaller sizes for 12-ounce bottles and larger ones for wine bottles. They are a must for removing caked-on residues. You'll want one or more of these, too.

Corker

Corking a bottle of mead is a reward in and of itself. While corks as closures are actually under commercial pressure from newer materials like plastic and twistoff caps in the winemaking industry, there is still something romantic about the sight of your homemade mead tucked safely away behind the closure that we all associate with fine wine. That, I'm sure, is why corked bottles of mead make such nice gifts.

Corkers are not cheap, but they are beautiful machines. Almost all of the manual designs are lever operated. With pressure from the sides, they compress the cork and then push it into the bottle with a plunger. Handheld lever corkers are the least expensive but most difficult to operate. Bench corkers are often fixed to a work surface. Floor corkers sit on the floor and are operated with foot power.

Corks are available in many grades and in lengths from 1¼ inches up to 2 inches. If you intend to age your meads in the bottle for anything longer than a few months, better corks are worth the investment. Corks should be soaked for 60 minutes in a gallon of water treated with two Campden tablets before using. A few drops of glycerin in the bath will lubricate the corks so that they will slip smoothly into the bottle. Drying the bottom of the cork before insertion is a common practice.

Just a few notes on corking practices: Use only wine bottles with a straight neck for cork closures. Some home winemakers reuse corks, but I don't like that practice. Make sure that your corker is driving the cork flush with the lip of the bottle or $\frac{1}{16}$ of an inch below it. Leave the newly corked bottles upright for about 72 hours to allow the compressed air to escape, then lay them on their sides until they are to be consumed. Foil bonnets and wax sealing materials are available from winemaking shops, for those with a flair for presentation.

Larger Vessels and Fermenters

As you advance in your meadmaking, there can be real advantages to scaling up the size of your meadmaking equipment. The ability to boil or heat 5 gallons at a time is very helpful. Taken to an even grander scale, the economies of scale become a blessing. A number of fabricators convert 15.5-gallon stainless steel kegs into kettles and fermenters. If you find you like melomels, a large kettle can make it possible to make two or three different 5-gallon batches with only one round of preparation. Kettles can be outfitted with valves and spigots to simplify the handling of liquid.

If you purchase a converted keg, make sure it has ball valves as opposed to gate valves. Ball valves are simple mechanisms with a few moving parts and a small surface area that will come in contact with your must. Gate valves have a large surface area, a complex valve mechanism, and are inherently very difficult to get completely clean. They are fine for plumbing but don't make the transition to beverage hobbies well at all.

Aside from converted kegs, food service vessels can be great for meadmaking. They can often be obtained at liquidation sales. An industrial-quality stainless steel stockpot can outlive several owners. Restaurant and food service liquidations are also great places to obtain large utensils, strainers, lids, and storage containers.

If you do move to larger batch sizes and containers, you will need to begin working out the logistics of moving the mead around, not the containers. You may need to work with tubing, or valves on fermenters, and let gravity do your work for you. Moving around full 15-gallon vessels is not an option; you'll need to plan ahead.

Propane Burner

Sold for use with large pots as fish boilers or turkey fryers, these high-BTU burners make heating large quantities of liquid quick work. They are available at sporting goods outlets and department stores. They are for outdoor use only. If you are planning on pairing one with a converted keg, make sure you take a few measurements and buy a burner with a grate surface large enough to support the bottom of your keg with some room to spare.

Odds and Ends

There are a few other things that will prove helpful that you probably already have around the house. You'll want a long-handled spoon or two, preferably made of stainless steel or food-grade plastic. A ladle will come in handy, and a skimmer or strainer that can be cleaned thoroughly and sanitized. You'll want a large colander or stainless steel mesh strainer, especially if you are interested in braggots that use barley or other grains. A large slotted spoon is also helpful at times.

I have commented to my wife that it must be a pretty harmless hobby if its enthusiasts are folks whose idea of a real thrill is a new, obscure, food-service grade stainless steel implement. We stand above it with steam from the must clouding our eyeglasses, oohing and aahing. As you get into meadmaking further, you will undoubtedly end up modifying a whole cadre of household and culinary items to meet your meadmaking techniques.

Additives

I'm all for making meads that are free from anything save what nature has given us. But as a practical person, I am also willing to take advantage of the fruits of human intelligence. There are some chemical treatments that can make a positive difference in your meads.

Clarifying Agents

Clarifiers, also known as fining agents, work to remove haze from a mead. Haze can be the result of suspended yeast, particles of protein, or polyphenols in the mead. Clarifiers bind to the proteins and other compounds and precipitate them out. Because they each work differently, no one fining agent can remove every possible cause of haze. In most cases, one agent on its own will provide satisfactory results. For difficult musts, the most effective approach is to use one positively charged agent and follow up later with one negatively charged agent.

Positively Charged Fining Agents: Gelatin, Egg Whites, Isinglass, Sparkolloid®

All of these agents work by bonding with negatively charged substances in the must. Both the gelatin and the albumen in eggs are colloidal in nature, and work by bonding to tannins, which in turn causes other compounds to clump together and drop out of suspension. Sparkolloid® is a form of diatomaceous earth. It requires some preparation before use. Isinglass is derived from the air bladder of fish. In the prepared, bottled form it is easy to use, but is gentler and may not work as effectively on stubborn hazes.

Negatively Charged Agents: Bentonite, Keiselsol (Silicon Dioxide)

Bentonite and keiselsol precipitate out yeast and proteins very effectively due to their negative electrostatic charge. Bentonite is, in fact, dried and powdered clay. It works well, but in my experience may require an additional racking to prevent an unattractive sediment in the bottle.

Pectic Enzyme

Another source of haze in melomels is pectin. Pectin is the compound in fruits that will gel when heated. Some fruits, like peaches and apples, have an abundance of pectin, and some less, but all fruits have enough to cause a problem in your mead. Pectin "sets" at 180° F (82° C). Pectic enzyme, or pectinase, breaks down the long polysaccharide chains that form the pectin. You can use pectic enzyme as a good insurance policy against haze when using heat to pasteurize fruit. It is added with the yeast in melomels.

Citric, Tartaric, Malic Acid, Acid Blend

Acids are used to impart the tart twang on the tongue that balances the residual sugar in your mead. The primary acid in honey is gluconic acid, but you won't find that at your local winemaking supply store. The three most common prepared acids available in dried form are citric, tartaric, and malic. You may also find ascorbic acid, which adds less tartness but is an antioxidant. Citric acid is, of course, the acid produced in citrus fruits. Tartaric acid is the prevalent acid found in grapes. Malic acid provides the tartness in acidic apples: think Granny Smith. Each has its own place. You can find acid blends that contain two or more of these acids in just about any combination. My preference is a blend of tartaric and malic acid, as that is the blend most commonly found in finished wines (see "Post-fermentation Strategies: Adding Acid"). Employ it at bottling rather than in recipe formulation to avoid depressing your pH during the critical early stages of fermentation.

chapter five

YEAST AND FERMENTATION

Fermentation turns your must—that combination of honey, water, and nutrients that you prepare—into mead. When given sufficient water, sugar, and nutrients, as well as the correct temperature and an appropriate pH level and, most importantly, the absence of oxygen, yeast undertake fermentation. This magnificent process requires a complex chain of reactions in which yeast cells metabolize a single larger molecule (sugar) into two molecules each of two simpler compounds: ethanol and carbon dioxide (see Figure 5.1). With an appropriate honey selected and a promising recipe at hand, a healthy fermentation and some packaging are all that lies between you and a great batch of mead.

figure 5.1

THE FERMENTATION EQUATION

$$C_6H_{12}O_6 \rightarrow 2\ C_2H_5OH + 2\ CO_2$$

Fermentation converts sugar (in this case, glucose) into alcohol and carbon dioxide.

Fermentation, however, presents the greatest window of vulnerability to problems that could create off flavors in your mead. If the needs of your yeast population—especially aeration, nutrients, and suitable pH level—are not adequately met, your yeast will become stressed. When that happens, the yeast is prone to produce other unpleasant flavor and aroma compounds: higher alcohols like heptanol and octanol, and phenolic compounds. A healthy fermentation is also known as a "clean" fermentation, because it avoids those undesirables. That is what we will strive for.

From a meadmaker's perspective, fermentation begins as soon as you pitch a yeast starter into your prepared must. But biologically, the fermentation process includes four main components: 1) a lag period; 2) a respiratory (also known as aerobic or reproductive) phase; 3) the actual fermentation phase; and 4) the settling of the yeast, or flocculation. For an optimal fermentation, you want your yeast to move smoothly through all of these phases. For that to happen, you will have to make sure all of the yeast's needs are met at each stage of the game. If yeast population, nutrition, oxygen, and temperature in your must are all within a yeast culture's optimal range, your mead can move through all of these phases in about two weeks, and your finished mead will be free of major flaws or off flavors.

I will begin this chapter by reviewing the four stages of fermentation to see what the yeast is up to in each one. Then, with that background, I'll move on to discuss the important steps that meadmakers can take to ensure a good fermentation and a successful mead. I'll divide those steps into must preparation, yeast selection and preparation, and managing the fermentation.

Lag period. During the lag period, or lag phase, the yeast acclimatizes to its new home. When yeast encounter a growth medium—a must with an acceptable amount of sugar and an appropriate pH—it first prepares itself to replicate. It takes on the necessary nutrients and compounds needed to support the massive changes involved in reproduction. After adjusting to the new temperature and sugar content of the environment, the yeast cells essentially begin to "beef-up" for the task at hand. They thicken their cell walls and set about hoarding the nutrients they will need to make healthy offspring.

To understand the lag phase, it might help to know what the yeast cells are preparing for: reproduction on a massive scale. Let's look at what's coming.

Respiratory phase (aerobic phase). To reach the ideal concentration of yeast in the must, the initial population that you add must multiply several times over. Each yeast will reproduce until it depletes the reserves required for replication. During reproduction, the yeast cell creates a bulge, known as a bud, in its cell wall. The cell replicates its nuclear chromosomal complement, infuses it into the bulge, and finally cleaves the bulged bud, creating an independent new yeast cell. This asexual process of budding requires the yeast cells to create large amounts of new cell wall tissue. During the lag phase, the cells take on oxygen and make precursors of amino acids and lipids, the components of the cell walls they'll be creating. If conditions are right, the yeast cells create new cell walls that will be permeable by the types of sugars they will be metabolizing.

Producing this new cellular membrane utilizes oxygen, as well as nitrogen and other nutrients, at a rapid pace. The terms "aerobic" and "respiratory" phase arise out of the yeast's need for oxygen in this stage of the fermentation process. Different strains of yeast will require different levels of dissolved oxygen and nutrient in the new must, but all require these elements to some extent in order to replicate and thus perform well during the main fermentation. Providing these components will be a main focus of our discussion on managing fermentation later in this chapter.

Fermentation phase. The transition from the aerobic (with oxygen) to the anaerobic (without oxygen) or fermentation phase occurs as the yeast depletes the molecular oxygen needed to create new cell wall tissue. At this time, the population of yeast cells shifts from a focus on reproduction to a focus on fermentation. At the height of the fermentation phase, the yeast population can rise to 1.5×10^8 cells/ml.

This is not to say that reproduction ceases, or that fermentation will not occur at all in the presence of oxygen, but as the O_2 level falls, the yeast cells begin absorbing the sugars in the wort and metabolizing them into alcohol and carbon dioxide. Yeast cells can utilize alternative energy sources to oxygen to continue reproduction, and reproduction generally continues on some small scale until the fermentable sugars are completely depleted or the yeast reaches its alcohol tolerance.

Before the actual transformation of the dissolved sugars to alcohol begins, the yeast cells utilize transport compounds known as permeases to move the sugars across the cell wall. Through enzymatic activity of α-glucosidase, the maltose and other disaccharide sugars are reduced to glucose. The fermentation process begins in a series of metabolic steps that reduce the glucose to trioses. Through the glycolisis pathway, the trioses are then reduced to pyruvic acid, resulting in two molecules of ATP per molecule of glucose fermented. The pyruvic acid is then converted to acetaldehyde by the enzyme pyruvate decarboxylase; the acetaldehyde is in turn converted eventually to carbon dioxide and ethanol by the enzyme alcohol dehydrogenase. The cycle has many similarities to the metabolization of glucose in humans, including the use of ADP (adenosine diphosphate), ATP (adenosine triphosphate), and NAD/NADH (nicotinamide adenine dinucleotide), which alternately collects or contributes hydrogen molecules during the reduction process. The ability to sustain this reaction, and thus the amount of ethanol and carbon dioxide produced, varies from strain to strain.

Depending on the strain of yeast you use, and the nutrient content of your must, the fermentation phase may begin as early as 12 to 24 hours after pitching, or as long as 72 hours. In most cases, if you have pitched enough yeast and added enough nutrient, 24 hours will be about right. During the fermentation, the number of yeast cells will begin dropping once the population hits its peak at about six days. It will fall in a bell-shaped curve. The yeast cells that remain will be selecting themselves for the conditions that prevail in their medium: higher alcohol and lower nutrient levels, and lower pH (see "Feeding a Fermentation" below).

In a must with a healthy yeast culture, the fermentation should proceed strongly until the yeast has consumed all of the available sugar, or it reaches its alcohol tolerance. At this point, the cells become less active and enter the final stage of the fermentation process.

Flocculation. As the sugar supply is exhausted and fermentation trails off, the yeast cells die or prepare for dormancy. As the fermentation slows, the cells exhibit changes in their cell wall structure, and they clump together to form "flocs." With most yeast strains these days, the clumps generally sink to the bottom of the fermentation vessel.

The degree to which the yeast settles quickly and compactly, yielding a clear mead, will vary from strain to strain. A strain is said to flocculate well if it ferments to completion and then settles quickly to form a firm yeast pack at the bottom of the fermenter. A strain's flocculating behavior is genetically determined.

Equipped with this understanding of yeast activity, we can now take a detailed look at the various aspects that contribute to a successful beverage fermentation. We will begin by examining critical steps in preparation of the must, then move on to talk about selection and preparation of the yeast, and then conclude by looking at how to manage the fermentation itself.

Critical Issues in Preparing the Must

Because the yeast's activity during fermentation greatly influences the flavor of the finished product, we must do everything we can to ensure the healthy and successful completion of the process. Let's look at what a meadmaker can do in this regard while preparing the must that will be the yeast's food and home during fermentation.

Nutrient levels. The first critical element for a robust fermentation is the amount of nitrogen available to the reproducing yeast population. The type of nitrogen needed by yeast is known as Free Amino Nitrogen, or FAN. To ferment without difficulty, a minimum of 130 milligrams per liter (mg/l) of FAN is needed; yeast scientists in the United States and Europe recommend optimal pre-fermentation FAN levels for musts ranging from 300 to 500 mg/l. Honey contains little amino nitrogen, with the lowest levels found in the lightest honeys. Thus, the FAN content of a honey-only must is far below the 130 mg/l minimum. Unless you fortify your musts with nutrients, a prolonged and troublesome fermentation will result.

Probably the best research on the optimal nutrient levels for mead fermentation was done by two scientists from Cornell University, the late Drs. Roger Morse and Keith Steinkraus. They were both beekeepers and keenly interested in mead. In 1966, they did an expansive study of honey fermentation that indicated that dark honeys might ferment more quickly than light honeys. It can be inferred that darker honey may contain a larger percentage of the needed nitrogen, vitamins, and nutrients required for a healthy fermentation. In any case, Morse and Steinkraus did come up with two formulas for mead additives that they found would result in honey fermentations that would reach completion in two weeks.

Morse and Steinkraus added Formula I at a rate of 6.75 grams per liter, and Formula II at 0.25 grams per liter. What they found was that the two formulas in tandem yielded the best possible results. They were able to ferment meads consistently to completion in two weeks or less, a huge improvement on the fermentation times of several months accepted as the rule at the time.

Obtaining, measuring, and blending these chemicals may seem like a tremendous length to go to for an amateur meadmaker interested in securing a fast and healthy fermentation. Not to worry. Many commercial fermentation aids are now available. As an interesting note, Fermaid K™, the fermentation aid from Lalvin, contains a blend of nutrients very similar to Morse and Steinkraus' two formulas. You use it at a rate of 1 gram per gallon. The Beverage People (see list of suppliers), a California beer- and winemaking shop, markets a nutrient blend specifically for meads, as well. Red Star produces Superfood, which includes both nitrogen in the form of DAP

table 5.1

Additives to Enhance Fermentation

Formula I		Formula II	
Component	Weight (g)	Component	Weight (mg)
ammonium sulfate	1.0	biotin	0.05
K_3PO_4	0.5	pyridoxine	1.0
$MgCl_2$	0.2	meso-inositol	7.5
$NaHSO_4$	0.05	calcium pantothenate	10.0
citric acid	2.53	thiamin	20.00
sodium citrate	2.47	peptone	100.0
		ammonium sulfate	861.45
Total	6.75	Total	1000.00

(diammonium phosphate, more on this below) and other necessary nutrients. They also make yeast-derived nutrient supplements under the names Tastone 50, Tastone 154 (baker's yeast extract)—which both provide some additional nitrogen as well as other micronutrients—and Nutrex, which is also known as yeast ghosts.

If you don't utilize a commercial blend, you can get very good results using a combination of a good nitrogen source and yeast hulls as the source of the other necessary trace compounds. Diammonium phosphate, $(NH_4)_2HPO_4$ (DAP), is used more commonly as a nitrogen source in fermentation aids today than is ammonium sulfate. Many home wine- and beermaking outlets sell DAP. Products labeled as yeast nutrient (which is often simply DAP) and yeast energizer (a combination of yeast hulls, nutrients, and sometimes DAP) are widely available. Unfortunately, the terms "energizer" and "nutrient" are used interchangeably by both suppliers and some sources of winemaking and beermaking advice. Additionally, some yeast nutrient contains other sources of nitrogen, such as urea, which some mead- and winemakers find objectionable. Others sell DAP labeled as just that. It will pay to do some research about the products you obtain.

DAP will contribute 258 ppm of fermentable nitrogen to a must when added at the rate of 1 gram/liter. That amounts to roughly 1 teaspoon per gallon.

Yeast nutrient and energizer can be used to foster aggressive fermentation or to restart a fermentation that has stalled before fully attenuating the available sugars. It is far better to start off healthy and have a vigorous fermentation than to try to save a sluggish or stuck fermentation. If you use yeast energizer and yeast nutrient, use them both in your recipe formulation. Most commercially available yeast additives come with appropriate instructions for their use. Some may come with instructions for use in beer wort; if you have a choice, select additives with dosages and instructions for wine musts, which are much closer to mead musts than are beer worts.

Regardless of the product you choose, you will want to include a source of Free Amino Nitrogen and a micronutrient supplement in all of your meads. A balanced nutrient supply (and oxygen level) are critical to the production of the permeases that act to deliver the yeast cells their food. Even in the case of melomels or meads that have nutrient sources other than honey, a healthy supply of FAN and the other nutrients will provide a valuable insurance policy against sluggish fermentation, which is a good mead's greatest threat.

Aeration. Prior to fermentation, you have several ways to get the critically needed oxygen dissolved into your must. The simplest way is to splash the must vigorously before pitching the yeast. The oxygen requirements of strains differ, but this technique is certainly sufficient for many yeasts. It also works fine for melomels, which may have oxygen and other nutrients available from the fruit.

Meadmakers with more energy and money to apply to the problem may use compressed air or oxygen. This makes oxygenation easier and generally increases the amount of oxygen dissolved in the must. In a must of 1.092 at 68° F (20° C), compressed air bubbled vigorously from a hose run to the bottom of a 5-gallon fermentation vessel typically requires five to ten minutes to reach oxygen saturation; pure oxygen will achieve this in just a minute or two.

Winemakers and even some yeast professionals recommend leaving the newly fermenting must open to the air for up to four days at the beginning of the fermentation. This allows oxygen from the air to diffuse into the must to supplement the oxygen supply during respiration. Open fermentations are accomplished by using air-permeable cloth covers or stopping bung holes or carboy mouths with sterile cotton. While I haven't yet tried this procedure, the concept behind it is sound. A yeast's peak demand for oxygen may occur after the must might normally have been sealed under a fermentation lock. An open fermentation will provide the yeast access to additional oxygen. One concern of open fermentation is that during the warmer months, many areas of the country have significant blooms of airborne wild yeasts.

pH management. Some of the most important information to come out of Morse and Steinkraus' work regards the relationship between pH and the fermentation of mead musts. During the lag and aerobic phases of a fermentation, the yeast gathers many of the nutrients it needs from the mineral compounds and amino acids present in the honey. Those compounds, however, provide the buffering that keeps the pH of the must in the optimal range for yeast fermentation. Once they have been absorbed by the yeast, the pH of the must can drop to levels that inhibit fermentation: below 3.0, sometimes even below 2.5. Under those conditions, the yeast slows its metabolism. The result is a mead fermentation that can drag on for many months. As the fermentation hobbles along, the yeast loses its vigor and the resulting stressed yeast produce compounds that adversely affect the aroma and flavor of the finished mead. Morse and Steinkraus recommended a pH range of 3.7 to 4.6 for optimal yeast performance, and noted that 3.7 was high enough for yeast metabolism and low enough to retard or inhibit undesirable bacteria.

You can affect the pH of your must in many ways, starting with the preparation of the must. While many mead recipes call for acid additions, I strongly advise against acid additions prior to the completion of fermentation. Acid additions benefit the flavor profile of some meads, but to ensure a healthy ferment, they should be made once fermentation is complete. Also be aware that some fruit juices, including citrus fruits like lemons, limes, or grapefruits, and some berries, can also add a considerable amount of acid to your must.

We will examine the issue of pH measurement and adjustment in further detail later in this chapter when we consider how to manage fermentation.

Selecting and Preparing the Yeast

When people in the wine- and beermaking fields speak of yeast, they usually mean the species *Saccharomyces cerevisiae*. An organism widely used by humans, *S. cerevisiae* includes hundreds of different strains, scores of which find application in beverage fermentation. Winemakers also use many strains of the closely related *S. bayanus*, and *S. bayanus uvarum*. As DNA testing and other analytical technique has improved, the classification and nomenclature regarding yeast species and strains has changed repeatedly over the past few years. The terminology used here reflects the current scientific consensus at publishing.

As meadmakers, we select specific strains for use based on their fermentation characteristics. Most strains evolved in specific winemaking regions or breweries. They behave differently in musts, have different nutrient and temperature requirements and, most importantly, produce unique flavor and aroma profiles in the finished mead. Between homebrewing and winemaking shops, as well as on-line vendors, you will find many excellent strains of yeast available for meadmaking. Let's review some of the common alternatives before considering some of the techniques you can use in preparing the yeast for fermentation.

Buying yeast. Yeast strains for meadmaking can be purchased primarily in two forms: **dried yeast** in foil packets or sachets and **liquid cultures** in either foil pouches or in vials. For those possessing microbiology lab skills, yeast strains can also be purchased in culturing kits. Often the same or similar strains will be available in more than one form.

Generally, yeast suppliers market their strains in two broad categories: wine yeasts and beer yeasts. Among the wine yeasts, you'll also find several strains targeted to meadmakers and labeled as dry or sweet mead yeasts. When applied to mead musts, these wine yeasts give predictable and acceptable results.

Wine yeast strains do a good job of fermenting mead musts. The sugars in a mead must more closely match those of wine rather than beer. Beer worts contain a very high percentage of maltose, maltotriose, and other complex sugars not commonly found in similar quantities in wine or mead musts. Also, beers have comparatively high levels of Free Amino Nitrogen (FAN) and pH levels of 4.5 to 6.0, much higher than mead musts.

Wine musts often lack in FAN just like mead musts. The pH level in a fermenting wine must is generally in the 3.2 to 4.2 range. Wine yeast strains often highlight fruity and/or floral notes in the bouquet and flavor profile of a mead. That can be especially helpful in traditional meads made with very florally piquant honey varieties, melomels, and certain metheglins. Lastly, wine yeast strains often have higher alcohol tolerances, making them less likely than beer yeasts to peter out as a fermentation reaches its most difficult stages.

This is not to say that no good mead has ever been made from beer yeast. I have tasted and enjoyed several. Dave West of Milford, Michigan, has fermented several award-winning meads using Wyeast 1056 (the supposed Sierra Nevada Pale Ale strain). Several other Mazer Cup award winners have been made with beer strains. Among the beer strains, the ale yeasts will be a better fit for mead fermentations. Ale strains ferment better at higher temperatures than lager yeasts. They do, however, have a tendency to present a more estery profile in their bouquet—a trait that will increase the fruitiness of the aroma. The Sierra strain is one known for a relatively clean nose.

Several manufacturers market high-quality wine yeast strains. Some of those manufacturers produce primarily for the commercial winemaking market and package their yeast strains in quantities that are not practical for home meadmakers, typically 500 grams or 1 kilogram. In the sidebar, I discuss the manufacturers and strains available in home-use quantities.

As I mentioned before, yeasts can be purchased in dry or liquid preparations. The leading manufacturers of dry yeast commonly available in the United States are Red Star and Lallemand (which markets its yeast sachets under the brand name Lalvin). Throughout Europe, meadmakers can find many of the same strains available from Gervin, Unican, SB, and Vierka. Vierka yeast strains are also available from some retailers in the United States. The leading manufacturers of liquid yeast cultures are Wyeast and White Labs.

Please note the list of yeast strains presented in the sidebar groups strains by general names or classifications offered by multiple suppliers. Despite these groupings, the individual strains will not be identical. Enologists (wine scientists) classify strains broadly by their region of origin, but many individual substrains also have been isolated further based on fermentation behavior and characteristics in the finished wine. Around the world, there are yeast banks devoted to identifying, collecting, and preserving individual yeast strains. There are several in Europe, with the most comprehensive being located in Germany. In the United States, the University of California at Davis has the most extensive yeast bank. Wyeast, Red Star, and Lalvin may all have Pasteur Champagne strains, but they may well be different isolates, and each will give slightly different results.

Preparing Yeast for Fermentation

Although often labeled as "ready to use," both liquid and dry yeasts will perform better if you prepare them properly before pitching them into your must. For dry yeasts, this means proper rehydration; with liquid yeasts, a starter may be well advised. Let's consider these techniques in turn.

Yeasts for Meadmaking

Assmanshausen (Wyeast 3277, Lallemand AMH, White Labs WLP749)

A German yeast strain used for medium- to full-bodied red wines. Known for enhancing the varietal character and spicy aromas of the grape. Alcohol to 15%. Temps 68-86° F (20-30° C).

Bourgovin (Lalvin RC212, White Labs WLP760)

Burgundy yeast used for big, full-bodied red wines and fruit wines using darker fruits and berries. Enhances fruit character. Moderately fast fermenter. Alcohol 14-16%. Temps 70-90° F (21-32° C).

Cotes du Rhone (Lalvin ICV D-47)

I have used this yeast for meads with success, as well. It takes longer to age than 71B and is a better choice for medium to dry meads. It makes a good traditional mead but is not tolerant of low nutrient levels and should be given appropriate nitrogen. Flocs very well. Alcohol 12-14%. Temps 50-86° F (10-30° C).

Cotes des Blancs (Red Star, Wyeast 3267, White Labs WLP745)

Has a reputation for being a slow fermenter, with higher nutrient requirements in low nitrogen mead or wine musts. Accents fruit aromas; a good choice with varietal honeys. Red Star says this yeast is the same as Epernay but with less foaming. This was a favorite yeast of Bill Pfeiffer, winner of many mead competitions. Alcohol 12-15%, less if fermented cool. Temps 64-86° F (18-30° C).

Epernay (Red Star, Lalvin DV10)

A Champagne yeast that also has been pressed into service for other white wines, meads, cider, and even reds. Another competitive factor yeast, and can handle low pH and other stresses better than most other strains. Clean, fast fermenter, notably lacking in edgy, bitter characteristics. Alcohol 16-18%. Temps 50-95° F (10-35° C).

Flor Sherry (Red Star, White Labs WLP700)

Actually a different species of yeast, *Saccharomyces fermentati* (syn. *Torulaspora delbrueckii*), which has considerably different fermentation behavior than *S. cerevisiae*. A flor is a pellicle of yeast organisms that forms after primary fermentation. The flor grows downward from the surface of the must. The flor is aerobic—it moves oxygen from the airspace into the must and is responsible for the production of the aldehydes and acetals, all which contribute to what we identify as the "sherrylike" character.

Montrachet (Red Star, Wyeast 3244, White Labs WLP755)

Very popular red wine strain. Reputed to have difficulty with higher-gravity musts, it is nevertheless able to tolerate high alcohol content. Montrachet is valued for its complexity in big, dry wines. Appropriate for melomels with big mouthfeel. Alcohol and temp info N/A.

Montpellier (Lalvin K1V-1116)

The definitive and original "killer" yeast strain, known for it strong competitive factor, which pushes out potentially infectious organisms. Known as a good white wine and

Yeasts for Meadmaking *Continued*

light fruit wine yeast, retains fruity attributes longer than other strains. High nitrogen requirements. Alcohol 16-18%. Temps 50-95° F (10-35° C).

Narbonne (Lalvin 71B-1122)

My preferred yeast for melomels with big, dark fruit such as cherries, plums, or raspberries. Used in making nouveau red wines. Strongly enhances fruit character, matures quickly. Enhances softer, estery fruit aroma profiles. Can metabolize malic acid to ethanol, reducing total acidity and producing a more rounded profile more quickly than many other yeast strains. Alcohol 14%. Temps 60-85° F (15.5-29.5° C).

Pasteur Champagne (Red Star, Wyeast 3021)

Quick starter, tolerant of high alcohol content. This was at one time one of the more commonly used strains for mead, but it has become less prominent as more varied and specific strains have become available to home meadmakers. Ferments to complete dryness and can require more extended aging in meads. Temps, alcohol info N/A from manufacturers, but alcohol can reach 16%.

Pasteur Red (Red Star, Wyeast 3028, White Labs WLP735)

A.K.A. French Red, Pasteur Red is derived from a strain from the Institute Pasteur in Paris. This yeast may produce considerable heat during fermentation; care should be used to avoid temps high enough to produce off flavors. Used in Cabernets and Merlots, this yeast will accent fruit flavors and will be best suited for big-bodied melomels. Temp and alcohol info N/A.

Prise de Mousse (Lalvin EC-1118, Wyeast 3237)

Red Star previously marketed a Prise de Mousse labeled strain, which it has relabeled Premier Cuvee. The strain they use is Davis 796, which has many similar characteristics to Prise de Mousse strains. High alcohol tolerance, strong fermenter, strong yeast profile in the finished product. Fast fermenter. A Champagne yeast that is tolerant of high sugar content and a wide range of temperatures. Temps: 50-95° F (10-35° C). Alcohol to 18%. Can be used to restart stuck or sluggish fermentations.

Rudisheimer (Wyeast 3783)

The traditional Riesling yeast, producing fruity, aromatic wines with an alluring balance of sweetness and acidity in the finish. Excellent choice for traditional meads or white wine pyments in which a balance of sweetness, acidity, and fruitiness is desired. Alcohol 11-14%.

Sauternes (Vierka, Lalvin R2)

French white wine yeast known for liberating fruity and floral aromas. A good yeast to highlight intensely aromatic honeys in traditional meads with some residual sweetness. Needs nutrients to stave off flawed fermentation characteristics. Can ferment to as low as 40° F (4.4° C). Alcohol 12-16%. Temps 50-86° F (10-30° C).

Yeasts for Meadmaking *Continued*

Steinberg (Red Star, Wyeast 3237, White Labs WLP727)

German yeast strain used in making whites with high levels of both residual sugar and acidity. Suited very well to traditional metheglins or pyments seeking big, fruity aromas and mouthfeels. Pushes tropical fruit esters. Temps, alcohol info N/A.

Tokay (Vierka)

Another good yeast for meads in which a medium to sweet finish is desired. Can be a bit flaccid when used with indistinct honeys. Works better with big-profile honeys and with metheglins. Temps, alcohol info N/A, but from my experience alcohol will be 12% or less.

Rehydration. Rehydration adds water to a dry (dehydrated) yeast culture to prepare it for pitching. This simple process usually requires just 15 or 20 minutes and can be accomplished while you are chilling the must. Please note that if you choose Vierka dry yeasts, the rehydration and starter procedures are more involved than those listed for Lalvin and Red Star—see below for more details.

When rehydrating freeze-dried yeasts, use 2 ounces of water at the temperature recommended on the yeast package for each 5 grams of yeast to be rehydrated. Add the yeast to the water but do not stir. Let sit 15 minutes, then stir well to suspend the yeast.

Vierka yeasts are not freeze dried. Some meadmakers in the United States have reported difficulty with Vierka yeasts, and I suspect that they may not have followed the correct procedure for getting them under way. To rehydrate and reactivate Vierka dry yeast, mix ½ cup water at 104° F (40° C) with ½ teaspoon (2.5 ml) sugar and a pinch of yeast nutrient until dissolved. Transfer to a sanitized vessel, add yeast, and stir. Stopper with a cotton ball or other air-permeable barrier. It will take one to two days for this starter to grow and become active. When preparing your must, add ¼ cup to your starter to acclimate the yeast to its new medium. Pitch two to four hours later, but do not stir into the must until signs of fermentation appear, then stir only shallowly. Stir deeply when vigorous fermentation is apparent.

Starters for liquid yeasts. If you choose to use a liquid yeast culture, you will probably want to increase the number of yeast cells before you pitch it into your must. A starter is a small fermentation grown up prior to pitching to ensure that you pitch an appropriate quantity of yeast. Getting your fermentation off to a vigorous start requires that you populate your must with a lot of yeast cells. In healthy musts, there can be up to 10×10^6 (that's 10 million) cells of yeast per milliliter, and typical starter populations for musts should be at least 1×10^6 (1 million) cells/ml. While most hobbyists won't be counting yeast cells, many use starters to ensure that their culture will have the ideal conditions needed to create healthy and vigorous parent cells, which then build a pitchable quantity of yeast.

In an ideal situation, you should plan on creating a starter that will provide a volume of yeast cells equal to approximately 1% of the total volume of your must. That is the volume of yeast slurry, the actual thick layer of yeast on the bottom of your starter. For a 5-gallon batch, that would equal about 6 or 7 ounces (~0.2 liter) of yeast slurry. To achieve this you'll want to create a starter of must that is approximately 10% of your batch size, or half a gallon. Although some recommend using a gallon of starter, I've always considered that a bit excessive, and I've had perfectly acceptable results with 10% starter volumes.

Many authors advocate the use of a starter solution that is very close if not identical to your must. In the case of meads, I feel that a starter solution with a gravity of between 1.040 and 1.050 works best. Dan McConnell of YeastLab advocates the use of a lower-gravity starter medium rich in nitrogen and other nutrients to insure the most robust parent cells possible. To paraphrase, he likes his starter healthy but hungry, and I agree with his logic.

Once you have selected a yeast, preparing the starter can be a straightforward task. If you are using a foil "smack pack," you'll need to burst the interior seal and allow the foil packet to swell according to the package instructions. When the packet is fully swollen, proceed with the following instructions.

You will need a clean, sanitized container capable of holding about 2 liters. A 2-liter plastic pop or sparkling water bottle works beautifully. You'll also want to sanitize the bottle cap, a funnel, a drilled stopper and airlock, and some scissors if you are opening a foil pouch. If you are using bleach for sanitation, make sure everything that will come in contact with the yeast is thoroughly rinsed with hot tap water until no smell of bleach remains.

Prepare your starter solution by boiling 6 cups of water with ¼ teaspoon yeast energizer and ¼ teaspoon yeast nutrient, and 1 tablespoon of dry malt extract for 5 minutes. Add ½ cup honey, stir, remove the pan from the heat, cover, and allow to cool to room temperature. When the liquid has cooled, use the sanitized funnel to pour the starter solution into the sanitized bottle. Cut the corner of the pouch or open the liquid yeast vial, and carefully pour the yeast into the bottle. Cap the bottle and shake it vigorously for about a minute. If you bubble oxygenate, now is the most critical time in the life cycle of your yeast to do so. Once aeration is complete, seal the bottle with the airlock. Your yeast starter should show signs of fermentation in about 12 to 24 hours or with some luck, less.

If you seek to boost the volume of yeast slurry in your starter (which I strongly recommend for higher gravity musts—1.100 or higher), you can easily accomplish that without much work. When the activity in your starter has slowed, (1 to 3 days), repeat the process of preparing and cooling a starter solution and sanitizing the cap and funnel. Unseal your now slowly fermenting starter and decant the spent liquid carefully off the yeast sediment and down the drain. Again using the funnel, pour the newly cooled starter solution into the bottle onto the yeast sediment, then cap and shake. In two to three days, you will have a substantial population of yeast with which to start your batch of mead.

When you go to pitch your yeast, carefully pour most of the spent liquid off the slurry. Swirl the remaining liquid and slurry vigorously to make it pourable, and pour it into your prepared must. It can be worthwhile to have some distilled or preboiled water on hand to rinse the remaining yeast from your starter vessel so you can add it to the must.

Once you have prepared your must and prepared and pitched your chosen yeast, your fermentation should begin fairly shortly. Let's look at what a meadmaker should be doing during fermentation to ensure good results.

Managing Fermentation

Once the yeast and the must have come together, the process of fermentation begins. Much of what you observe about your fermentations will be qualitative: bubbles through the airlock, the smell near the fermenter, the look of the liquid. But alcoholic fermentations don't always go as planned, so it is nice to have some objective, quantitative measures that we can use to assess the condition of our meads. In this section, we'll discuss both specific gravity and pH. After talking about pH, we'll examine the related concept of acidity and talk about when you might want to measure and adjust the acid content of your mead. Finally, we'll take brief look at the topic of malo-lactic fermentation.

Gravity. Gravity indicates the quantity of solids dissolved in must or mead. The more of any given solid you have, the higher your gravity will be. Several systems of measurement exist for gravity: specific gravity, degrees Balling or Plato, and Brix. (Brix is actually more of a system for determining the percentage of sugar in a fruit or fruit juice and does not represent the effects of alcohol on a finished must.) All of these measurements can be made with a suitably calibrated hydrometer or using techniques such as refractometry, which may be more suited to laboratory or commercial operations than to home meadmakers.

The common reference point for all of the systems is water with no dissolved solids. Pure water at 68° F (20° C) is represented by 0° Balling, Plato, and Brix, or by a specific gravity rating of 1.000. Some older hydrometers may be calibrated at 60° F (16° C), but 68° F, or 20° C, has become the present-day standard. For reference, in a 5-gallon batch of must intended to produce 10% alcohol by weight or more, 1 pound of honey should raise the specific gravity by approximately 8 points of specific gravity, or 2 degrees Plato or Balling. A must consisting of 1 gallon of honey (11.75 lbs.) and enough water to constitute 5 gallons will have a specific gravity of about 1.094 or 22.5° P. Another useful fact: 1 pound of honey produces approximately 1% alcohol by weight in the finished mead, up to the selected yeast's ethanol tolerance.

Perhaps the most important gravity consideration is the gravity tolerance of your yeast strain. Some strains may have difficulty beginning the fermentation process in a must with a gravity of 1.140 or greater. When pitched, they will simply revert back to a dormant state. If you intend to start a fermentation with a high starting gravity, select a yeast strain that is known for high gravity tolerance.

As your must ferments, the sugars that account for most of the gravity are converted to alcohol and carbon dioxide, reducing the gravity of the must as it becomes mead. Ethanol is lighter than water, and thus a fully attenuated mead may have a specific gravity lower than 1.000.

By measuring the specific gravity of your must before fermentation, you can assess the extent of fermentation and alcohol content of your mead. Musts should finish up about 0.100 gravity points lower than where they started, and maybe a bit lower still if a strongly attenuating strain of yeast was selected. Of course, any mead starting under 1.090 will be an exception. Typical final gravities for different types of meads are as follows:

Dry meads: 0.990–1.006

Medium meads: 1.006–1.015

Sweet meads: 1.012–1.020

Dessert meads: 1.020+

If fermentation has stopped and the gravity has not dropped by roughly 0.100, then you probably need to consult the "troubleshooting" section of this chapter to see about getting things going again.

Feeding the fermentation. One of the versatile aspects of mead musts is that with honey, additional fermentable sugar can be added quickly and easily at any point in the fermentation. Meadmakers have been taking advantage of this for many years now by adding small amounts of honey—1 or 2 pounds—as the fermentation progresses. The honey is generally added as the initial vigorous fermentation slows.

This procedure is especially useful to meadmakers seeking to create meads with *lots* of alcohol. By waiting until the fermentation slows, you effectively create an artificial selection process, isolating the cells in the culture that can tolerate higher alcohol levels. Through continued feeding of strains like Lalvin EC-1118, it is possible to attain alcohol levels of 20% or more. Even with strains with a lower alcohol tolerance, there will be a small population of cells that push the higher end of the range, and can be encouraged to continue fermenting beyond their expected tolerance.

I have to admit, I don't actually do this. Most of my reluctance has arisen from the fact that the alcohol levels in many of the "fed" meads I have tasted have seemed out of balance—hot, in the vernacular. I also theorize (granted, without any empirical evidence) that by significantly prolonging the fermentation, the yeast cells that are left become stressed. While the yeast may not require additional oxygen at this stage, the other nutrients that aid in healthy yeast metabolism already will have been depleted in the must. My anecdotal evidence suggests the prolonged fermentation may produce off aromas and flavors, which may or may not diminish with age.

My preference is to identify a profile of sweetness and alcohol that you desire, then match a yeast with a starting gravity that will finish up fermentation right in your target range. On the other hand, if you seek to prepare a particularly high-alcohol mead, for a celebration or just to have around as a novelty, this procedure will certainly do the trick.

pH. As I mentioned earlier in the section on preparing your must, pH is an important parameter of fermentation. If the pH drops too low, the yeast will slow fermentation to a crawl. Fermentation problems resulting from pH appear more commonly in traditional or show meads and sometimes in metheglins. The use of fruit in any quantity in meads will dramatically change the amounts and types of acid and buffering compounds in solution, making pH problems far less likely.

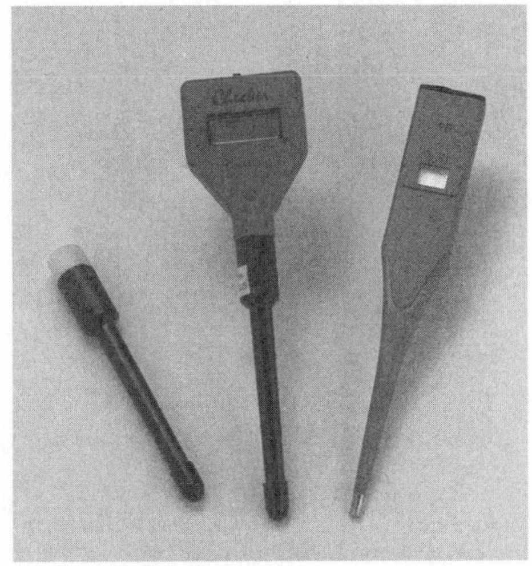

Digital pH meters eliminate mess and judgment calls in pH measurement.

The best tool I have found for measuring pH is a handheld, battery-powered pH meter. They can be obtained from many winemaking and brewing supply shops and on the World Wide Web. Paper test strips for measuring pH are also available from pharmacies, winemaking and homebrew shops, and health food stores, but may not offer as much accuracy as you desire.

I recommend that you test the pH of your must before fermentation to ensure that it is not too low. Do not immerse your meter or test strip in the fermenter. Rather, draw a sample from the must to test, and discard it after testing. Keep an eye on your fermentation activity, and test again if the fermentation seems to have slowed dramatically during the first seven to nine days.

If you use a honey with a high acid content, or have noted a slowing of fermentation activity and find that the pH of your must has fallen below 3.5, you can adjust the pH upward (reduce the acidity) by adding calcium carbonate. When adjusting the pH of a must, it is important to understand that pH is not simply a measure of the amount of acid in a solution, but rather expresses the ratio of the amounts and strengths of acidic to alkaline compounds in that solution. As such, the addition of a given amount of a buffering compound can produce a great change in the pH of a solution, or may produce almost none at all. The method of pH adjustment I prefer is to add calcium carbonate, $CaCO_3$, ½ teaspoon at a time, stir, test, and repeat as necessary to bring the pH up to about 3.8.

You can use other alkaline compounds such as sodium bicarbonate to change pH, but I would advise against them. Any sodium compound in sufficient quantity will lead to a salty taste in your mead. Due to its low solubility, calcium carbonate also will precipitate out well. Obtain calcium carbonate from a winemaking shop or on-line supply operation, and use it judiciously.

Fermentation problems. If you heed the nutrient and pH guidelines I provide and ferment within the temperature ranges recommended for the yeast strain you are using, you should rarely, if ever, encounter fermentation difficulties. From time to time, however, fermentation problems may crop up even for an experienced meadmaker. These difficulties manifest themselves as sluggish or stopped fermentation. The four most common problems experienced by meadmakers are: too high an initial gravity (fermentation activity never begins), too little nutrient (prolonged slow fermentation), too low a pH (fermentation slows dramatically after two to five days—see earlier instructions on pH control), and stuck fermentation (fermentation stops completely before all sugars are attenuated).

Troubleshooting Problem Fermentations

When fermentation problems arise, they generally stem from the four common sources listed here. Under each, you'll find suggestions for how to get things back on track.

Fermentation Activity Never Begins

If you are sure you pitched a viable starter or a rehydrated dry yeast and an appropriate dosage of nutrients, but your mead never starts fermenting, there is a good likelihood that you have exceeded the gravity limit of your yeast. If you have room in your fermenter, you can try adding water, although this may not be sufficient to rouse your yeast from its renewed dormancy. A better solution would be to pitch a culture of a strain tolerant of higher sugar levels.

Meadmakers in haste may fail to remove bleach or other sanitizers from their fermenter, and their yeast may be killed when it is pitched. It is a pretty speculative diagnosis, but I have seen instances in which no other justification for a complete lack of activity could be found. Far more common is the use of fruit juices or concentrates containing preservatives such as potassium sorbate or sodium benzoate. These compounds will render a must unfermentable and have caused the waste of more than a few batches.

Prolonged Slow Fermentation

If your fermentation gets under way but never hits anything close to a fever pitch, you have probably provided too little nutrient. You can add additional nutrient at 1 gram per gallon, and be sure to agitate the must thoroughly to push some air into it. Stirring, splashing, and swirling are good, but putting a portion of the must into a clean blender and whipping the living snot out of it is better. Do not get too uptight about sanitation at this point; if you don't get some oxygen and nutrient into your must, you are going to have a lost batch anyhow. You don't have much to lose.

Stuck Fermentation

Every so often, you may be faced with a fermentation that poops out well before you expected. You have provided adequate nutrient and your pH is above 3.5, but your must

TROUBLESHOOTING PROBLEM FERMENTATIONS *CONTINUED*

has quit fermenting after attenuating only a portion of the fermentable sugar available to it. You have taken gravity readings that account for attenuation of enough sugar to produce 6-7% alcohol; the yeast should still be well below its alcohol tolerance. You will need to take corrective action.

Try aeration and a small dose of nutrients. If fermentation does not resume, the most reliable solution is to switch to a yeast strain with a higher alcohol tolerance, such as Lalvin EC-1118 or Red Star Pasteur Champagne. This can have the effect of producing more alcohol and a drier mead than you had originally intended, but you can sweeten it up later if needed.

Another possible cause of arrested fermentation is the stratification of the must. The fermenter becomes layered into two different viscosities of liquid. I am not aware of the cause of this phenomenon, but I have witnessed it and had several communications from mead- and cidermakers seeking to correct the problem. If the problem occurs early in the fermentation, I have simply stirred with a racking cane. Later in the ferment, a racking will serve to blend the must sufficiently to reinvigorate the yeast activity.

POST-FERMENTATION STRATEGIES

Once fermentation is complete, you have a mead that should resemble in many ways the finished product that you hoped to produce. In addition to assessing the gravity and pH, meadmakers sometimes look at residual sugar and acidity, and they may take steps to adjust these characteristics. Another step they may consider is a malo-lactic fermentation. Let's consider these issues now.

Acidity. Acidity and pH are related but not interchangeable. Of the two, acidity has by far the greatest impact on the taste and mouthfeel of your mead. Total acidity refers to the amount of acid in a solution, irrespective of buffering compounds that may affect pH. In your must or mead, total acidity (TA) measures the combined amounts of malic, citric, and tartaric acid present. In the United States, total acidity is expressed as grams of tartaric acid per 100 milliliters of mead or wine. This convention stems from the fact that tartaric acid is the predominant acid in wine. The amount of acid in commercial red wines is about 0.6 g/100 ml (0.6%). White wines average about 0.7g/100 ml (0.7%).

The total acid content of a must or mead is measured by titration. Titration is a means of accurately quantifying acidity by using an alkaline reagent (0.1 normal sodium hydroxide—NaOH) to neutralize the acid in a specified quantity of must. An indicator (phenolphthalein) is used to show exactly when the neutralization has occurred. By precisely measuring the amount of base needed to fully neutralize the acid, the total amount of acid in the solution can be calculated. See the sidebar for details of this measurement.

Measuring Acid by Titration

Acid titration kits can cost anywhere from a few dollars for home kits to hundreds of dollars for high-quality laboratory-grade glassware. They consist of flasks for mixing, a pipette, burette, or syringe graduated to 0.1 ml, a stirring rod, phenolphthalein, and sodium hydroxide. You'll also need some distilled water. Most kits include instructions, but if you assemble the items yourself, here is the procedure:

1) Make sure all glassware is thoroughly clean.

2) Fill the syringe or burette with the NaOH solution. Disgorge a small amount to bleed off any air and/or check the stopcock function. Record the level of NaOH.

3) Put about 75 ml of (hot) distilled water into the flask.

4) Using the pipette, add exactly 15 ml of the juice, must, or mead you are testing to the flask.

5) Add five drops of phenolphthalein to the flask, stir well.

6) Begin adding NaOH one drop at a time, swirling/stirring after each drop. Stop when you reach a point at which the pinkish color does not dissipate after stirring. The color may change from amber or reddish to blue/black in darker musts or fruit juices. You have reached the end point. Measure and record the level of NaOH, and subtract it from the initial reading.

It is prudent to repeat the test and average the results. If they are dramatically different, there was a problem with your testing, and you should repeat the entire process.

7) Divide the number by 20. This will give you the total number of grams/100 ml of tartaric acid.

Since fermentation does not change the amount of acidity in a mead (with the exception of malo-lactic fermentation by cultures or as in Lalvin's 71b-1122 strain), it should not matter when you measure your acidity.

The purpose for acidity testing is the impact on your mead's flavor. Meads with a titratable acidity over 0.8-0.9% will express considerable tartness. Some dry melomels made with highly acidic fruits can be almost unbearably dry or tart. To balance an overly acidic mead, you may need to add sweetness. Meads with too low an acid level (0.3% or less) can be cloying and flaccid in the mouth. In that case, you may need to add acid tartness to give the mead some "backbone" (see above).

I need to make note of some interesting research done by Dan McFeeley. McFelley has extended work done earlier by Dr. Jonathan White and others, which isolated "pH drift" in neutralized honey solutions. McFeeley has noted that both pH modification and acidity testing in mead are also difficult to perform accurately. Honey contains both gluconolactone and gluconic acid. When the pH of honey or mead are raised (as one would do by adding sodium hydroxide in a titration), the gluconolactone hydrolizes to gluconic acid, and the pH begins to fall. The higher the pH, the faster this reaction appears to occur. This causes what is known as a fading end point reaction, in which the neutralization point in the titration occurs later than expected.

This could affect the results of even a quick TA titration as performed by a hobbyist. I know winemakers often complete the procedure in just a few seconds, but the color change that occurs would not be stable in a mead. McFeeley has found that the reaction can occur quite rapidly, becoming apparent in less than a minute. This would indicate that the closest accurate TA reading might occur at the first instance of a color change that lasts more than a few seconds, even if it does fade shortly thereafter.

These findings throw an interesting wrinkle into the mix and are further evidence of the remarkable properties of honey. This research with mead must should be repeated soon. McFeeley has published information on alternative methods of acid analysis for mead and honey, which will certainly be of interest to those making mead on a commercial scale.

Residual Sugars

Residual sugar provides complexity and balance in your mead. The "correct" amount of residual sugar in your finished mead is a matter of personal preference, and I am not one to dictate what is good or bad. Make what appeals to you or those around you whom you are hoping to please. You can test the residual sugar content of a mead with a reasonable degree of accuracy by using glucose test strips, which are available at pharmacies and medical supply facilities.

Commercial wines have residual sugars ranging from below 1 to 3%, with higher levels for dessert wines like German Ausleses, ports, and madeiras. Some commercial dessert wines have residual sugar levels of 20% or more. I find meads with higher levels of residual sugar very pleasant. I also feel that sweet meads can convey the character and aroma of the honey in a way that meets the expectations of uninitiated mead drinkers.

Matching your desired profile with your finished product is a matter of combining the correct amount of fermentable sugar with an appropriate yeast. Remember that it is easy to sweeten a finished mead that is too dry for your tastes, but it is difficult to dry out a mead with too much residual sugar and still have it fall into the profile you sought in the first place. Let's take a look at some of these techniques.

Sweetening. To sweeten a mead, you must first ensure that the remaining yeast will not resume fermentation when additional sugar is added. You can accomplish this in a few different ways, but in my experience the most reliable and consistent is to use potassium sorbate, $C_6H_7KO_2$. Potassium sorbate does not kill the yeast but rather prevents the fermentation process from continuing.

When the normal fermentation has ceased, add potassium sorbate at the rate of ½ teaspoon per gallon. Stir it in and allow it to work for at least a day. At that point, additional sugar (honey) can be added without the risk of the fermentation resuming. I prefer to add honey 1 cup at a time, stirring thoroughly and tasting after each addition until the desired sweetness level is attained.

Malo-lactic fermentation. Winemakers often use a bacterial fermentation, known as malo-lactic fermentation, to reduce the real and perceived acidity of wines. After primary fermentation, winemakers pitch the species Oenococcus oeni. This bacteria converts malic acid to lactic acid, creating a rounder, less grating impression on the tongue. As with yeast, you can choose from several strains of malo-lactic bacteria available commercially.

Some care must be taken with these cultures as they are notoriously persnickety, and must be handled and added according to a specific regimen. They will not work in a must with a pH below 3.0. They will also ferment remaining sugars. Malo-lactic fermentations are used primarily in dry wines that finish with too much acidity. Because malo-lactic fermentations produce CO_2, they can be used to carbonate meads that are intended to finish dry but with a reduced acidic profile.

I must admit to having no experience with M-L fermentation. Certain fruit melomels would be well served by reduced acidity in the finished profile, most notably currant, blackberry, and raspberry meads, or cysers made from apples with particularly high malic acid content. If you elect to try a malo-lactic fermentation, follow the manufacturer's specifications precisely. Cultures can be obtained at winemaking supply shops and on-line.

Drying out a mead. The only method I know to reduce the amount of residual sugar in a mead is to repitch using a yeast with higher alcohol tolerance than the strain used in the primary ferment. The strain commonly used for this is Lalvin EC-1118, which has a high alcohol tolerance and is known for finishing fermentations that have not consumed all of the available sugar. The drawback in repitching is that higher alcohol levels also affect the mouthfeel and overall profile of a mead. In my estimation, the best dry wines and meads strike a delicate balance between bouquet, flavors, mouthfeel, and alcohol. Fermenting a mead to its highest potential alcohol level can risk throwing that balance off.

Increasing acidity. Medium to sweet meads will be cloying if there is not enough acid present. I have found taste to be the best guide when adding acid to a mead. At bottling, taste some of the mead. If it is sweet without any bite of acidity on the tongue, I recommend adding an acid blend. The most commonly available blends consists of malic, citric, and/or tartaric acid. Dissolve ½ teaspoon of the blend in ¼ cup of water, stir into the mead, and taste. Repeat the process until the tartness and sweetness balance into a flavor profile that you enjoy. My rule of thumb is that I am in the right range if I find myself desirous of a second glass.

chapter six

Conditioning, Aging, and Using Oak

The natural processes that yield mead from honey, water, and yeast are not finished when fermentation ends. Mead, like beer and wine, will change and improve over time. Unlike most beers, however, wine and mead often continue to improve over months and years. This is the process of conditioning or aging, and its benefits are many.

Not to sound too much like an alchemist, but the details of the chemical changes that occur in wines during the aging process are not understood as well as they could be, and the specific changes that occur in meads have not been documented or studied scientifically at all, to the best of my knowledge. In wines, the reactions that occur in aging are reduction reactions, meaning those that occur without oxygen. They result in a "softening" of a wine—a reduction or diminishing of the tart, harsh, and angular characteristics that make a young wine unpleasant. Certain compounds—harsh phenolics and esters, for example—lose their edginess. Monoterpenes become "mature" and more appealing. These changes generally take three to six months for white wines and one to two years for reds. White wines are generally consumed young. Reds, particularly big ones, are often allowed to age for periods of five years or more.

A similar softening occurs in meads. Young meads can possess a strongly astringent element, sometimes described as Listerine® or dry cleaning fluid. This detractor falls off markedly in the first year of aging, but can require even longer aging in some cases. Truly flawed examples—those that were fermented too warm or too cool, or had prolonged fermentations due to weak yeast cultures or poor nutrient levels, leading to excessive esters or higher alcohols—may never grow out of this harshness. Fruitiness can become "closed," meaning that fruit character or aroma can seemingly run and hide for a time, only to re-emerge and become distinctive.

The effects of aging become even more pronounced if some or all of the bulk aging is done in (or with) oak. Simply put, oak and mead are a match. Whether or not oak barrels were actually designed for the aging of fermented beverages, the effects they have on wine and mead border on evidence of a higher power. Oak contributes vanillin and tannins that add distinct aromas and complexity and fullness to the mouthfeel. Barrels provide the opportunity for gaseous exchange—a slow oxidation that mellows some of the harsh flavors in young wines and meads. At the risk of sounding too gushy, you know how a really good mead can seem like it has attained a level of deliciousness that is nigh on to impossible to improve? Well, oak can grab it by the scruff of the neck and haul it three rungs up the ladder. The use of oak in a mead can be accomplished in a two ways: oak barrels and oak chips.

Oak barrels have been considered difficult to manage for home wine- and meadmakers, but that is not necessarily the case. The main reason for trepidation about their use is the geometry of small barrels. For many years, commercial winemakers have known that barrels of around 200 to 225 liters (50 to 60 gallons) would provide just the right amount of contact between the wine and the oak for prolonged aging. The surface-to-volume ratio for a 200-liter cask is about 90 cm^2 per liter. The ratio for a 20-liter cask (just slightly larger than 5 gallons) is 190 cm^2 per liter. Shorter barrel contact is dictated for smaller barrels.

White oak (from America and Europe) is the primary source of barrel wood, although other types of barrels have been and in some places still are being utilized for wines and distilled products. Oak from different regions will have regional characteristics. French and Eastern European oak is reputedly lower in assertive character, while delivering more extractable solids and tannin, while American oak is noted for more distinct aromatics.

The oak is open-air aged for periods ranging from nine months to two years or longer. Wood for staves is graded by the density of the grain—broad, medium, or fine. Broader-grained wood will give up its oak flavors and aromatics earlier and produce a stronger, more assertive oak profile. Broad-grained barrels are often used in blending regimens. Medium-grained wood is the middle ground, with medium levels of oak flavor and aroma constituents, imbuing the mead with nutty/vanilla, butterscotch, and apricot flavors. Fine-grained oak staves provide higher levels of tannins, but release other oak components more slowly. Flavors and aromas include hazelnut, toasted grain, and fruity esters.

The other critical variable in oak barrels is the toast level. Barrels (and oak chips) can be purchased at toast levels from untoasted to charred, and at every increment in between. Heavily toasted barrels will reduce the definition of the oak character and deliver higher levels of vanillin. Medium toast will release some wood sugars, as well as vanilla, and at higher toast level (medium-plus), almond. Lightly toasted barrels provide lower levels of vanillin and more pronounced oak character. Obviously, a huge vineyard purchasing thousands of barrels will be able to exert far more control over the degree of toasting provided by a cooperage, but it is possible for a meadmaker to purchase a barrel of at least a broadly specified toast level.

If you are seeking a general-purpose barrel, medium is probably the way to go. Lightly toasted barrels can overwhelm light meads with their profound oak influence.

Commercial wineries dedicate barrels to one style of wine for their useful life. If you progress more deeply into meadmaking, you may want to have one barrel for lighter meads and one for heavier, more full-bodied meads.

Barrels need to be treated before use. They need to be filled with clean water for at least 48 hours, and sometimes several days, to swell and become watertight. They should then be cleaned with a cleanser such as Barolkleen to remove any debris and lower the tannin levels. Next, fill the barrel with hot water and treat the barrel with five to ten Campden tablets (some advise a cursory five-minute treatment, others overnight). Rinse the barrel with hot water thoroughly and repeatedly until the water runs clear. Most winemakers will advise filling the barrel with a lower-quality wine or mead the first time it is used for an hour or up to a day to two to soften the impact of the new oak on the first high-quality mead you will age in the barrel. Even after such treatment, you will want to check your first mead in a new barrel every day or two. A good dose of oak may be in evidence after five days to a week.

You should always keep your barrel full between meads. If it dries out, it will shrink and be rendered unsound. Equally hazardous is the plethora of evil microbiota just aching to set up shop in your moist barrel. Once mold or other infection sets in, a barrel cannot be restored to useful quality. Fill it with a light sulfite solution (2.5 tablets in 5 gallons or 18 to 20 L), and keep it completely filled and bunged. Change the sulfite solution every three months.

Winemakers expose white wines to oak for short periods, ranging from a few weeks to six months and, rarely, a full year. White wines are also often aged in huge casks with even smaller surface-to-volume ratios. Big, full-bodied red wines in (225-liter) 60-gallon casks can see up to three years in oak, but 16 to 24 months is more the norm. In a small, young barrel, one month may provide more oak than even a bombastic mead can withstand. It is critical to keep the barrel completely full, pretty much all the time. Airspace creates risk of oxidation. Taste the mead regularly, and be prepared to move back into glass or bottles for additional aging.

Oak chips are the other alternative. They can be purchased from many wine and beer supply shops, and are available in French, American, and Eastern European oak, some even in specified toast levels. There is an especially intriguing system available from StaVin that allows you to use a tubular enclosure to house the oak chips while they are being used in your mead. Chips should be treated by bringing to a boil and soaking in water for a few hours—some producers recommend an eight- to twelve-hour soaking. Many varieties of chips are available in pre-sanitized pouches; they can be added directly to a fully fermented mead. Again, check the mead regularly to insure that it does not become over-oaked. One or two weeks to a month are often all that is needed. Proponents of oak chip use are backed up by the argument that surface-to-volume issues are much more controllable with chips than with a small barrel.

All barrels and chips for winemaking are white oak. Don't try to economize by using scrap oak from construction projects—there is a great likelihood that they are red oak and will do your mead a great disservice.

Proper Aging

So how long should you age a mead? Well, there is no one answer to that question. With or without oak, aging periods for meads are not uniform, and are dependent on ingredients and treatment of the must, but experience has provided me with several practical observations that I apply when deciding when to drink my own meads.

Meads that have been produced by the no-heat method are generally drinkable sooner that those produced through heating. Meads produced by sulfiting will have similar aging curves. No-heat meads are frequently very drinkable in six to eight months, and should be free of any harsh or unpleasant characteristics in a year. They may continue to improve for another one to four years, and longer, if good attention was paid to oxygen exposure. Oxidation causes a sherrylike flavor in meads. It can be appealing at low levels in some meads, but is a real flaw in light traditional meads made from mildly flavored honey. That means keeping your airlocks filled at all times. If you have access to carbon dioxide gas, blanketing with CO_2 during the racking and bottling process will help in this regard. In meads that will be bottled and aged, preventing oxidation can be aided by the use of at least 25 ppm of potassium metabisulfite (one-half Campden tablet per gallon) at the last racking. Aging away from bright or direct light and at cellar temps between 50° F and 60° F (10° C and 16° C) are highly recommended practices.

Meads that have been heated or boiled will generally require a full year to become drinkable, and will become more rounded between 12 and 24 months. Again, if produced with diligent care to avoid exposure to oxygen, they may continue to improve for several years. I have several meads in my cellar of more than ten years of age. Some have passed their prime, while others, in particular one "Mambo in Your Mouth" Melomel, have continued to mature gracefully and have lived up to their promise with each sampling.

Regardless of your choice of production method, in high-gravity meads and dark pyments, this improvement can continue for years. It is my experience that in lighter traditional meads and metheglins, there is a point of diminishing returns. One or two years may be the apex of the mead's drinkability.

The use of stainless steel soda kegs for aging and serving meads is a method that will help you prolong the span during which your mead will continue to improve. Kegs and the required hardware are available at many retail and on-line homebrew stores. By kegging your finished mead, you can keep it under a protective blanket of CO_2, and thereby eliminate any chance of oxygen absorption. I have kept meads in kegs for several years without signs of deterioration. Mead on tap is a blessing well worth the effort and expense.

The equipment needed for kegging is: a CO_2 canister, a regulator, a keg or two, and supply and tap hoses. The carbon dioxide can be obtained from any commercial gas supplier, which can be found in your local phone book. Regulators are metered valves that enable you to adjust the exact amount of pressure applied to the interior airspace of the keg. Regulators and hoses can be obtained from many gas suppliers as well, or can be purchased from homebrew shops.

For still meads, only about 8 to 10 pounds of pressure per square inch (psi) is needed to dispense the liquid. Pressure levels higher than that may cause the mead to absorb some gas and develop a level of carbonation. Sparkling meads should be held and dispensed under about 14 psi. Still meads can be carbonated artificially by applying 20 psi of CO_2 and rocking the keg gently for a period of about 30 to 40 minutes. Vent the keg to approximately 14 psi (if you dispense at 20 psi, you'll get nothing but foam), and test a serving to assess whether the degree of carbonation is satisfactory. Add more carbonation if desired.

There are few more gratifying moments than the tasting of a self-made mead at the peak of its bouquet and flavor. It is the culmination of good process, selection of top-quality ingredients, and adherence to proper handling technique. Proper aging is one of the keys to hitting that mark. Patience *is* a virtue, and satisfaction is its reward.

part three

INGREDIENTS

chapter seven
ALL ABOUT HONEY

Mead is inextricably linked to honey. And at least linguistically, it appears that the reverse may be true as well. The Indo-European word "medhu" meant both mead and honey. This may lead one to believe that meadmaking developed simultaneously with the discovery of honey as a food.

People attribute many mythical properties to honey, and its fascinating creation makes it a remarkable and cherished foodstuff. But what has all this talk of honey got to do with making mead? Plenty. For to really understand mead, we really need to understand honey.

In this chapter, we'll tackle the subject of honey from flower to flavor. To start out, we'll take a look at bees and their life and move on to the art of beekeeping. Once we understand how bees and beekeepers influence the process, we'll move on to examine honey characteristics including its chemistry and the resulting flavors and aromas. The chapter ends with a review of common varietal honeys and leads into the next chapter by giving a detailed chemical analysis of different types of honey.

A Bit About Bees

Although bees come in many variations, most folks have a good idea of what they look like and also what they do. Of course, the bee's most important activity from the meadmaker's perspective involves production of honey. But bees don't produce honey simply to please their human neighbors or handlers. Honey production plays a central role in the bee's life. Let's take a look at that life and how honey comes into existence.

Bees and flowering plants enjoy a classic symbiotic relationship: Each benefits from its interaction with the other. Most plants cannot make the seeds needed to reproduce unless bees visit their flowers and transfer pollen from plant-to-plant in the process. To encourage these visits, the plants make colorful flowers that offer a succulent nectar rich in nutrients. Bees collect the nectar and other substances

Lavender is a favored bee forage plant.

from the plant to use as food. They consume a portion of the nectar during collection, but their real goal is to create a stored reserve of concentrated nectar, otherwise known as honey.

A bee collects nectar by thrusting its proboscis deep into the flower's corolla (sounds kind of erotic, doesn't it?). There, it ingests the nectar and, as it performs this act, it ends up covered in the plant's pollen. As bees move from plant to plant and blossom to blossom, they transfer pollen along the way and pollinate flowers in the process.

A bee continues collecting nectar until loaded to capacity. "So," you may be asking, "exactly how much is one bee-ful of nectar?" Well, as best as we can tell, it's about 50 to 60 milligrams—perhaps as much as 75 milligrams. Incidentally, that's 90% of a female bee's body weight—an incredible load for a flying insect, or any creature, for that matter.

The worker bees, which are all female, have a honey sac at the head of their digestive tract that holds the nectar. The sac contains enzymes that act on the nectar to begin the process of curing it into honey. Water from the nectar is also absorbed in the honey sac.

The bee's honey sac connects to the remainder of the digestive tract by a one-way valve and serves as a kind of gas tank. Using this valve the worker bees absorb just enough nectar to provide for their nutritional needs. Bees outbound from the hive fill up with just enough honey to fuel the trip to the nectar source. Upon return to the hive, they regurgitate the collected nectar for further processing and storage.

When the honey sac is emptied, it may be deposited either into a comb or into another bee. The bees at the hive continue the process of ingesting and regurgitating the collected nectar, adding enzymes and removing water. Moisture also is removed by forced evaporation. Chains of bees fan air across the unsealed combs by beating their wings. The bees test the unripe honey regularly to determine its moisture content. When moisture drops below about 17 to 20%, the honey will remain stable and the bees seal or "cap" the combs.

Southernwood has a distinctly spicy, perfumed aroma.

Bees produce most honey from nectar, but another source bears mention in case you run across it. Bees occasionally frequent deciduous or coniferous trees that have been beset with aphids. The aphids suck sap from the trees and leave small sap droplets on the branches and leaf stems when they depart. The bees may collect this sap and process it just like nectar. The resulting product is called honeydew and is considered inferior to real honey by just about anybody familiar with the stuff.

During nectar collection, bees also collect pollen to provide the protein portion of their diet. While pollen is essential to the hive's survival, it is not integral to the production of honey. Pollen needs are highest during the peak periods of brood rearing. Foraging bees gather the pollen, and form it into pellets that attach to their legs. On return to the hive, the foragers hand off these pellets to hive bees, who store them for later use. One-quarter to one-third of the foraging bees from any given colony are actively collecting pollen, and this can account for much of the hive's pollination activity.

Bees obviously do much of their work in the summer, collecting nectar when it is plentiful and storing it as honey for use during other parts of the year. Bees do not die off or become dormant in the mammalian sense during the winter. Over the winter months, bees swarm about the queen, protecting both themselves and the matriarch by beating their wings and generating heat to keep the swarm alive. They utilize their stores of collected honey for food, and leave the hive periodically on warm days to excrete waste.

In the spring the bees again begin to collect nectar but then use it rapidly to restore the strength of the hive and to feed the brood, which were laid over the winter. These young restore the strength of the hive and populate it for the rest of the summer. As a result of this life cycle, crops that blossom in the spring, such as fruits in northern climes, will not produce harvestable honey, since the nectar is consumed as fast as it is collected.

It takes about twenty thousand trips by a bee, and roughly four million stops at blossoms, to produce a single pound of honey. The average colony of European honeybees produces about 70 pounds of honey per year. Depending on the health of

A beekeeper uses smoke to tranquilize bees and drive them into the brood chamber. He can then remove the super loaded with honeycomb (note the lack of arm protection). Photo courtesy National Honey Board.

the hive and the availability of nectar, some hives have been known to produce 200 pounds or more in a given season. The National Honey Board estimates total international honey production over recent years at about 400 million pounds.

Our Friends the Beekeepers

The presence of a beekeeper defines the difference between wild bees and domestic bees. These folks do plenty to see to it that we get honey for our mead without being stung or having to fight with bears. Along the way, they gather a ton of information that meadmakers will find interesting and useful.

The vast majority of beekeepers are hobbyists with fewer than twenty-five hives, who do not make a living keeping bees. Hobby apiarists account for 50% of the bee colonies in the United States and about 40% of domestic honey production.

I strongly encourage you to develop a relationship with a beekeeper, and it will most likely be one of these hobbyists. Your local beekeeper may already know a few meadmakers and will likely be somewhat familiar with mead. He or she is invariably proud of his or her honey and can tell you when it was collected, the nectar sources, and any other properties of interest. But perhaps the best reason to befriend a

Nectar production soars during pollination periods. Hives can reach impressive heights as successive supers are added and filled. Photo courtesy National Honey Board.

beekeeper is that they are, by and large, very interesting people. Like bees, beekeepers toil ceaselessly at their craft, and they deserve our vocal admiration and support.

If you find that beekeeping interests you, you might take a crack at it yourself. It isn't really much of an option for the truly urban among us, but semi-rural and even suburban areas can provide plenty of forage for a colony, and the rewards are substantial. You may need to bribe your neighbors into cooperating ("Suppose you might have a use for this half-gallon of honey, Mrs. Harrington?"), but done right, beekeeping can be a safe activity on even an average-sized lot. As with most hobbies these days, there is plenty of literature on the subject in print and on the Internet. In addition, you can build most of the equipment you will need yourself if you so desire. Local clubs and extension services across the country can help you through the inevitable pitfalls.

Far beyond hobbyist beekeepers are the professional pollinators. If you establish contact with a professional pollinator, you create another way to obtain great honey for meadmaking. These individuals serve farmer and orchard owners by bringing colonies of bees to pollinate their crops. Many are small local apiarists, but some are massive interstate operations. Some of these people, known as migratory beekeepers, are truly amazing individuals. The real road warriors transport hundreds or thousands of hives via 18-wheeler truck across the country. To meet pollination demands and their hives' needs for food, they chase nectar flows wherever they can find them. Their stories are as remarkable as their lives (see Whynott, *Following the Bloom,* listed in the Bibliography), and they play a huge role in the agricultural landscape of the United States.

The Art of Beekeeping

Beekeepers in the United States keep European bees primarily, because of their many beneficial characteristics. The most popular strain is probably *Apis mellifera ligustica*, commonly known as the Italian bee. These are the striped yellow bees, and they are gentle, and very productive. *Apis mellifera carnica*, also known as carniolan or Austrian bees, are becoming quite popular in North America. Carniolan bees originate in the area of Bulgaria, Romania, and eastern Austria, and seem to winter better than Italian bees. These bees are extremely docile and well behaved, except for swarming, which the beekeeper must make efforts to control. Another strain, *Apis mellifera mellifera,* from northern Europe, is also raised in the United States and

A stainless steel radial extractor at work. The honey is driven to the side of the drum. Photo courtesy National Honey Board.

An uncapper and parallel design extractor. Photo courtesy National Honey Board.

Europe. This strain is known as the Dark bee, because of its dark, unbanded appearance. It is a large bee with very good cold tolerance, due presumably to its origins in northern France, the British Isles, and Europe north of the Alps.

Beekeepers around the world are facing a serious threat from two major pests: varroa and tracheal mites, which weaken bees and can kill off whole hives. Significant losses are being experienced around the globe, and the mite problem is receiving a good deal of attention from entomologists in an effort to find treatments for infected hives, or resistant strains of honeybees that can stem the tide of this insidious infestation. Among the resistant strains are Russian bees that are less subject to varroa mites, and the Buckfast bee, which is resistant to tracheal mites. The Buckfast bee has the interesting distinction of having been hybridized by the late master beekeeper and meadmaker Brother Adam of Buckfast Abbey. You would be well advised to discuss mite problems and their severity with beekeepers in your area or your local extension agency before you make a large investment in beekeeping as a hobby.

Beekeepers can keep hives in a number of ways, but the most prevalent method consists of a rectangular box hive with combs hanging vertically about ⅜ of an inch apart on wooden "supers," essentially a box with no top or bottom. A hive generally consists of two 10-inch-deep brood supers, and several 6-inch supers stacked above, which can be moved or removed as necessary. This arrangement facilitates hive management and eases collection and extraction of the honey.

Most beekeepers extract honey twice (once during the summer in northern climes) and may extract virtually year-round in tropical areas. In the warmer southern zones, beekeepers generally get three or four extractions per season. In deciding when to extract honey, the beekeeper considers the health of the hive and whether the hive has put up enough honey to support its needs. Once the beekeeper decides to extract honey, timing is important. If the supers are not pulled immediately after they are sealed, they will continue to ripen, altering the honey's final sugar blend.

Once the supers are removed, the beekeeper extracts the honey from the comb. He or she does this by removing the wax cap with a hot, knifelike metal implement. The now "uncapped" supers are placed in an extractor, a large stainless steel drum with a tap. The extractor has a frame in its center in which the supers are held, either like spokes on a wheel or tangentially. The frame is spun mechanically or manually, acting as a centrifuge to drive the honey from the supers onto the walls of the drum. The honey is generally passed through cheesecloth or a similar filter to remove debris and can then be packaged.

As honey users, we often like to get single-source or varietal honey. While this seems simple, it presents specific challenges for the beekeeper. The crop must meet several conditions before it will be capable of producing a varietal honey. For starters, it must occur at a point in the bees' nectar collection that will permit the bees to both fill and cap the combs.

Additionally, the crop or floral source must be large enough to secure the majority of the hive's attention. The plant variety must have a long enough pollination season to allow the bees to collect and cap full supers of the honey, and it must produce enough nectar to ensure that the bees will find it worth the effort to focus on the one source and not search for more attractive alternatives. No matter how prevalent the nectar source may be, some bees will inevitably seek out other sources. As a result, no honey is in the strictest sense a "single-source" product.

Professional pollinators move their hives to large areas of a given floral variety, both to take advantage of the nectar source and to collect the unique honey. In some cases, beekeepers do not even need to move their bees but simply keep track of the source their bees are frequenting. If they do this and separate the supers at appropriate times, they can collect several varietal honeys. Among the many floral sources collected this way are raspberry, star thistle, tulip poplar, tupelo, sage, and mesquite—and all of them produce truly unique varietal honeys that will make accordingly extraordinary mead.

From Nectar to Honey

As we have seen, bees turn plant nectar into honey. Let us now consider the composition of these substances and the process of transformation.

Not much is known about nectar—or at least less is known about nectar than, say, weapons-grade fissionable material. Perhaps the government does not think it worth the effort to collect the knowledge the way it pretty much has to be collected: one bee-ful at time.

Nectar is hard to characterize in detail because it varies a great deal. Many sources put water content at 70% to 80%, but the range varies from a low of 50% to a high of 90%. And because every plant adds its own special components, nectar is a complex blend of compounds.

Despite these variations, sugar constitutes the most important component of nectar. The primary sugar in raw nectar is sucrose with smaller quantities of fructose, glucose, and a number of other sugars. The exact ratio of sugars varies between floral species but does not seem to vary in the same species from one location to another.

The process of nectar production and its movement through the plant still prompts some debate. The current model has plants producing sugars in areas with lower sugar *utilization*, called sources, and moving them to areas with lower sugar *concentrations*, called sinks. Fruits, as well as nectaries in flowers, are sinks. The sugary sap flows largely through the phloem system of the plant and may be additionally modified by the tissues surrounding the nectaries. Apparently, some concentration of aroma and flavor compounds occurs during this modification of the sap near the nectaries.

Nectaries can occur in several locations in, on, and around the blossoms. Glands in the nectaries actually secrete the nectar to make it available to bees and other pollinators.

Honey and nectar are not the same thing. Two things happen when bees convert nectar into honey. First, they reduce the moisture content from more than 50% to less than 19%. Second, they add enzymes that change the chemical composition of the nectar. Two of these enzymes are of particular significance. First, the enzyme invertase converts sucrose (a disaccharide or double-ring sugar) into its constituent monosaccharides (or single-ring sugars), glucose and fructose. Second, the enzyme glucose oxidase acts on glucose, producing gluconic acid and hydrogen peroxide. We'll talk more about the implications of these changes as we discuss the properties of honey.

Interesting Properties of Honey

Since ancient times, the antibiotic effects of honey have been recognized by the medical community. Honey has been used to treat open wounds, has been mixed with whisky for throat and upper respiratory problems (the "hot toddy"), and has been mixed with vinegar and water as a tonic to ward off ills and maintain digestive health. Specifically, honey was known to inhibit bacterial growth. In 1937, Dold and others measured and documented the effect, and called it "inhibine." Twenty-five years later, Dr. Jonathan White and others isolated the exact cause of the antibacterial effect: The glucose oxidase in the honey produces hydrogen peroxide as it acts on glucose to produce gluconolactone and eventually gluconic acid. Glucose oxidase is heat sensitive, and the amount present in specific honeys varies with floral type.

The hydrogen peroxide produced is not present in significant enough quantities to affect flavor, but it is enough to retard bacterial growth in the honey. *The Compleat Meadmaker* National Honey Laboratories (a figment of my hopeful imagination) has not yet completed its research on the bacterial suppression capability of the hydrogen peroxide in the constituted must. My experience with the Mazer Cup and in general gives me cause to surmise that, given fundamentally sound sanitation with your brewing equipment, bacterial activity in mead musts may be sufficiently suppressed to prevent offensive bacterial infection characteristics. White's work actually indicates that the reaction producing the hydrogen peroxide is more prevalent in diluted honey.

Scientific research as to the antibiotic and medicinal properties of honey has continued in other areas. The use of honey in burn treatments has led to further research about possible bioactive components derived from the plants from which nectar has been gathered. Nature seems to hold many of the answers to the problems it poses, and some of them appear to be coming from honey. This comes as no surprise to many beekeepers and honey enthusiasts.

A Closer Look at Honey

Meadmakers must acquire honey before making mead. As a result, we must know everything we can about the characteristics of honey and the factors that influence its composition. Let's start with a general look at grading and honey composition before moving on to the flavor and aroma chemistry of this refined nectar.

As mentioned earlier, beekeepers harvest or extract honey from a hive at various times during the year. The flavor and aroma of each extraction differs from every other. The specific plants in bloom during collection produce the most obvious differentiating factor, but others exist. While the bees cure honey in the hive, it is open to the air and therefore susceptible to inoculation with wild yeasts and other airborne particles. In addition, ambient humidity—as influenced by things like temperature and rainfall—affects the relative moisture content of the nectar collected and the honey produced.

As a general rule, honey from the earlier flows tends to be lighter in color, milder in aroma and lower in wild yeast count than that of later flows. Most apiarists attribute this to the fact that wild yeasts tend to peak in airborne concentration later in the summer. If you can find honey from the first flow of the season, I highly recommend it for meadmaking.

The same variables that differentiate extractions from a single hive also account for the substantial differences seen in honey collected from the same areas from one year to the next. Beekeepers from my area have provided me with samples showing that honeys collected during drier times can have more striking and concentrated aromas. Honey is truly a "vintage" agricultural product—not all that different from wine grapes. The meads made from honey from the same relative extraction from the same hives in two different years will be readily identifiable as two different meads, even though they may have more similarities than differences.

The United States Department of Agriculture grades honey into four classes based on moisture content, flavor, absence of defects, and clarity. Honey meeting USDA Grades A and B must not have more than 18.6% moisture. The low moisture content keeps the growth of wild yeasts and other organisms naturally found in honey in check. In honey with a higher proportion of water, these organisms may begin to metabolize and grow using the honey's nutrients and adversely influence the clarity and flavor of the honey.

Grade C honey contains up to 20% water. Since fermentation activity may occur when the moisture content exceeds 19%, meadmakers steer clear of this grade when selecting honey. Grade C honey generally gets used for commercial food processing, so you may never run across any, but don't think you have found a great bargain if you do. Stick with a good beekeeper and his or her best product, and you will make better mead.

When it comes to assessing flavor, graders look (or *taste*) for smoke (used to pacify the bees during collection), fermentation, chemicals, and other off-flavors, and also for caramelization. Grade A honey has none of these components, but Grades B and C will be "practically free" and "reasonably free" from caramelization while remaining completely free of the other named characteristics and general off-flavors.

The "absence of defects" trait in honey is assessed by looking for visible defects and debris in the honey that would affect its "appearance or edibility", such as bits of comb or propolis, a gum that bees produce. Clarity is based on the presence of bubbles, pollen grains, and other suspended particles. Grades A, B, and C would be rated "clear," "reasonably clear," and "fairly clear," respectively. For meadmaking, I recommend using only Grade A (Fancy) or Grade B (Choice).

Beyond grade, the most apparent characteristic of honey is color. I warn you now however, that you should not judge honey primarily on the basis of color. First, the color of the honey tells you nothing about the actual quality of the product as measured by things like moisture content and flavor. Second, you'll find important exceptions to the intuitive association of milder flavors with lighter honeys. Some distinctive and strongly flavored honeys such as basswood are very light, while very mild and pleasant honeys such as tulip poplar can be quite dark. On the other hand, many beekeepers will have a first extraction of water white premium honey during the late spring, and I have found this to be an excellent source of meadmaking stock. They prize this honey as being of the highest quality, and I have to agree. The floral character of the samples I enjoyed was exceptional.

With that said, you'll want to know that inspectors grade honey color using seven categories: water white, extra white, white, very light amber, light amber, amber, and dark amber. These distinctions can be measured by optical density or using a device called a Pfund color grader.

table 7.1
Color Designations of Extracted Honey

Color Name	Pfund Scale (mm)	Maximum O.D.
Water White	<8	0.0945
Extra White	9-17	0.189
White	18-34	0.378
Extra Light Amber	35-50	0.595
Light Amber	51-85	1.389
Amber	86-114	3.008
Dark Amber	>114	no limit

Composition and Organoleptic Effects

Brewers and winemakers have deconstructed virtually every ingredient and process in brewing and winemaking, and it's time we did the same. As I am not quite ready to establish *The Compleat Meadmaker* National Honey Laboratories, I'll do the next best thing and look at the body of research already collected on honey and its constituent compounds and properties.

The Honey Investigations Unit of the Plant Products Laboratory of the USDA conducted one of the preeminent studies of honey. This information was collected and published by Dr. Jonathan White, who was the chief of the Plant Products Lab, and to whom I owe credit for much of the information here. The results of the study became USDA Technical Bulletin 1261 (see Bibliography). When I discuss the values of honey without mentioning a specific variety, those values are based on averages determined during that analysis of 490 samples of honey collected over two years. It remains one of the most comprehensive pieces of information on honey available.

The Amber Colloid

Honey is a colloid: a fluid system permeated with fine particles that do not settle out and that resist filtration. In honey, there are other "colloids within a colloid": proteins, waxes, pentosans, and inorganic constituents. They appear to originate both from the bees and from the floral source. Colloids can be removed from honey during aggressive filtrations. The most aggressive process, ultrafiltration, can remove substances of a given molecular weight (say 50,000, or 50 KiloDalton) and above.

Much of the flavor and aroma that we associate with honey is associated with these colloidal substances. Like the stems, seeds, and skins of the grape that create distinct variations in different varieties of wines, they add flavor and character to mead. Truly great wines are not all clean and sanitized. The same has been true of the really excellent meads I have tasted. They achieve distinction not from what you take out, but from what you leave in.

The fluid part of the colloid is composed of water, and additional compounds are dissolved in that water. Let's take a look at these constituents of honey.

Water

As mentioned in the discussion on grading, the moisture content of honey plays a critical role in its quality. Honey is hygroscopic and so readily absorbs moisture from the air. To prevent this in the hive, bees seal the combs over honey when it reaches an average of 17.2% water by weight. Of course, that number varies, and beekeepers report seeing moisture contents as low as 15% in dry times with honey from particular nectar sources. Although thick and difficult to handle, such low-moisture honey gives rich flavors and aromas and contributes more points of gravity per pound to your must than a thinner honey.

As a point of reference with regard to moisture, honey with 18% moisture by weight has a specific gravity of 1.417. Such a honey weighs about 11 pounds, 12 ounces per gallon.

Sugar

Honey contains many sugars, and their percentages and ratios vary from one honey to another depending on floral source, curing, and storage. During curing, enzymes break down the multi-ring sugars of nectar (disaccharides, trisaccharides, and oligosaccharides) into simpler products. For instance, sucrose breaks down to its constituent monosaccharides, glucose and fructose—the most prevalent sugars found in honey. Depending on processing and storage conditions, this enzymatic breakdown can continue until the honey is consumed or used. Thus, the actual composition of the honey may vary depending on its age as well as all the other conditions we have discussed.

Honey contains a wide list of sugars in addition to the major constituents we have already mentioned such as sucrose, fructose, and glucose. Other disaccharides include maltose, isomaltose, maltulose, turanose, and kojibiose. Longer chain sugars—oligosaccharides—include things such as erlose, theanderose, and panose.

table 7.2

AVERAGE SUGAR CONTENT OF HONEY

Dextrose (dextrorotatory glucose)	31.3%
Levulose (levulorotatory glucose)	38.2%
Maltose (and other disaccharides)	7.3%
Higher sugars	1.5%
Sucrose (table sugar)	1.3%

Acids

Sweetness masks honey's acidity, but honey *is* acidic. The pH of honey ranges from 3.4 to around 6.1, with the mean and mode both being around 3.9. In making mead, we will need to know both the pH and total acid content of honey and the resulting must. These factors play a role both in the rate and character of fermentation and in the flavor of the finished mead.

Acids account for 0.57% of honey by weight. The primary acid in honey is gluconic acid, produced by enzymatic breakdown of glucose as mentioned earlier. Other important acids include citric, malic, succinic, formic, acetic, butyric, lactic, and pyroglutanic, as well as various amino acids. As you saw when we looked at fermentation, the amount of acid in honey and the specific varieties present are very important to a mead's flavor profile.

Nitrogen and Protein

Proteins constitute about 0.26% of honey by weight. These proteins include the enzymes added by the bees during curing as well as compounds contributed by pollen, yeasts, and other materials incorporated in the honey. Not surprisingly, the amount, variety, and nature of honey protein content is complex, with wide variations seen between honey varieties.

All proteins contain nitrogen—an element that yeast require to grow and thrive—and the average total nitrogen in honey is about 0.043%. Unfortunately, yeast require what is known as Free Amino Nitrogen and much of the nitrogen in honey is bound in proteins. Thus, most honey fermentations require nitrogen supplements to meet the needs of the yeast.

Minerals

Minerals and ash content contribute 0.17% by weight to the average honey. While the absolute amount is very low, minerals have a big impact on honey character. We'll talk more about this when we discuss the flavor attributes of honey in the next section.

This gives you a sense of the overall composition of honey—a look at the "whole," if you will. Now, let's delve deeper into the composition of honey to try to understand better what makes it taste the way it does.

Flavor and Aroma Chemistry

Sadly, the finest reference materials on honey prove inconclusive on the actual flavor-producing substances in honey. Still, a good bit has been learned, so let's run through what we do know.

Obviously, the dominating flavor of honey is the complex sweetness arising from the blend of fructose, glucose, maltose, and other sugars. The exact blend of sugars varies substantially by floral source. For instance, maltose runs from below 4% to above 12%, and higher (longer-chain) sugars range from 0.13% to 8.6%. These variances impact honey flavor, body, and mouthfeel, as well as the fermentation process and its flavorful by-products in mead.

Of course, we know from practical experience that honey takes on many different flavor and aroma characteristics depending on its floral source. A portion of this results from variations in the mineral and acid contents of the honey.

The range of mineral content in honey is quite wide. In general, we find higher mineral contents paired with darker color and higher pH readings. These darker honeys often have stronger flavors, which may result from the higher mineral content. Sulfur, for example, has been shown to exceed aroma thresholds in dark honey. The averages for potassium run more than eightfold higher in dark honey than in light. To compound the situation further, sodium (a flavor enhancer) can reach 400 ppm in darker honeys—a level more than four times that of lighter honey.

In addition to having a flavor impact, minerals provide valuable nutrients for the yeast, especially during its earliest fermentation stages. The range of minerals found in honey include potassium, chlorine, sulfur, sodium, iron, manganese, and magnesium.

The acids found in honey also affect flavor. Citric and malic acids give tart but not unpleasant flavors sometimes associated with citrus and green apple. Acetic acid tastes like (and actually *is*) vinegar. Butyric acids convey a buttery or even cheesy flavor. Various other organic acids also appear in honey and probably contribute to the flavor profile in some extractions. Various amino acids, tannins, and glycoside or alkaloid compounds contributed to the mix by the floral source may also affect flavor.

Some unwanted flavors in honey come from a substance called 5-hydroxymethylfurfural, or HMF. Described as a stale flavor similar to vegetable oil, HMF results from sugar decomposition under acidic conditions. Some HMF inevitably occurs in all but the youngest honeys, but it becomes detrimental to honey flavor at higher concentrations.

As a rule, HMF should be below 40 ppm in honeys, but you will rarely know its concentration in the honey you buy. This simply adds another reason for using fresh honey in meadmaking.

Aroma Compounds

While our tongues can only detect a small number of flavors, the nose can identify hundreds if not thousands of different scents. Thus aroma chemistry is inevitably more complicated.

In honey, the aroma substances lean toward the phenyl alcohols and carbonyls. Using chromatography, the researcher ten Hoopen isolated dinitrophenylhydrazones (DNPH's) in honey. DNPH's are an indicator of aldehydes and ketones. He identified formaldehyde, acetaldehyde, acetone, isobutyraldehyde, and diacetyl. Formaldehyde and acetaldehyde are aliphatic aldehydes. Formaldehyde is obviously going to be astringent, but most aldehydes are described as having fruity flavors and aromas. Isobutyraldehyde is perceived by most as having a malty aroma. Acetone is described as sweet and fruity; diacetyl is associated with buttery or butterscotch aroma and flavor.

Cremer and Riedmann identified phenylethyl alcohol, propionaldehyde, and acetone, and later n-pentanol, benzyl alcohol, and 3-methyl-1-butanol. Propionaldehyde is another aliphatic aldehyde that is fruity with green grass characteristics. Benzyl alcohol is in the same group of flavor and aroma compounds with phenyl ethanol and presents itself with bitter and almond notes. These compounds were present in all of the honeys that they found to be organoleptically recognizable as honey. Phenylethyl alcohol has long been associated with pleasant aroma, being described as perfumed, floral, or roselike. Phenylethyl alcohol oxidizes down to phenylacetic acid, and nearly all phenylacetic esters have been described as having a honey taste and odor.

Other aroma constituents identified include the carbonyls butyraldehyde, isovaleraldehyde, methacrolein, and methyl ethyl ketone. Alcohols include isopropanol, 2-butanol, ethanol, and beta methylallyl alcohol. Esters identified were aliphatic esters—methyl and ethyl formate. Aliphatic formate esters are described as fruity, light, and flowery, and most aliphatic esters have fruity and pleasant descriptors.

All of this makes the point that honey flavor and aroma are neither simple nor straightforward. Many natural flavors can be emulated through the use of one or a small number of "principal" flavor compounds. For example, methyl anthranylate is the principal peak in grapes and it is used in artificial grape flavor. But honey aroma involves a complex blend of subthreshold and above-threshold compounds in delicate balance. The overall character of honey cannot be broken down to replicable formulas or easily copied chemical blends. There just isn't any "principal" flavor compound for honey.

Conclusion

Honey is a variable, dynamic agricultural product, the sum of both botanical and animal processes and subject to the influences of Mother Earth. Most of the compounds that contribute to the flavor and aroma of honey are volatile and have boiling points below 180° F (82° C); they would therefore be subject to rapid blow-off during boiling. It also would stand to reason that the character these compounds create also would be bound to the colloidal substances held in suspension in unheated and unfiltered honey. Putting it plainly, the closer to the hive (in terms of time and treatment), the more complex and flavorful your honey, and thus your mead, are likely to be.

Variation of Honey Composition by Floral Variety

Unless you are buying honey directly from a beekeeper, you'll usually get little information about exactly what you are getting. Hopefully, you'll know the grade (A or B), the floral source, and perhaps the color. Beyond that, you'll be left to your own senses to assess the character of the product. Even when you can talk to the beekeeper to understand the product better, you still won't get a chemical analysis that tells you the balance of sugars, acids, and minerals.

What follows is information that can help to fill the usual information void with regard to honey. To do so, I'm relying on two sources: one published, one personal.

The published data comes from the previously mentioned USDA Technical Bulletin 1261—a worthwhile reference for most meadmakers. Whenever I discuss chemical composition of honey without mentioning a specific variety, those values come from the averages determined during White's analysis of 490 samples of honey. Certain floral varieties of honey may differ markedly from these averages, and I will make an effort to note when those differences should have noticeably good or bad effects on your meadmaking efforts.

The second source of information on varietal honey is personal experience. I served as competition director for the Mazer Cup Mead Competition for several years, and each year provided me with the opportunity to taste and learn about meads crafted from different varietal honeys from around the world. I have tasted and enjoyed my first tulip poplar and tupelo meads there, as well as sage, mesquite, and so many others. This experience has led me to begin accumulating honeys and "banking," as it were, my perceptions on their aromas and flavors. I have tasted more than a hundred varieties, and without being too immodest, I generally have a gallon—or more—of three or four varietal honeys waiting in storage for their transformation into mead. I have begun collecting a "honey library" that currently numbers about twenty-five different varieties from North and South America, Australia, and New Zealand.

In 1993, I embarked on a meadmaking experiment with Dr. Dan McConnell, a close friend, research microbiologist at the University of Michigan, and co-founder of the Mazer Cup. Our goal was to understand the flavors that would be imparted to meads made from the same basic recipe by different varietal honeys and also by different yeast strains on a mead of one varietal honey. We made 65 gallons of mead in one day, using clover, wild raspberry, fireweed, Michigan wildflower, orange blossom, snowberry, and star thistle honeys. We divided a large batch of clover mead and inoculated it with six different yeasts. Tasting and comparing the fruits of that one effort provided me with a deep appreciation for the tremendous impact ingredients have on the profile and impression of a finished mead.

Lastly, over the past several years, I have been regularly visiting with and learning from the South East Michigan Beekeepers Association, or SEMBA. Getting to know beekeepers has helped me to understand how the world of beekeeping and honey revolves, including their practices in beekeeping, how honey gets to market, and the important role hobbyist beekeepers play in agriculture and the honey industry. Along the way, I have shared my knowledge of meadmaking with them, and I hope the relationship has been mutually beneficial.

Varietal Honeys

The nectar source affects most of the variable characteristics of honey, including sugar balance, color, scent, and flavor. FDA guidelines hold that a plant or blossom must serve as the chief floral source in order for the honey to be labeled as such. Beekeepers extract varietal honey by placing new supers or combs in their hives before the hives go out to the crop to be pollinated. By removing these supers from the hive after crop pollination, a "single source" honey results.

Single-blossom honeys possess unique characteristics and often resemble the blossoms or fruit of the plant in aroma and even flavor. For instance, raspberry and cranberry honeys display striking aroma and flavor similarities to the fruits of these plants. Like the fruit, nectaries are a sugar sink for the plant. Thus, it seems logical that the same botanical processes that create sugar, aroma, and flavor in the finished fruit could deliver those characteristics in the nectar used to entice bees.

As mentioned earlier, there are many factors that affect honey character, and many of those factors will play a role in your meadmaking. From honey to honey, the variations largely break down as differences in the levels of the sugars that make up the honey and in the levels of the other components. The data on the substantive differences in composition between honey varieties is presented in Table 7.3.

Honey with a lower moisture content will have a higher sugar content, yielding higher gravity. The dextrose/water content ratio is also important: Lower dextrose levels reduce the chance of crystallization and possible spoilage (see "Storage and Stability" below). Dextrose-to-water values below 1.7 indicate that a honey will not granulate readily. Ratios above 2.1 are indicative of honey varieties that will granulate rapidly. Honey with a complex sugar blend (high levels of maltose and other sugars) will yield complexity in flavor and aroma after fermentation.

The pH of a honey will carry over to the must, and will affect fermentation substantially; try to keep the starting pH of your must above 3.6. That doesn't rule out using honey with a pH below that, but adjustment may be needed. Total acid content will have a big impact on flavor. Higher ash and mineral content will affect aroma and flavor, and also will provide important nutrients and nitrogen content for fermentation. In the same vein, lower mineral and ash levels may dictate the need for additional nutrients.

Table 7.3 expresses the total acid content of the honeys measured as millequivalents/ kilogram. The use of meq./kg provides a more accurate assessment of the acidity than does the method used for acid analysis used by home winemakers. It reflects the amount of cationic charge produced by the acids in the solution. The average for the 490 samples was 29.12; I have weighted my comments relative to each honey's acidity as being either low or high against that value.

Let's look at how the values for different floral source honeys may affect their use in mead.

Citrus. By analysis of the numbers, citrus honey appears to be an excellent candidate for mead. While the glucose level is a bit high, moisture is low, pH is in the middle, and ash content is very low. The low nitrogen content might dictate higher-than-normal yeast nutrient use. Citrus honey of any blend is marketed as "orange blossom," and is light in flavor and very aromatic. Mead made from orange blossom honey remains true to the honey's character, and is both striking in profile and quite delicious.

Clover. The values in Table 7.3 are for sweet clover honey; the USDA has several dozen specimens profiled in the technical bulletin. Moisture levels tend to run on the high side, making clover honey a candidate for quick use. As with most of the lighter-flavored honeys, ash content is low, as is total acid content. The consensus on clover honey is not clear. There are many types of clover, including crimson, white, and red. Many beekeepers report that truly single source clover honey has a strong flavor and aroma profile, which some of them consider too strong to be appealing. They report that a percentage of clover honey sufficient to make it the "primary source" of collected nectar is often mixed with other honeys of mixed or unknown origin to produce a palatable blend with the distinct clover aroma and flavor. This blended honey is then marketed (completely within the rules) as clover honey.

Fireweed. Other than slightly lower than normal total acids and ash, fireweed honey looks like a very average honey. Fireweed honey did not express a dramatic nose or flavor and doesn't seem to create much of a stir as a varietal traditional mead.

Mesquite. Not one of our experimental honeys but a good candidate by the numbers. Produces mead with a strongly distinctive flavor and aroma. High pH is due to lack of total acid, not high ash buffering. This honey should ferment well with a healthy dose of nitrogen and no pH adjustment. Low moisture and acid content make for higher sugar content by weight. Low ash should mean light color and minimal offensive odor or flavor. Might require some acid before bottling for balance, especially in sweeter meads.

table 7.3

Composition of Honeys by Floral Source

Sample	Color	Granulation	Moisture	Levulose	Dextrose	Sucrose	Maltose	Higher Sugars	Undetermined	pH	Free Acid	Lactone	Total Acid	Lactone/ Free Acid	Ash	Nitrogen	Diastase
Alfalfa	4	6	16.2	39.11	33.4	2.64	6.01	0.89	2.8	3.88	20.19	10.16	30.35	0.501	0.093	0.033	17.5
Aster	7	2	17.4	37.55	31.33	0.81	8.45	1.04	3.5	4.68	20.22	2.17	22.39	0.106	0.302	0.043	—
Athel Tree	8	8	15.3	39.75	37.65	1.3	4.24	0.27	1.5	4.09	30.15	5.86	36.01	0.198	0.305	0.063	—
Basswood	4	3	17.4	37.88	31.59	1.2	6.86	1.44	3.6	4.05	16.78	6.58	23.7	0.382	0.084	0.022	—
Blackberry	8	0	16.4	37.64	25.94	1.27	11.33	2.5	5	4.5	27.37	1.76	29.11	0.112	0.399	0.055	—
Blueberry	8	2	17.4	37.2	31.08	0.79	9.09	0.83	3.6	4.36	16.36	4.92	21.29	0.301	0.163	0.059	—
Buckwheat	10	2	18.3	35.3	29.46	0.78	7.63	2.27	4.3	3.97	35.07	6.99	42.06	0.213	0.224	0.064	38.9
Chinquapin	10	1	15.8	33.63	23.93	0.89	12.27	4.79	5.3	4.95	28.57	3.36	31.93	0.121	0.761	0.052	25.3
Clover Alsike	3	1	16.8	39.18	30.72	1.4	7.46	1.55	2.9	3.83	15.82	7.19	23.01	0.44	0.067	0.025	—
Clover Crimson	2	2	17.4	38.21	30.87	0.91	8.59	1.63	2.4	3.74	15.65	6.04	21.68	0.39	0.57	0.029	22.7
Clover Sweet	4	2	17.7	37.95	30.97	1.41	7.75	1.4	2.6	3.77	19.55	6.98	26.53	0.365	0.084	0.039	20
Clover White	5	3	17.9	38.36	30.71	1.03	7.32	1.56	3.2	3.84	22.95	8.71	31.66	0.366	0.156	0.046	—
Coralvine	11	0	16.8	34.86	28.46	0.61	6.11	3.03	7.9	4.32	46.21	8.9	55.11	0.193	0.592	0.057	—
Cotton	5	8	16.1	39.28	36.74	1.14	4.87	0.5	2.3	4.29	24.61	5.21	29.82	0.207	0.339	0.037	—
Cranberry	9	1	17.2	35.59	28.13	1.02	8.03	2.95	7.1	4.37	23.82	6.32	30.14	0.274	0.33	0.041	—
Eucalyptus	6	3	17	39.35	32.27	1.43	6.84	0.8	2.4	4.14	18.96	7.51	26.46	0.383	0.204	0.05	21.9
Fireweed	4	4	16	39.81	30.72	1.28	7.12	2.06	2	3.83	19.3	7.47	26.77	0.374	0.108	0.032	—
Gallberry	5	2	17.1	39.85	30.15	0.72	7.71	1.22	3.2	4.2	16.19	4.46	20.65	0.269	0.163	0.028	18.1
Goldenrod	6	4	17	39.57	33.15	0.51	6.57	0.59	2.6	4.45	19.93	2.11	22.05	0.091	0.263	0.045	37.4
Grape	12	0	21.2	34.4	25.42	1.12	11.47	1.55	4.8	4.03	35.83	8.64	44.47	0.241	0.239	0.082	—
Heartsease	6	4	19.6	37.23	32.98	1.95	5.71	0.63	1.9	4.06	20.7	2.6	23.3	0.123	0.161	0.06	—
Horsemint	4	1	18.8	37.37	33.63	1.01	5.53	0.73	3	3.72	28.51	13.74	42.24	0.483	0.221	0.045	—
Locust, Black	3	1	17.3	40.66	28	1.01	8.42	1.9	2.7	4.03	11.88	4.03	15.94	0.328	0.052	0.018	11
Manzanita	5	7	17.9	34.88	37.1	0.8	6.26	1.4	1.8	4.3	13.86	4.26	18.12	0.308	0.208	0.029	—

Table 7.3

Composition of Honeys by Floral Source *Continued*

Sample	Color	Granulation	Moisture	Levulose	Dextrose	Sucrose	Maltose	Higher Sugars	Undetermined	pH	Free Acid	Lactone	Total Acid	Lactone/ Free Acid	Ash	Nitrogen	Diastase
Marigold	4	4	19.3	37.08	34.22	0.93	5.3	0.44	2.7	3.6	23.42	12.26	35.68	0.524	0.076	0.034	27.3
Mesquite	5	7	15.5	40.41	36.9	0.95	5.42	0.35	3.8	4.2	13.74	2.59	16.33	0.193	0.129	0.012	—
Mexican Clover	9	0	18.2	38.28	29.42	0.75	7.94	1.38	4	3.9	42.23	13.56	55.79	0.321	0.268	0.067	27.8
Mint	1	2	18.8	38.84	33.33	2.1	4.93	0.96	1	4.01	15.9	7.85	23.75	0.494	0.123	0.019	15
Orange	4	4	16.7	39.26	31.83	1.87	6.5	1.33	2.5	3.67	24.23	13.21	37.35	0.54	0.082	0.03	27.8
Orange/grapefruit	6	4	16.5	38.89	32	2.78	7.16	1.37	1.2	3.84	21.47	8.87	30.34	0.415	0.073	0.012	11.9
Palmetto, Saw	7	2	16.6	38.24	30.92	0.83	6.48	1.69	5.3	3.98	26.54	14.71	41.25	0.57	0.352	0.022	14.4
Peppermint	9	5	16.5	42.11	31.04	0.51	6.37	0.89	2.7	4.71	34.11	3.16	37.22	0.096	0.473	0.045	—
Prune	8	6	19.4	36.94	28.09	0.42	10.47	0.77	3.9	6.1	11.8	0	11.8	0	0.694	0.095	—
Raspberry	8	0	17.4	34.46	28.54	0.51	8.68	3.58	3.5	4.04	33.64	5.55	39.19	0.192	0.471	0.047	—
Sage	4	1	16	40.39	28.19	1.13	7.4	2.38	4.3	3.81	19.9	9.19	29.1	0.458	0.108	0.037	—
Sourwood	5	0	17.1	39.79	24.61	0.92	11.79	2.55	3.2	4.53	13.52	3.43	16.95	0.263	0.23	0.02	15.3
Spearmint	6	3	16.6	41.09	32.58	0.43	5.98	0.6	2.7	4.3	32.76	5.67	38.43	0.173	0.313	0.045	—
Sumac	10	2	17.6	31.46	24.39	1.77	8.21	6.9	9.7	4.42	37.74	6.36	44.1	0.168	0.931	0.056	34.1
Thistle, Star	4	3	15.9	36.91	31.14	2.27	6.92	2.74	3.9	3.54	27.67	13.98	41.65	0.52	0.097	0.055	32.9
Thyme	8	1	16.8	37.13	31.2	0.85	8.83	1.7	3.2	4.8	22.41	5.47	27.88	0.244	0.384	0.057	—
Tulip Tree	10	0	17.6	34.65	25.85	0.69	11.57	2.96	6.6	4.45	38.28	4.71	42.99	0.121	0.46	0.076	21.7
Tupelo	7	0	18.2	43.27	25.95	1.21	7.97	1.11	2.3	3.87	25.46	11.2	36.59	0.435	0.128	0.046	17.8
Vetch	3	3	17	38.33	31.67	1.34	7.23	1.83	2.5	3.68	20.46	9.69	30.15	0.469	0.094	0.033	16.4
Vetch, Hairy	2	2	16.3	38.2	30.64	2.03	7.81	2.08	2.5	3.73	15.51	7.51	23.02	0.481	0.056	0.03	12.9
All Honey	5	3	17.2	38.19	31.28	1.31	7.31	1.5	3.1	3.91	22.03	7.11	29.12	0.335	0.169	0.041	—
Lows	0	0	13.4	27.25	23.08	0.14	3.66	0.13	0	3.4	6.5	0	8.68	0	0.017	0	2.1
Highs	12	9	22.9	44.26	40.75	6.54	15.98	8.49	14	6.1	47.19	19.37	59.49	0.95	1.028	0.133	61.2

Raspberry. The very high ash content may seem to make this honey somewhat suspect, but it expresses a dynamite nose and flavor out of the jar, and this character carries over impeccably to finished mead. The interesting sugar blend may be responsible for this honey's complexity, and the higher nitrogen is of benefit during fermentation. Dan McConnell and I took 5 gallons of this mead to the 1994 American Homebrewers Association conference, and it was the most popular of the thirteen meads we brought. The meads we have made and tasted from this honey have all been of very high quality.

Sage. Another low ash, near-the-mean sugar blend honey. It is light in flavor with a delicate and inviting aroma.

Tulip poplar. Tulip poplar honey is a very distinctive honey in aroma, and although it is one of the darker honeys, it has a mild and appealing flavor. Tulip poplar honey has a high maltose content, lending to its complexity, and, like other dark honeys, is high in ash content. It is widely available from the north to the south throughout the Midwest. The tulip poplar mead entered in the Mazer Cup was very characteristic of its constituent honey and was very appealing.

Tupelo. White tupelo is the primary source for the light unblended honey sold as tupelo honey. It has a very high levulose content, low glucose, and a high maltose count, which make it attractive to meadmakers. It is low ash, high in acids, and has a moderate pH. Tupelo honey creates deep complexity in meads, possibly from the elevated levels of maltose. Tupelo mead is distinctly characterful, both in flavor and in a profound bouquet, which hangs in the glass even after the mead is long gone.

Wildflower. The range of honeys sold as "wildflower" is too great to be characterized by one broad brush statement. The USDA included 57 "blend of floral source" honeys in its study, with pH values from 3.67 to 5.30, ash contents from 0.054 to 0.615, and other swings in other categories. Our experience with the wildflower honey in our batch was not particularly favorable, and I suspect too much mineral content, but some of the honeys had values that looked very conducive to good mead. *Caveat Emptor.*

Commercially blended honey. The drawback to much commercially blended honey is that it has been heat pasteurized, albeit at temps in the 145° F (63° C) range. The upside is that the honey is generally buffered through blending to a pH around 3.9, is light amber in color and therefore free of excessive mineral content, and has been blended to have a neutral palate and nose. It makes a good base honey, frequently providing quality grading that assures low moisture content and color grading for ease of use and good recordkeeping.

A quick look through the National Honey Board's *Honey Suppliers Directory* provided me with a list of various suppliers who were marketing a total of 35 identified source honeys. Many of the suppliers listed several honeys. Several other honeys stood out in the study as having interesting characteristics.

Japanese bamboo: high maltose, higher pH, low to medium ash, high nitrogen.

Alfalfa: high glucose, low ash, low nitrogen.

Blackberry: high pH (5.0), high maltose (11.3%), high ash, high nitrogen.

Blueberry: high maltose, low acid, higher pH, high nitrogen.

Chinquapin: low moisture, low glucose, high maltose, very high other sugars, very high ash (0.761%).

Gallberry: low acid, higher pH (4.2).

Black locust: high maltose, very low acid (15.54), very low ash (0.052%), low nitrogen.

Peppermint: high pH (4.7), high acid, very high ash (0.473).

Prune: high moisture, high maltose, pH 6.0!, acids very low (11.80), ash 0.694%.

Sourwood: glucose low, maltose very high, pH 4.53, acids 16.95, ash slightly high. Very interesting candidate. Highly respected among honey authorities.

Vetch, hairy: average sugar values, low pH, low total acids, very low ash, low nitrogen.

Sources of High-quality, Fresh Honey

Due to its instability, the finest honey for meadmaking will be fresh. Quality is further enhanced if it has been extracted and packaged by a beekeeper concerned with the parameters of moisture content and attentive to floral variety documentation. The more you know about your honey and the more accurate that information, the more success you are likely to have as a meadmaker.

With more than 200,000 small-scale beekeepers in the country, you should find at least one in your area. If you have a local beekeepers' supply retailer, he should be able to give you the names of reputable local beekeepers. I also suggest that you call your state's agricultural extension service. It can provide information on potential honey suppliers, as well as information on beekeeping clubs, which in turn can provide information on varietal honey production in your area.

Beyond local relationships, you can secure fresh varietal honey in bulk at reasonable prices from additional sources. Farmers markets generally have at least one quality honey provider; my area actually has four. Local suppliers are unlikely to provide a full range of floral varieties, and for that you will need to contact a good packer. And if you develop a relationship with a packager, he or she may keep you up to date on what is fresh and which honeys are particularly attractive during any time of the year. You may be able to arrange bulk purchases of the exact quantities you desire, and my suppliers also appreciate when I give them the chance to reuse/recycle their packaging materials.

The National Honey Board's *Honey Suppliers Directory* provides tremendous information. I have found good bulk suppliers to include the Bees Knees Honey Factory in Portland, Oregon; the Glorybee Sweetener Company in Eugene, Oregon; Dutch Gold Honey in Lancaster, Pennsylvania; Sandt's Honey in Easton, Pennsylvania; McClure's Honey and Maple Products in Littleton, New Hampshire; Highs Hill Honey in Crossville, Tennessee; and Drapers Super Bee Apiaries in Middleton, Pennsylvania. I'm sure that this list will change with time, but based on my research all of these companies offer good selections of varietal honey.

Storage and Stability

Most people think of honey in much the same way they think of sugar or flour: It's something you can keep around at room temperature until you use it without much thought of spoilage. For really fine meadmaking, however, we advise a different approach. Honey should be thought of in the same way you would think of any other agricultural product you use—the fresher the better. We already know that the volatility of the aroma constituents makes pasteurization an unappealing option, but a number of other problems can also result from age and improper storage.

From the time the honey production begins, it changes constantly. Invertase breaks down sucrose content to its constituent sugars. Evidence suggests that as much as 9% of the glucose in honey also may be converted to more complex sugars, thus changing the balance of sugars. In addition, gluconic acid forms by enzymatic degradation of glucose, affecting both the acidity of the honey and its sugar balance. As a result of this and other actions, some honeys show an appreciable increase in acid content during storage. Finally, honey stored at room temperature will darken with time.

One particular hazard of storage is granulation or crystallization. Honey granulates by building up glucose around a "crystal nucleus" such as a dust particle or pollen grain. Honey crystallizes most rapidly when stored at temperatures between 50° F and 60° F (10° C and 16° C). The optimal temperature for initialization of crystallization is 41° F to 45° F (5° C to 7° C). Crystallization in and of itself is not the cause of any deleterious effects. Great mead can be made from crystallized honey, and many varieties of untreated honey will crystallize very quickly after they are packaged. Honey varieties that have higher glucose concentrations will crystallize more quickly, some in a matter of a few short weeks.

The problem with crystallization is that it creates small localized areas where moisture content exceeds the "safe" level for honey. When solids concentrate into a crystal, the surrounding fluid contains a higher moisture content. The nearby uncrystallized honey becomes, in effect, more watery. Under these conditions, fermentation can occur, resulting in the formation of alcohol and then acetic acid (vinegar). Thus, if crystallization is present and a distinct separation of solids and liquids is apparent, your honey is at risk for off flavors. The end result is honey that is definitely not conducive to making premium mead.

All of these problems can be avoided through immediate use of fresh honey or through proper storage of your honey. The ideal temperature for long-term honey storage is at or below 0° F (-18° C). At these temperatures, honey shows little or no degradation of flavor, color, aroma, or its other physical properties, even when stored for prolonged periods. If freezing is not an option, short-term storage between 61° F and 80° F (16° C and 27° C) is the best option, as this will not promote crystallization. Just be sure it doesn't get too hot: Storage above 80° F will cause particularly rapid deterioration of color, flavor, and enzyme content.

chapter eight
FRUIT AND MELOMEL

Judging from the number of melomels entered in the Mazer Cup each year, meadmakers make more melomels than any other individual style of mead. Fruit can add a host of interesting and beneficial flavors and aromas to mead. In this chapter, I will talk about how to find good fruit, and give recommendations for specific varieties that should yield flavorful results. Then, I get into the specifics of making melomel: when to add fruit and how much to put in.

The nature of individual fruits places them into one of several categories. These categories describe the basic characteristics of fruit and help us decide how to treat the fruit in meadmaking. The commonly available tree-grown fruits are divided into *pomes* (apples and pears) and *stone fruits* (peaches, plums, apricots, and cherries). The *soft fruits* cover berries, further subcategorized into brambles (raspberries, blackberries), vine fruits (melons), ribes (currants), and ground fruits (strawberries). Some fruit enthusiasts include *grapes* here, but because of their substantial influence on alcoholic beverages, I consider them a category—and chapter—of their own. Lastly, we have *tropical fruits,* a category so broad as to offend tropical fruit growers, to be sure. Here we find a diverse and enticing range of options for the meadmaker. Each of these fruit groups presents its own set of challenges, and each should be dealt with appropriately so as to yield optimal results.

I am firmly committed to the notion that wherever possible, meadmakers should pursue the best fruit available for their meadmaking. Just as with honey, you'll find dramatic flavor variations between fruit varieties. Careful selection will dramatically affect the finished quality of your meads.

Supermarkets select fruit for reasons often antithetical to your goals as a meadmaker. Supermarket fruit buyers buy first based on appearance (good-looking fruit moves faster), shelf life (less capital thrown away due to spoilage), and lastly, flavor (it has to taste *kind of* good, or you'll buy your produce elsewhere). You, on the other hand, want fruit that tastes great, smells terrific, and is at the peak of ripeness and freshness. It wouldn't hurt if it was cheap, either, but five years down the road you won't remember if you spent an extra few dollars for that bushel of plums, but you will be able to taste the difference in your crowd-pleasing plum melomel.

With a little effort and legwork, meadmakers can find great fruit varieties. Prior to the advent of the huge grocery chains, a massive amount of work was put into developing fruit with rich flavor and aroma, as well as high sugar content, thin skin, and high juice content. A few farmers still grow these older cultivars, and you also may find them as nursery stock for homegrowers. If you are interested in growing your own fruit, bear in mind that almost any fruit grown with care and harvested at its peak will be of markedly higher quality that store-bought fruit, since proper fertilization, watering, and plant care will yield better fruit from every variety. Once you do some work to obtain good fruit for your mead, you may not be willing to go back to Red Delicious apples or rock-hard grocery store plums again.

I will discuss good varieties of fruits later, but the work of finding them or other high-quality fruit for your mead will be up to you. Try starting with the local farmers market or your phone book. If a grower knows which varieties he or she grows or sells, you are on the right track. Any grower who is growing the high-quality varieties listed below will be happy to help you select good fruit and will probably enjoy talking to someone who knows the difference and appreciates the effort an orchardist puts into growing really tasty and aromatic fruit. Learning to find and recognize good fruit will yield wonderful dividends not only in your meads, but in your pies, desserts, and fruits you eat out of hand. I also feel that the growers of these fruits deserve to be rewarded with our business. Theirs can be a tough go. They are doing the work that suits our needs, and they have earned our business.

Finally, remember that the flavor of mead made with fruit can and often does differ dramatically from the flavor of the fresh fruit itself. Just as a fine Cabernet tastes markedly different from grape juice, so will a blueberry melomel contrast distinctly with the fruit from which it was made. Of course, the finished product will be enjoyable, but those with a taste for alcoholic fruit juice would do well to add a shot of Absolut to their Welch's, if that is the goal.

Pomes

No other fruit receives so much attention from horticulturists around the globe, and the number of apple varieties available to the meadmaker is staggering. For many years, in both the United States and Great Britain, the consumption of cider (hard cider) equaled or surpassed the consumption of beer and other alcoholic beverages. The many uses for apples, as well as their nutritional value and long cellar life, as compared with other fruits, have given the apple a high place in the hierarchy of fruit science. Orchard owners around the globe choose from several thousand apple varieties, each with its own merits and shortcomings.

With few exceptions, meadmakers add apples to their must in the form of pressed apple cider. There are two options for creating a cider to ferment. The first uses a single variety of apples in the pressing. Here the meadmaker seeks to find a variety with good flavor, tannin levels, and a desirable sugar-to-acid balance. Use of just one variety offers consistency by eliminating the variances that occur in blending. Several traditional European varieties have been used for this practice: Dabinett, Medaille d'Or, Stoke Red, Yarlington Mill, Kingston Black, Foxwhelp, Harry Master's Jersey, and a few others. Unfortunately, unless you grow or press your own apples, these single variety ciders will likely be quite difficult to find. In the United States, some fruit growers press single-variety ciders out of necessity (they only have one kind of apples), and others are experimenting with varieties they consider promising. I have tasted single-variety ciders fermented from Northern Spy, Gravenstein, and Wolf River apples, and all were distinct and quite pleasant. As this practice grows, and the results become better known, some American apple varieties will likely be welcomed into this exclusive single variety club. Roxbury Russet, Golden Russet, and Spigold are apples with pronounced character that merit consideration.

Show time in the orchard: a branch of Jonathan apples ready for harvest.

The Roles of Tannin

The term "tannin" is used to describe a family of chemical compounds with a variety of astringent properties. Among them are the chemicals derived from tree barks used in the leather tanning process, hence the term. Most of compounds in the tannin group are harmful if ingested, except for a group known as the proanthocyanidins.

Proanthocyanidins (PAs) are derived from the stems, seeds, and occasionally flesh of fruits, including grapes, apples, and pears. They are of particular interest to us; when wine- and meadmakers refer to tannin, they are speaking of PAs. Tannin contributes a mouth-drying or puckering effect. By itself, tannin is not a pleasant substance to taste, but in wines, meads, and ciders it balances the sweetness from sugars and glycerine in the honey and fruit. Tannin also juxtaposes with the perfumed or flowery characteristics of many fruits. Full-bodied red wines and dry ciders both derive much of their character from tannin. As meadmakers, we can obtain a desirable level of tannin in our meads by using high-tannin fruit varieties or by adding tannin to the fermented mead before bottling.

Fresh-picked Royal Gala apples have a nearly blossom like floral character.

The second approach to cidermaking blends a number of varieties, with each contributing its distinctive and beneficial characteristic. Individual varieties may add sweetness (sugar content), tartness, tannin, or exceptional aroma or flavor. Cider mills continuously adjust and tinker with their blends, both to improve flavor and to account for the changes in availability of given varieties during the picking and pressing season. For those interested in blending or pressing their own, cider blends (both for sweet and hard cider) generally contain about 40% sweet or dessert apples (Red or Golden Delicious, Macintosh), 40% tart apples (Jonathan), 10% aromatic apples (Winesap, Roxbury Russet), and 10% highly flavored apples (Mutsu, Northern Spy, Pitmaston Pineapple). Some varieties of so-called "crab" apples are added to hard cider blends as sources of acid and tannin.

In *The Art of Cidermaking,* Paul Correnty offers considerable guidance about blends of apples for cidermaking. The blending of cider for meadmaking has largely been driven by the blending of sweet cider for unfermented consumption, and the truth may be that blends of apples that make for great mead may be entirely different from those used for the table. Good cysers, I have found, must retain a substantial amount of apple aroma and flavor to balance the body and aroma from the honey, as well as the alcohol. At a minimum, I would advise that you take the time to find and taste a selection of different ciders from your area. Try to select a cider that has a distinctive and bold taste that will carry over to your mead.

A groundswell of interest in antique apple varieties has been occurring over the past few years, and this will be of benefit to meadmakers. Some of the more elegant and distinct commercial hard ciders are being blended from Russets and other antique varieties. Many of these varieties are highly flavored apples whose appeal in the past was based on flavor and aroma, and not on appearance. This is all to the better for those who are most interested in the juice. Finding these varieties, or a cider mill that uses them in their blend, may prove to be a bit of a challenge in your area, but it should be worth the effort. Growing your own may be another alternative.

Pears have not had nearly the impact on meadmaking that apples have. Much of this is due to the difficulty in dealing with pears in the fermentation process. Whole pears in a fermenting mead tend to turn to sludge and create huge problems with racking and clarity. Pressed pear nectar would be far easier to deal with in the meadmaking process. I have had a few very well-received pear melomels in the Mazer Cup competition, and they were both well made and very representative of the fruit. Seckel, Passe Crassane, Sheldon, Magness, and Winter Nelis varieties are noted for their robust and distinctive flavors. These are dessert varieties, and meads made with them will probably require the addition of some tannin to avoid being bland or flaccid.

The pear-based counterpart to hard cider is perry, the fermented juice of pears, reportedly named for Sir Geoffrey Perry, one of Henry VIII's favorite cidermakers. Perrymaking is largely, but not exclusively, a pursuit of the French and English. As with apples, there are many European varieties of pears that are cultivated for this purpose. These pears, like cider apples, have higher levels of tannin and acid and are considered "dry" pears, often both in taste and moisture content.

European meadmakers will have far better luck obtaining both fruit and trees, as orchard stock of many of these varieties has not passed though the elaborate process of quarantine required for their introduction into the U.S. agricultural market. Rock, Moorcroft, and Yellow Huffcap are among those still available from nurseries in Britain. Blakenely Red, Brandy, and Normannischen Ciderbirne are also available in the United States.

Many of the varieties grown in the heyday of cider and perry production have disappeared from the horticultural landscape, often rightly so. Like antique apples, some of those with finer merits are being rescued from extinction through diligence and field research by fruit enthusiasts. By tapping the memories of aging fruit aficionados, these orchard sleuths have found nearly forgotten trees of many unique and tasty varieties of fruits. They have located these trees growing unrecognized on abandoned farms and in the yards of newly developed subdivisions, and grafted their progeny to new stocks, preserving their blessing for at least one more generation of fruit lovers.

Stone Fruits

Since the resurgence of meadmaking, stone fruits have enjoyed considerable popularity among meadmakers, with good reason. Cherries, peaches, plums, and

Tart cherries may produce treasures for meadmakers.

apricots all provide wonderful complementary tastes and aromas to the honey in mead. As summer fruits, their flavors and aromas readily evoke the warm, comfortable sensations of the season. In season, you can buy them at very reasonable prices and freeze them for later use without tremendous loss of quality, especially for use in meads. Alternately, you can purchase them frozen.

Cherries come in two types; tart (also known as sour, acid, or pie) and sweet. Foods such as pies and preserves generally use tart cherries, as do juices and flavorings for candy. Sadly, U.S. cultivation of high-quality tart cherries lags far behind that of Europe, particularly in eastern countries such as Poland, Germany, and the Slavic countries. Red tarts commonly grown in the United States include English Morello, North Star, Early Richmond, Montmorency, and Meteor. Of these, the late Robert Kime of Cornell University, a Mazer Cup best-of-show winner, recommended Meteor for its strong cherry character. My tastings with Amy Iezzoni at the Michigan State University Agricultural Experiment Station showed me, however, that these common U.S. varieties lacked the almost explosive mouth-filling flavor and complexity of character and aroma of the European cherry varieties I tried. I found that Oblacinska and Pozog worked well in mead, and would be good choices for homegrowers. They also possessed an intensely rich purple coloration, which looked beautiful in the finished mead. The diversity of European tart cherry varieties offers an untapped treasure trove for meadmakers.

Tree-ripened peaches are far more flavorful and juicy.

Sweet cherries receive much more attention in North America. Bing and Napoleon (a.k.a. Royal Anne) cherries are widely available and generally are of high quality, but other varieties may offer more intense flavor, aroma, and color. Stella, Van, Lambert, and Black Tartarian have excellent flavor and may be easier to find. Not as common but worth the trouble are Merton Bigarreau, Kirtland's Mary, and Downer's Late Red. Sweet cherries are not as flavorful, pound for pound, as their tart cousins, and so may require more fruit per gallon, but their soft fruity bouquet blends marvelously with honey aromas. They also go very well in dry to medium meads, since their acid content does not demand as much sweetness to provide balance as tart cherries might.

Cherries can be added to a must either pitted or unpitted. The pits are an issue of some debate. Some people will tell you that pits add an astringency to the mead that they find unpleasant. I have added small amounts of unpitted cherries to a must and found that they added a vanilla/nutty and perhaps even woody character that was very pleasant. If you kept 15 pounds of unpitted cherries on a must for a prolonged period, however, it would, in all likelihood, become offensive. Another concern is that the flesh of the pits of stone fruits contain cyanide compounds. The question lies in whether or not the concentration of these compounds poses any threat. The topic has been debated at length in other arenas, and you might study those arguments in deciding whether or not to use pits.

Good peaches differ dramatically from those you get off the shelf at the store. Peaches ripened on the tree attain a profound flavor and sweetness that store or kitchen-ripened fruit cannot approach. The peach family splits into cling and freestone varieties, depending on whether or not the flesh clings to the stone or is easily separated. For meadmaking purposes, the cling varieties tend to be more highly flavored and, unfortunately, harder to deal with. You also will find white and yellow fleshed varieties; this distinction does not affect flavor, but may have an effect on the color of your mead.

Reliable peach varieties for flavor include Late Crawford, Zachary Taylor, and Harbinger (yellow fleshed), George IV, Oldmixon Free, and Peregrine (white fleshed), and Cresthaven (for warm climates). Apricots also stand up well in meads, and good varieties are Blenheim and Moorpark. Blanching (dipping for 40 to 60 seconds in boiling water) makes peaches and apricots very easy to peel. For use in a mead, sliced or halved peaches will hold their form better; mashing yields a mess. I would advise removing the pits.

Lift the boughs when picking raspberries. Berries often hide beneath the foliage.

Plums make some of the finest melomels I've tasted but can be tricky to use. For starters, they are unwieldy to work with. In addition, they offer a delicate character that can become unrecognizable after fermentation and aging. Perhaps more so than any other fruit, plums will be of dramatically higher quality if allowed to ripen on the tree. Store-bought plums will rarely be of anything more than passable quality. Plum skins become thinner and more fragile, and the fruits become very soft as they ripen, making them a storekeeper's nightmare. Plums are therefore picked very "green" or unripe and are kept in controlled storage until sold. A tree-ripened plum is a joy for the eye, the nose, and the tongue.

Plums fall into three categories: Japanese, Japanese American, and European. Japanese plums tend to be larger and are the type eaten out of hand in most areas of the country. European plums are often used in canning or are dried as prunes. Good European varieties include Coe's Golden Drop, Count Althann's Gage, Pearl, Sugar, Kirkes, Mirabelle, and Mount Royal. Japanese plums tend to be slightly juicier and also ripen better after they are picked. Good choices would be Formosa, Shiro, Starking Delicious, Methley, and Elephant Heart. There are some varieties that are crosses between American and Japanese types. Kahinta, La Crescent, Perfection, Superior, Tecumseh, and Toka all have very good flavor.

Soft Fruits

Homegrown strawberries – ripe all the way to the stems. Though small, they are packed with flavor.

Pound for pound, the soft fruits bring more flavor to the table than any other type of fruit that I know. Raspberries, blackberries, blueberries, and currants pack a wallop on your palette, and they also make for some dynamite melomel. These fruits are popular with meadmakers because they are easy to use during fermentation and aging and also because they taste so good. With the exception of the melons, soft fruits tend to have a lot of acid in their acid-to-sugar ratio.

Raspberries may be the most common fruit added to mead. In sweet meads they retain much of the character of the fresh fruit, but in dry meads they can add a significant acidity and can almost over-accentuate the dryness. They retain their aroma well, and always add a deep, rich color. They are universally available, either fresh or frozen, but are never cheap to buy, and so make a good choice for home cultivation or pick-your-own farm procurement. If you choose to grow or pick your own, good varieties are Bababerry, Royalty (Purple), Heritage, Latham, and Fall Gold (Yellow).

Blueberries in season are far less expensive than raspberries, but again, fresh-picked or homegrown berries will outstrip their store-bought cousins in flavor intensity by a long shot. Good options for the quality conscious would be Bluecrop, Earliblue, O'Neal, Patriot, Sharpblue, Blueray, Northblue, Northland, Northsky, Coville, and Jersey. Cultivating blueberries requires substantial soil treatment in most geographical locations, so some research and preparation are in order for the aspiring blueberry grower.

Currants will be much harder to obtain fresh. They require a cool climate, and home cultivation of black currants is still prohibited in many areas of the country due to diseases they can harbor. Black and red currants fairly burst with flavor and color and contribute tremendous fruit aromas and esters. Even vine-ripened currants are very high in acid, which will carry over to your mead; adjust your recipe accordingly. The finished melomels can be very vinous in character. Try Magnus, Consort, Mendip Cross, and Champion black currants, if you can find them. Among the red varieties, Red Lake is a reliable producer, and Johnkeer van Tets has a reputation for excellent flavor. Jostaberries are a cross between a gooseberry and a currant and are also a good berry to try. Meads of this sort may not do well in competition, due to the judges' lack of familiarity with these fruits, but don't let that stop you. They will go beautifully with food or after a meal.

Melons may seem perhaps an unusual addition to a fermented beverage but are not really out of place, and they retain their fruit character in the finished mead

Growing Your Own

If you do choose to start growing fruit, bear these thoughts in mind. Selecting the right varieties can be of critical importance. Find cultivars that grow well under your soil conditions and in your climate. A highly touted variety grown under less than ideal conditions will probably not bear fruit of as high a quality as another variety growing in its peak conditions. Find a nursery or an orchard supplier with a friendly proprietor—one who is knowledgeable about your area and willing to make suggestions and offer growing insights. Learning to graft can provide a means of increasing the number of varieties available to you on a small piece of property. Grafting permits you to put multiple varieties of a fruit on one tree, and can provide the added benefit of extending the season during which you will have fresh fruit.

remarkably well. They have a much lower acid level than berries, and so can work well across the dry-to-sweet spectrum. They're very easy to deal with, and they contribute distinct and pleasing aromas. Lastly, they are not all that hard to grow at home, requiring only careful attention to your planting schedule and a healthy dose of compost. Good cantaloupes: Ambrosia, Burpee Hybrid. Good muskmelons: Classic and Sweet Dream. Honeydews are particularly aromatic and sweet; Earlidew and Sweetheart are solid choices. Kiwis are another vine fruit, but one with considerably more acid than melons. In fact, a great deal of the kiwi's flavor comes from its acidic nature, and thus the delicate flavor of kiwi can be difficult (but not impossible) to capture recognizably in a finished mead. Kiwis require a good deal of processing, but often bear generously, and can make for a fun crop to grow. Kiwis require both male and female plants in order to bear fruit. Good varieties are Blake, Monty, and Saanichton (female), and Chico #3 (male).

Strawberries make a great crop to obtain from a pick-your-own farm, if you can. Call ahead. If they know the varieties, you know you've got a serious grower; if they don't, try around until you find one who does. Growing enough strawberries to make a batch of mead can take some territory, and unless your family is particularly appreciative of your meadmaking efforts, it can also be difficult to convince them that they don't belong over ice cream, in jam, or on a shortcake. If you are growing or picking strictly for flavor, try Earliglo, Honeoye, Veestar, Cardinal, Catskill, Kent, Raritan, Secord, Allstar, Lateglow, or Sparkle. Grow-your-own Everbearing berries (nice for extending the season) are Autumn Beauty and Ogallala. If you are looking for little jewels that are packed with flavor, you might try the Alpine varieties. They are small in size, but long on taste. Try Mignonette or Pineapple Crush. Strawberries are also lower in acid content than are raspberries. They are also a bit timid when it comes to adding color; they often yield soft blush or pinkish colors. You might consider matching them with light-colored and -flavored honeys, such as alfalfa.

Tropical Fruits

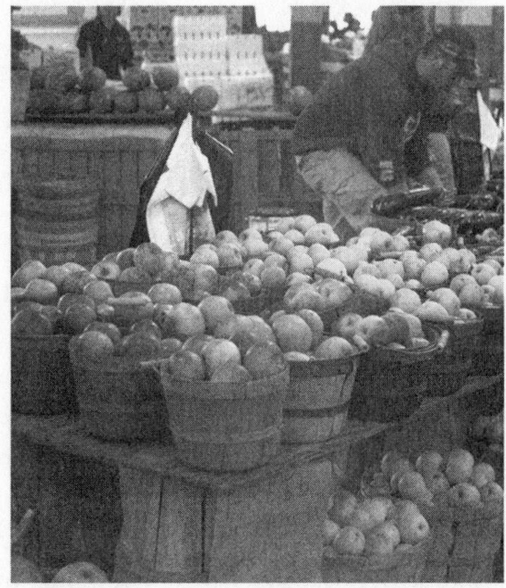
To find the highest quality at the Farmers Market, look for local growers.

The availability of some excellent and exotic honey and some truly luscious fruit in the tropical climes make tropical fruit and mead a great match. Mangos, pomegranate, passion fruit, as well as the citrus fruits, will all make delicious melomel. Some of the best dessert mead I have ever tasted was a sweet pineapple mead that dripped with the taste and aroma of pineapple. Guavas and papaya all make fine additions, too, especially if they are plentiful in your area.

If you elect to make a citrus mead, you should know that the average acid levels in citrus fruits are high enough to be a challenge to meadmakers. Grapefruit varieties average about 3% acidity, lemons and limes about 5%. Those are averages across several varieties; you could find yourself with a crop of lemons with acidity of 7% or higher. That is a level nearly ten times higher than is found in most commercial white wine grapes. Even if you become adept at acid reduction, you can end up with very tart mead. If you are interested in making mead with fruit that has very high acid levels, you will want to monitor pH during fermentation and consider sweetening post-fermentation.

If you are fortunate enough to live in an area that will permit you to grow your own, here are a few recommended varieties that are highly regarded. Mangos: Tommy Adkins, Cooper, and Villasenor. There are three groups of pineapples: Cayenne, Queen, and Spanish. Try Smooth Cayenne, Natal Queen, or Singapore Spanish. Guavas come with pink or white flesh. Beaumont, Patillo, and Ruby are good pinks; Parker's White, Mexican Cream, and Supreme are noted whites. Passion fruits are technically a vine fruit, but require tropical conditions; try *P. edulis*. Papayas can make fine meads. Fairchild, Higgins, and Waimalalo are known for good flavor.

All of these fruit are soft in nature and will require additional preparation before adding to your must. The use of a hop bag to contain the fruit in a plastic fermenter can yield very good results and reduce your cleanup dramatically.

Prickly Pear

Prickly pear is the fruit of a cactus. It isn't the most friendly of fruits—its thorns are barbed and will embed themselves into your skin. Leather gloves are recommended. In addition, prickly pears must be boiled for a half-hour or more before adding to your fermentation, or they will become a bubbling, foaming, slimy, and difficult-to-clean mess. If you can press or otherwise extract the juice, it can be boiled on its own.

Finding Good Fruit

With all of my commentary on fruit varieties, you may think that the only way to acquire good fruit is to grow it yourself. That's really not the case. Knowing your way around fruit retailing can get you into very high-quality fruit. With a little research, good fruit can be found almost anywhere. Orchards and homegrowers offer some of your best options. Check out your phone book, or call your local extension agent. Traveling the back roads in orchard country while fruit is in season will generally reveal more than a few small growers plying their crops (and often their honey, too) at roadside stands.

Farm markets also offer good opportunities, but you'll need to know the difference between a grower and a reseller. Altogether too often, the resellers will have the prime spots at farm markets, with gorgeous boxes and baskets of fruit displayed proudly right near the entrance. The fact of the matter is that all they are doing is buying fruit in bulk at a produce terminal and then reselling it to the public at a profit. Growers, on the other hand, operate on a much more fragile margin and cannot afford the high-profile locations. They will, however, be much more knowledgeable about the fruit they are selling, and since they are picking it and transporting it short distances themselves, their fruit may spend more time on the tree or vine, and be sweeter and more flavorful. Beware the beautiful fruit at farm markets, unless you're just buying it to look at. Usually the best-tasting fruit will not be the prettiest, and may take some finding. Another trick that I have found to be worthwhile is to shop farm markets late in the day, as they are preparing to close. The farmers will be clearing out their stalls in order to keep from transporting their crop back from whence it came and may be willing to unload large lots of very good fruit at bargain prices.

Produce terminals are a possibility, as well. For the most part, terminals sell only to businesses, and in case lots. They keep some odd hours, too, usually operating at night so that grocery store and other retail buyers can buy at night and get shelves stocked during off hours. The variety at produce terminals can be staggering, and the demeanor is all business. There can be great fruit there, though, and bargains, too, for the stout of heart.

As I have demonstrated in this chapter, fruit can become an obsession equal to or greater than mead itself. As with any mead, ingredient quality drives finished product flavor, so when you make melomels, any time that you spend finding good fruit will be repaid with palate-pleasing dividends. Once you have good fruit, you'll be ready to add it to your mead—and that is the topic of our next section.

Making Melomel

Adding fruit to your mead recipes opens up a cadre of possibilities, both in the fruits you choose and in how you add them to your mead. Below, I will discuss many techniques for getting fruit flavor into your meads. Please bear in mind that any method that you perceive to deliver satisfactory results following a workable procedure is a good method. Dogmatic adherence to strict and ungainly procedures can turn your efforts from enjoyable to burdensome, and defeat the whole purpose of your hobby in the first place.

Making mead with fruit can be accomplished in many ways. For the most part, I prefer to use fresh, whole fruit whenever possible. However other forms of fruits can yield very impressive results while being quicker, easier, and more consistent. Let's consider the various forms of fruit you can choose from, including juices and concentrates, elixirs and fruit liqueurs, and fresh and frozen fruits.

Juices and Concentrates

Pasteurized juices can be used at any stage of the meadmaking process: in primary or secondary fermentation or at bottling. The upside of fruit juices is their ease of use. The downside of juices is that the concentration of flavor and desired specific gravity can be hard to hit exactly. Use of fruit juices in combination with a thick, heated honey solution—10 to 15 pounds of honey and 1 gallon of water—can make this problem easier to overcome. To hit a targeted specific gravity, start with a defined amount of pasteurized juice, say 1 or 2 gallons, add the honey solution, and then dilute the combined liquid with distilled water up to your desired gravity.

Fruit extracts and concentrates also can be used effectively and can make for far greater control of fruit flavor and aroma. They generally do not require sanitation and are best added after fermentation or at bottling. I frequently tinker with my meads right up to the point at which they are bottled or kegged, and sometimes even after that. Extracts and concentrates give the meadmaker the opportunity to adjust or strengthen the flavor of the fruit across a huge spectrum. If this is going to be your method of adding fruit or other flavors to your mead, I recommend "naked" meadmaking, meaning that you start with a show mead and ferment it to completion without flavorings or acid adjustments. This leaves you with maximum flexibility when you go to create your flavored mead. You will then know if your mead is too dry and needs sweetening, or is too sweet and requires acidity to balance the sugar and provide complexity.

Concentrates can also be tricky to deal with. The two most commonly available concentrates are fruit concentrates sold for brewers and frozen juice concentrates. Both work well and should be added after secondary fermentation has ceased. Use the sorbate technique explained in "Sweetening" in the chapter on Yeast and Fermentation to prevent re-fermentation. My favorite method is to use several 4-ounce samples of the base mead and to add different measured amounts of the fruit flavoring to the individual samples. If the desired amount of flavor works out to 2 milliliters of flavoring per 4 ounces of base mead, then 4 into 128 gives 32 glasses per gallon; 2 ml x 32 = 64 ml of flavoring per gallon of base mead. It's also not a bad idea to hold back a gallon or so of the base mead when blending. Since you can't take out the fruit concentrate once it's in, a little margin of error can be a saving grace. Another highly advisable practice is to add the concentrate a week or so before bottling, thus giving the additional sugars an opportunity to ferment out, should the yeast still have anything more to say on that subject.

Elixirs and Fruit Liqueurs

Elixirs and liqueurs are not much different from the extracts and concentrates I mentioned above, except that they contain a fair measure more alcohol, and in the case of liqueurs, a lot more sugar. They can be added using the same procedure (and I speak from experience when I say that you should give them a chance to work off the extra sugar before bottling). Others have preached adding a small amount of liqueur to each individual bottle at bottling time, but I am uneasy with this approach. Liqueurs should, in my opinion, be reserved for dessert meads, as they will add so much sugar. They are quite nice in recipe formulation, however; if you want to nail a nice orange blossom honey and Grand Marnier® mead, you can get the exact flavor and balance you want with very little difficulty. Whether or not you think that's cheating, I will leave to your conscience.

You can easily make an elixir for flavoring mead. Start with a large, sealable glass vessel (the half-gallon or gallon honey jars you may have hanging around will work beautifully), and some inexpensive vodka, preferably with as little recognizable taste as possible. Put a fifth of vodka in each gallon jar, and then add fruit to fill the remaining space. After a month or so, taste some of the fruit (yowee!); if it still tastes strongly like fresh fruit, seal it back up for a few more weeks. If the fruit is bland and uninspiring, pour the liquid off into a separate container, discard the fruit, seal up the fruity liquid and use as needed (you might try "discarding" your raspberries or pitted cherries into a blender with some ice cream).

Homemade liqueurs can be an excellent method of having both a fruit flavoring for your mead and something nice to share after a meal with a loved one or to pour over vanilla ice cream. Or maybe even to pour over a loved one. Homemade liqueurs make terrific gifts, too, and after sharing a bottle with friends, you'll know exactly who will appreciate them. They are very easy to make, and will keep, either on the fruit or in the bottle, for an indefinite amount of time. Friends of mine have decades-old jars of this stuff lingering around their houses that they haul out only for nearly sacred annual ritual samplings. I don't take it quite that far. I just like to make and drink the stuff. Here's a sample recipe of a good dual purpose (multi-purpose?) liqueur that I have made and enjoyed.

Cherry Euphoria

1	**fifth (750 ml) cheap vodka**
4	**c. (1 qt., or 0.97 L) fresh or frozen Red Tart pitted cherries**
2	**c. (0.474 L) table sugar**

You simply toss all of the ingredients into some type of sealable glass or plastic container, stir it occasionally for two or three days until all of the sugar has dissolved, and then wait. In three or four months, strain out the cherries and bottle (you don't have to be as compulsive about your sanitation in bottling; the alcohol will take care of anything stupid enough to venture into this stuff). For those of you using commercially available frozen tart pitted cherries, you might be interested to know that a 10-pound box of cherries equals roughly 28 cups, and for that much fruit you'll need about four half-gallons of cheap booze. Not that any of us would ever make that much of this stuff once a year. Optional adjuncts for complexity include vanilla beans, honey, cinnamon stick, and anything else you think might improve the basic recipe. The Euphoria treatment does work with raspberries, too, but you don't need quite as much fruit.

Commercial fruit liqueurs are widely available, and will provide consistent, repeatable results, but can cost an arm and a leg. Chambord (raspberry), Midori (melon), cherry kirsch, and apple and peach schnapps will all offer strong fruit character, but the cheap schnapps in particular seem to add an almost artificial edge to meads, and they don't do much to support your local high-quality fruit orchardist, either.

Fresh and Frozen Fruits

Given the opportunity, I would chose to use fresh, whole fruit for every mead I make. That isn't always the case, and I have made many fine meads from frozen fruits and concentrates, but the level of control and the overall quality and flavor of the mead cannot match what is possible with fresh fruit. Some also find a mystique in working with fresh fruit. It can be messy, and yes, it does require some timing on your part, but working with fresh fruit instills a sense of connection with winemakers and meadmakers from generations far back in time. Obtaining and using real fruit connects me with the earth and with the people who work so hard to grow these tasty ingredients. Of course, it also gives me an excuse to make some pie!

Frozen fruits provide some real advantages for meadmaking. Frozen fruit is easy to obtain and handle, and you can use it whenever the spirit moves you. Freezing fruit also breaks down much of the cellulose between the cells in the flesh of the fruit. This liberates the juice more readily, and makes the job of the yeast much easier. Some fruits, such as tart cherries, freeze well, and retain much of the character of the fresh fruit when used, but this is not true of all fruits. Raspberries, strawberries, and peaches all experience subtle or not-so-subtle changes in aroma and flavor after being frozen.

Fruit can be added to your must anywhere along the line, but when it goes in will determine how it must be treated, and the volume of flavor and aroma the fruit will contribute. Pre-fermentation additions raise some concerns about sanitation. Unsanitized fruit generates risk of bacterial contamination, but perhaps more alarming is the presence of large quantities of wild yeast on the surface of the fruit. I have made pre-fermentation additions of fruit to meads and beers several times using a hybrid technique I call the "Plastic Fermenter and Immersion Chiller Method."

With your immersion chiller in place in the boiling kettle, bring 3 to 4 gallons of water to a rolling boil. Boil the water for 10 to 15 minutes, then put the fruit and the chiller in a previously sanitized plastic 7-gallon fermenter. You can place the fruit in a muslin bag in the fermenter, if you would like, for easier cleanup. Add your honey to the boiling water in the kettle, and carefully pour the mixture into the fermenter, over the fruit and immersion chiller. Cover the fermenter with aluminum foil, and allow the whole mess to sit for 20 to 30 minutes as it falls from about 150° F (66° C), then chill to pitching temp.

A concern when using heat and fruit is the potential setting of pectin(s). Different fruits have different amounts and types of pectin. Pectin is the component in fruit that causes it to gel when heated and cooled. When heated, the pectin sets—chains of pectic acids form—and causes a haze that can be difficult to remove.

There are some other downsides to this process. The fruit in a primary fermentation gets beaten up pretty substantially. The carbon dioxide expelled during a vigorous ferment will carry with it a generous amount of the aroma from the fruit. You also need to take great care with the hot honey solution. A boil kettle with a spigot is a blessing for this procedure. The large amount of head space in a plastic fermenter leads to concerns about oxidation due to the larger surface area. Lastly, you are putting a lot of faith in your recipe formulation. Other than blending, there is little you can do to change the outcome of this method.

On the other hand, you do have the peace of mind of guaranteed sanitation, and you have good control of fruit handling. You aren't squeezing fruit into a carboy or stainless steel keg, and getting both the mead and the fruit out later is much easier. After a fruit fermentation, a plastic fermenter is, by comparison to glass or stainless steel, a breeze to clean. I have used this procedure repeatedly with excellent results, and I am sure I will use it again.

Two types of mead that largely dictate use of the fruit or pressed juice in the primary are cyser and pyment. In the instance of cyser, fresh cider is mixed with honey, and the fermentation is permitted to proceed. In pyments the honey is mixed with the crushed grapes or pressed juice. Many meadmakers utilize potassium metabisulfate for sanitation of both cysers and pyments made with real fruit. If you choose not to sanitize your must at all (and great mead can be made this way) you are taking a risk of producing either bad mead or vinegar. You can minimize the risk by utilizing a press that is clean and has been used repeatedly before your fruit is pressed. After nearly a full year's disuse, cider and grape presses can be loaded with bacteria or wild yeasts, which pose a huge threat to your must. True sanitation of such a large and complex piece of equipment is a virtual impossibility, so the next best option is dilution, so to speak.

My favorite method of adding fruit is secondary or post-secondary addition. In this method, the fruit is added to the secondary fermenter after signs of fermentation have slowed dramatically or stopped. The fruit can also be added to an empty fermenter, and the must can then be racked onto it. The best way to accomplish this feat that I have found is the use of stainless steel soft drink kegs as fermenters, but I have used plastic fermenters and glass carboys with very acceptable results, as well. After the must has reached an alcohol content of 10% or thereabouts, fruit additions can generally be done without sanitation but still require good attention to cleanliness.

table 8.1

SUGGESTED FRUIT ADDITIONS FOR 5 GALLONS OF MEAD

Fruit	Mild Fruit Character	Medium Fruit	Strong Fruit
Apples (cider)	3 gallons in primary 0.6 L cider/L must	4 gallons in primary 0.8 L cider/L must	4 gallons + 3 (16 oz.) cans apple juice concentrate in secondary 0.8 L cider/L must, plus 1.6 L concentrate
Blueberries	5-7 lbs. in secondary 120-168 g/L	7-10 lbs. in secondary 168-240 g/L	11 lbs. or more 265 g/L or more
Cherries (sweet)	4-6 lbs. in secondary 96-144 g/L	7-9 lbs. in secondary 168-216 g/L	10 lbs. or more 240 g/L or more
Cherries (tart)	3-5 lbs. in secondary 72-120 g/L	6-8 lbs. in secondary 144-192 g/L	9 lbs. or more 216 g/L or more
Citrus Fruits (less for lemons and limes than for oranges and grapefruits)	3-5 lbs. in secondary 72-120 g/L	6-8 lbs. in secondary 144-192 g/L	9 lbs. or more 216 g/L or more
Currants	2-4 lbs. in secondary 48-96 g/L	5-7 lbs. in secondary 120-168 g/L	8 lbs. or more 192 g/L or more
Melons	3-5 lbs. in secondary 72-120 g/L	6-8 lbs. in secondary 144-192 g/L	9 lbs. or more 216 g/L or more
Peaches	5-7 lbs. in secondary 120-168 g/L	8-12 lbs. in secondary 192-288 g/L	13 lbs. or more 312 g/L or more
Pears	5-7 lbs. in secondary 120-168 g/L	8-10 lbs. in secondary 192-240 g/L	11 lbs. or more 265 g/L or more
Plums (use the skins)	4-6 lbs. in secondary 96-144 g/L	7-9 lbs. in secondary 168-216 g/L	10 lbs. or more 240 g/L or more
Raspberries	2-4 lbs. in secondary 48-96 g/L	5-7 lbs. in secondary 120-168 g/L	8 lbs. or more 192 g/L or more
Strawberries	5-7 lbs. in secondary 120-168 g/L	8-12 lbs. in secondary 192-288 g/L	13 lbs. or more 312 g/L or more

The biggest advantage of this method is the retention of the true fruit character in the flavor and aroma. I am also fond of this method because it gives me the flexibility to make large batches of show mead during the winter and spring, and then to add the fruit to them when it comes into season. It is much easier simply to add fruit to a fermenter and rack on some mead than to deal with both mead and fruit in the same meadmaking session.

Without sounding like I am avoiding the question, I would like to assert that there is no one fixed standard for how much fruit you should add to your mead. The amount of fruit you should add depends on the amount of fruit flavor you desire. Bear in mind that some fruits are more flavorful than others. Raspberries, blackberries, currants, and

Raspberries make a flavorful addition to any mead.

cranberries are little flavor-bombs, and they can overwhelm a mild honey and dominate the flavor and aroma of a melomel quite handily. And if that is exactly what you want, then you will have succeeded. For those who want a more defined set of information on how much fruit to use, I have provided Table 8.1 for various fruits showing how much of each could be used to create mild, medium, and strong fruit characteristics in 5 gallons of a medium mead. You should plan on using a little less for dry meads, and a little more for sweets.

The character of both fruits and meads vary, and so will the required contact time between them. You can obtain entirely recognizable fruit flavor and aroma from just a week or two in a primary fermenter. At the other extreme, I have left meads on fruit (in a secondary fermenter) for periods approaching a year, and I was not sad that I did. Generally, you want to get the mead off the lees of its primary fermentation before setting it to work on fruit for an extended period. I definitely recommend at least one and perhaps two additional rackings after the mead has been on the fruit to help the mead to clear (to get the big chunks out). That means you're going to have to get either the fruit or the mead out of the fermenter, or both.

Using a plastic fermenter or stainless steel keg gives you the option to contain your fruit in a muslin bag or a nylon stocking inside the fermenter. When you have obtained the amount of fruit character you desire, just lift out the fruit bag, and empty the contents onto your compost heap. If you don't use a bag you can sanitize a plastic or metal kitchen strainer, and scoop the fruit out gently.

Glass carboys and stainless steel kegs without a bag pose more of a problem, but not one that is insurmountable. Set your fermenter in position for siphoning one or two days before you plan to rack. That will give the mead a chance to settle down and separate before you rack.

You can buy some devices to make racking easier, or you can glom something together yourself. Phil's Sparger is a tube of stainless steel screening that attaches to the end of your racking hose and helps filter out the fruit and sediment. Use it on the fruit side of your siphon hose. You can accomplish the same effect by affixing a hop strainer bag to the bottom of a racking cane; wrap it on solidly with a section of copper wire. You can improve your clarity by putting a hop bag on both sides of your siphon hose. Insert the racking cane gently under the fruit pack, siphon gently, and don't get greedy. Conical siphon tools for winemaking have a plastic mesh bottom and piston-style plunger that fit right on the end of your siphon hose.

Another trick I have used with plastic fermenters is to sanitize a strainer and push it down into the fruit, creating a pool of clear liquid inside, from which to siphon. Getting that process started is definitely a good job for four hands. With any of these techniques, you may have to restart your siphon a few or even several times during the racking process. Be patient and deliberate, and your efforts will be rewarded.

Some fruits, particularly strawberries and raspberries, will pass along a solid dose of seeds, small bits of pulp, and flecks of "hair"—actually small bits of cellulose used by the plant to hold the fruit together—to the next fermenter. Mesh hop bags and sparge filters are no match for these little buggers. In some instances, you may just be forced to live with them. If you are really picky about it, several rackings will diminish the problem, but each progressive racking will claim a little more of your mead, and somewhere in there you will have to determine your own point of diminishing returns. Peaches, plums, and pears become extremely mushy in the fermenter. The resulting must will take at least one extra racking—and some time—to clear. Patience is a virtue, and you have no need to rush things. I am talking about mead here. The longer you wait with the mead in the carboy, the shorter you'll have to wait with it in the bottle.

More than any other adjunct, fruit adds the opportunity for self-expression and diversity in your mead. It offers the chance for the melding of two of nature's most perfect and complete gifts, fruit and honey. I hope you will take the opportunity to explore this juxtaposition in your own meadmaking.

> *"Fine fruit is the flower of commodities. It is the most perfect union of the useful and the beautiful that the Earth knows. Trees full of soft foliage; blossoms fresh with spring bounty; and finally, fruit, rich, bloom-dusted, melting, and luscious—such are the treasures of the orchard and garden, temptingly offered to every landholder in this bright and sunny, though temperate climate."*
>
> Andrew Jackson Downing, 1845, "The Fruits and Fruit Trees of America"

chapter nine GRAPES AND PYMENT

No one can say when mankind first combined grapes and honey in a fermented beverage. It most likely occurred prior to recorded history. Egyptian, Greek, and Roman references cite wines made with or sweetened with honey. Whatever the case, the spectrum of grape and honey blends ranges from mead with fleeting grape highlights at one end to wine with a hint of honey complexity at the other. In any part of this range, the two complement each other magnificently.

Today, the word *pyment* commonly describes a fermented product made from grapes and honey. Historically, the term pyment appears to have come from the Middle Ages. Gayre cites Chaucer's references to *pyment* and *clare* or *clarre* in phrases intimating wines sweetened with honey before serving. Further, Gayre describes the Roman "mulsum" and Greek "melitites" as the same sorts of beverages. Similarly, *hippocras* appears to have been a wine sweetened with either honey or sugar and then spiced. Thus the beverages we make today are paired somewhat incongruently with the names we attach to them.

In any case, fermenting honey and grapes together produces wonderful mead. Spices present a whole new canvas for expressing your creative energy. And rhetorical jousting about the semantics of mead nomenclature still leaves us thirsty! For now, let's accept mead made with grapes or grape juice as pyment, and pyment to which spices are added as hippocras, and get on to the fun part: making and drinking mead.

Meadmakers can use grape extracts, pressed juice, or real fruit to get grapes in their mead. As with most food, getting the best, most authentic flavors in your finished product requires that you get as close as possible to the pure, unprocessed raw material—in this case, grapes.

Personally, I prefer pyments made with high-quality wine grapes. But to each his own. You may make a pyment from Concord or Niagara grapes that you enjoy. I find that pyments crafted from good-quality wine grapes present more complex, refined aromas and flavors. In addition, they seem more likely to deliver an enjoyable balance of body and sweetness to acidity.

That said, dealing with whole grapes is no small task. Grapes have to be crushed and pressed, either before or after fermentation. Both crushing and pressing require specialized equipment. You can get manual and motor-driven crushers and threaded gear presses, as well as bladder presses, which squeeze the juice from the grapes by using hydraulic pressure to inflate a bladder inside a tubular mesh grate. If you come to meadmaking from the world of winemaking, you may have a press and experience in using it. If not, the expense can be substantial.

An alternative to pressing your own grapes is to purchase pressed juice from a vineyard or winery. Crushed grapes are also available from some sources. Purchasing high-quality grapes or juice from a local or mail order supplier dramatically increases your chances of making pyment of award-winning caliber. Every year, more vineyards offer this product/service. You can locate them using the Internet or explore local options by contacting your state's extension service or Department of Agriculture. Local vineyards or vintners can be a good source of information on grape varieties and quality.

Concentrates represent another alternative with many grape varieties available for home winemaking. This avenue gives you the opportunity to make pyment with specific varietal grapes that might not be available in other forms. You'll find concentrates easy to obtain and use and generally less expensive than fresh fruit or juice. The problem with concentrates is that everything that started out in the grape doesn't necessarily make it into the can. To make concentrates, producers remove the water from grape juice. Along the way, many of the desirable constituents of the fresh grape go with it. The highest-quality concentrates come from vacuum distillation. The more complete the vacuum (or the lower the pressure at the surface), the lower the boiling point becomes, resulting in less trauma to the juice and removal of fewer aromatic compounds. Concentrate producers can capture some of the volatile flavor and aroma compounds from the escaping steam and reintroduce them to the finished product. In the end, though, the aroma and flavor of the reconstituted juice will change—and not for the better. With all that in mind, the better your concentrate, the better your pyment.

When you first make pyment, I recommend that you purchase pressed juice. I'll warn you that it is expensive. But you recover the expense in quality and you will get a true impression of the depth of character that can be obtained with good ingredients. To find fresh juice, check the World Wide Web, your local extension service, and look for U-pick/press growers in your area. Fresh, high-quality varietal grape juice is also packaged in batch-sized lots, with or without sulfites, and sold at homebrewing and winemaking stores. You'll need to remember that fresh juice is available on a seasonal basis only, so some planning and consultation with your source will be necessary.

Vintners want grapes with a peak ratio of sugar content to acid level. As grapes mature and ripen, their acid level drops as the sugar content rises. At peak ripeness, grapes pass through a window where acid levels drop to around 1 percent while sugar content continues to rise, reaching a peak of 20 to 26%. Grapes in this window make the best wine, so vineyards move quickly to harvest the grapes before the moment passes. Weather drives this ripening process. Inclement weather at the harvest, or a cool or shortened growing season, may keep the crop from reaching its potential. When this happens, vintners may make adjustments to their standard practices. They may blend varieties or make changes in the recipe or process. Since you are free of their economic constraints, you will be best served to select the varieties that have reached peak ripeness, even if it means changing your plans slightly. Some winegrowing regions traditionally have difficulty ripening their grapes, and certain styles of wine have been developed to compensate for these unique characteristics. Champagne-style wines made from underripe grapes demonstrate an excellent use of tart juice.

Many, but not all, wines take their names from their grapes. Certainly the grape varieties I list below account for a large percentage of the fine wine produced in the United States and abroad. This list simply represents grapes I know to be useful in creating excellent wine and pyment—other varieties may serve equally well. The grapes you choose will depend on the region where you live and the type of pyment you seek to create.

The first criterion for grape selection must always be growing region. For example, certain regions in California have the long growing season required to ripen Cabernet Sauvignon and other hearty red varieties. When grown in the Great Lakes region, these same varieties virtually never ripen completely. If you purchase grapes or juice from a local supplier, do some research into the types and varieties of grapes that prosper and yield high-quality fruit. If growing conditions in your area produce abundant and extraordinary crops of Baco Noir, then by all means, take advantage of that.

Don't hesitate to blend varieties. Almost all of the world's red wines and a significant percentage of the whites result from blending. Some varieties, such as Cabernet Sauvignon, are used as the sole source of juice for a wine, but in many instances even varietally named wines are blends. Blending allows a wine or pyment maker to capture the beneficial characteristics of one grape (big aromas, complex fruitiness) with those of a second or even a third (higher acid levels, deep coloration, long finish). Vineyard owners and winemaking shop owners happily share this sort of grape knowledge with sincere, polite inquisitors.

Grape Varieties

The list that follows begins with white wine varieties and moves on to those used for red wine production. While I haven't had the chance to make or taste pyments made from each of these varieties (more's the pity), their reputations for superior wines make them all worthy of consideration in pyment, depending on your tastes and preferences. In addition to traditional varieties, I have included a couple of newer hybrid white and red varieties that have shown promise for their quality in areas away from California, France, and the popular winegrowing regions of Australia and South America.

White Wine Varieties

Pinot Blanc. A French offspring of Pinot Gris, which is a clone of Pinot Noir. This grape is known for high acid levels. It has been described as indistinct in aroma and neutral in flavor by some, and better than Chardonnay by others. Plantings in Italy, France, Germany, and Austria, as well as South America, and in Monterey County, California. Pinot Blanc lends itself to blending with strongly characteristic honeys such as fruit blossom (raspberry, orange) or with full-bodied varietal honeys such as tupelo. Takes oak well. Apple aromas predominate. Nutty, vanilla flavors.

Riesling. Prized German variety, with highest quality coming from Mosel River valley and the Alsace region of France. More suited to cooler areas such as the Great Lakes and New York than to California. Can attain very high levels of sugar, and is valued for its development of noble rot (*Botrytis cinerea*), a non-toxic mold that concentrates the sugars in the berries without destroying them. The grapes are allowed to hang on the vines and then are selectively harvested. Riesling grapes can retain a higher acid level even at appropriate sugar concentrations, and thus the wine finishes with a fruity sweetness and a distinctive tweak of acid on the tongue. In some areas, Riesling grapes may have higher tartaric acid levels than normally desired in white wines. This makes Riesling an excellent candidate for pyments, which balance the acid level with honey, providing sweetness and complexity in both the bouquet and flavor. Can also be finished dry. Colors range widely from light straw to golden. Aromas: apple, floral (rose and violet). Flavors: big fruit—apple, peach/apricot, and pear.

Gewürztraminer. This is a very full-bodied grape capable of producing quite high levels of sugar. It is produced best in the Alsace region, but is also in successful production in some areas of New Zealand, California, and the Pacific Northwest states. It is an early bloomer, and is difficult in some other aspects of its viticulture (including a very precise picking window to avoid flaccid-tasting, low-acid grapes), and so can be a challenge to the grower. Often finishes sweet but can be dried out with higher alcohol yeast strains. Pink to rose-colored skins, it is golden to copper shaded in the glass. Rose and honeysuckle aromas. Lychee, peach, mango fruit flavors.

Sauvignon Blanc. Some consider this the finest of the French white varieties, as it is possessed of good aromas, full and distinct mouthfeel, and it bears well, notably in California, France, Chile, Argentina, New Zealand, and South Africa. Sauvignon Blanc wines will stand up to spicy foods, strong cheeses, and even tomatoes and dark meats. This grape has the authority to handle a wide variety of honeys, and the acidity to be finished sweet without becoming cloying or flaccid. Just as some honeys beg to be made into mead, this grape makes a compelling case for use in a pyment. Citrus fruit, herbal/grassy, and green pepper aromas (among others!). Vanilla, butter, and unapologetic tart acidity in the mouth.

Sémillon. Another French variety, more delicately balanced than the dramatic high sugar/high acid levels of Sauvignon Blanc or the German white wine grapes. Grown in France and California. Component of many fine French wines. American examples finished dry can lack backbone. Could serve in a blend with other high-acid grape varieties, or as the base for a pyment that features an assertive honey such as sourwood. Acid correction may be needed at bottling.Aroma: floral, some herbal notes. Flavor: fresh fruit.

Chardonnay. In huge production now, as the wine-drinking masses have turned to this as the generic "white wine" in vogue. Originated in Burgundy, it produces the most distinct varietal character when produced under less-than-optimal conditions. Some regions of California are reaching world-class quality now, as are some Australian vineyards. For pyment, Chardonnay will be best matched with light, early-season honey. Chardonnay produces light and fragile aromas and flavors, which can be overpowered if blended with other grape varieties. It is the complex blend of aromas and flavors that give Chardonnay such appeal: apple, peach, and pear scents juxtaposed with citrus and tropical fruit flavors. Chardonnay will pick up oak flavors very rapidly and also can express some nuttiness and diacetyl (buttery aroma and flavor).

Vignoles (Ravat 51). A newer variety seeing considerable planting and use in the Traverse Bay area of Michigan and in New York. It is being used in domestic Champagne-style sparkling wines, as well as in blends and as a varietal. Very light in color. High acid, complex herbal and citrus fruit nose. This grape has been receiving very high praise from growers and winemakers. Can be finished dry, or has the acid to make a good medium to sweet pyment with light to amber honeys. Herbal/grassy aromas. Citrus (grapefruit), apricot, peach, and melon flavors.

Seyval (Seyve-Villard 5276). Also referred to as Seyval Blanc, the moniker under which the varietal wines are sold. Another comer, now among the most widely planted in the East. Reaches maturity earlier (mid-season). Has a reputation for crisp but somewhat thin-bodied wines; could be balanced with a medium- to full-bodied honey and perhaps oak aging. Used in dry whites and sparkling wines, frequently compared with Chablis. Aromas of melon, grass/hay. Apple, pear flavors.

Red Wine Varieties

Cabernet Sauvignon. Among American vintners, this is the Big Daddy. Actually the offspring of Cabernet Franc and Sauvignon Blanc. Cabernet Sauvignon has a long growing season, and produces up to its quality potential in France and California, as well as in warmer South American growing regions (Chile, in particular). Takes to oak like a duck to water, and has enough acidity, tannin, and body to balance strong, even aggressive honeys. This grape packs a wallop in the nose, with an array of aromas that can challenge the vocabulary and are variable by region and by vintage. Most notably, it delivers black currant and dark berry and cherry aromas, as well as green pepper, pimento, and spices, ginger in particular. It also throws impressive fermentation bouquets of cedar and other woods, leather, earth, tobacco, and musk. Fruit/berry and spice flavors, including plum/prune as well as the above, occasionally smoke, cinnamon, sandalwood, and on and on.

Cabernet Franc. Parent of the widely heralded Cabernet Sauvignon, Cabernet Franc is a venerable powerhouse in the winemaking world in its own right, holding a prominent place in the blends of many high-profile French Bordeaux vintners. Franc is in widest distribution throughout France but also is cultivated across Europe, and, to a lesser extent, in California and South America. This grape is particularly suited to blending with other varieties, adding deep color and layers of flavor complexity. Cabernet Franc lacks the acidic and tannic backbone of its offspring but presents itself with many of the same aroma, bouquet, and flavor descriptors.

Merlot. Coming on strong in the red-wine-drinking set, Merlot is also one of the most widely planted of the French varieties. It is grown ubiquitously in warmer regions worldwide. It is a major component of some of the most famous French estate bottlings. Some describe Merlot as more accessible to the new red wine drinker than Cabernet Sauvignon. It is not quite as high in tannin and acidity, comes across more softly, and finishes rounder, with less astringency. Merlot has black currant and berry notes, along with more floral aromas. Wood, earth, and leather flavors come through here, too, as well as coffee.

Pinot Noir. Like many antique fruit varieties, this is a grape that produces extremely high-quality fruit if given lots of TLC. In cultivation in Roman times, it is now in production around the globe. It is subject to a number of frailties and yet creates wines of clarity and distinction. The grapes have a very high amino acid content, providing sufficient nitrogen and nutrients to generate strong, almost violent fermentations. Lower in acidity and tannin than the big boys, and commensurately smoother/softer, yet with a long finish. Also noted as the variety highest in resveratrol, the compound credited with causing the "French Paradox" effect of lowering cholesterol. Lighter in body than Cabernet, Pinot Noir expresses lighter berry aromas (raspberry, cherry, strawberry), rosemary, mint, and cinnamon spices, and deeper vegetal notes. Complex palate includes earth, leather, ripe tomato, and barnyard flavors, along with whatever this wine picks up from oak (highly recommended).

Syrah. The biggest of the big, this is the grape at the heart of Chateauneuf du Pape, the Rhône blend. Old variety of uncertain (debated) heritage. Grown in France, California, Australia (as "Shiraz"), and Argentina. Nearly black in color, this variety is known for intense wines, which fairly explode with vibrant aromas and flavors. This grape can stand up to big honey aroma and flavor (it might have to be big just to get a word in edgewise), and has the acid to balance more sweetness than is customary in drier red wines. Black currant and blackberry aromas, along with deep herbal/grassy/cedar/incense notes. Everything said before in the mouth, plus smoke, toast, musk, oak, and truffle.

Maréchal Foch. A French-American hybrid grape, also known simply as Foch. Produces wines that are lighter in body that Merlot or Cabernet Sauvignon. Maréchal Foch has a shorter growing season, making it possible for growers in cooler areas, such as the Great Lakes and Oregon, to produce red wines with the body and acid balance that comes from mature grapes. Can mature with high sugar content. Blackberry aroma, leather, earth, but lighter/lower impact than Syrah or the Cabernets.

DeChaunac (Siebel 9549). Similar to Foch, in that it has a shorter growing season and is in more regular production in cooler areas, such as the Northwest and Great Lakes. Known for having a lower tannin level with a pronounced fruitiness. Not regarded as one of the most impressive varieties, it will still provide a good base for Midwesterners seeking to create a pyment in the vein of a very passable table wine. Well-served by a solid dose of oak. Aromas and flavors similar to Foch.

Gamay Noir (formerly Gamay Beaujolais). Better Northwest alternative variety. Shorter growing season, very narrow ripening/picking window. Clone of Pinot Noir. Very high quality if picked promptly. Color: Rosé to light burgundy. Strawberry/raspberry and floral aromas. Fresh, bubblegum estery, fruity flavors complemented by wood, coconut, and toast (if oaked).

Chambourcin (Joannès-Seyve 26-205). Another French-American hybrid that has seen a decrease in acreage in Europe due to restrictions on hybrids. Plantings in North and South America. Often blended with other varieties with very good results, making this a good candidate for pyment. Lower in tannins and can benefit from being left on the skin or from oak aging. Longer growing season than other popular hybrids (mid-October). Aromas: spicy, herbaceous. Flavors: big, dark fruit and berries, with strong earthy component.

If you make pyment using fresh fruit or fresh-pressed juice, follow the sulfite regimen directed by the vendor. Lacking other instructions, you can treat red grape juice with 50 ppm of sulfite (one Campden tablet per gallon or 3.785 L) 24 hours before pitching. You can sulfite white grape juice at double this amount. Most winemaking references also recommend an additional sulfite treatment at first racking.

It can be fairly simple to create a pyment from juice, especially when using a plastic fermenter. Place 3 to 4 gallons (11.4 to 15 L) of juice in the fermenter, and add 4 to 8 pounds (1.82 to 3.64 kg) of honey. Then dilute the mixture with water until you reach the desired starting gravity. In areas of the country with shorter growing seasons, you may be able to use a higher portion of juice, as the fruit may not reach the expected sugar level for the variety. There are pyment recipes in the "Recipes" chapter for reference.

The delightful fruitiness and balancing acidity of wine grapes provide a terrific foil for the complex fresh aromas and flavors of honey. The possibilities for matching varietal honeys with varietal grapes and with different yeast strains intrigue the mind of even the most experienced vintner or mead artisan. Making pyment opens a door to a new realm of inquiry and exploration. It is a door laid open long ago but passed through by only a fortunate few. It kindles the flame of imagination just thinking about it.

chapter ten
Spices and Metheglin

In some circles, "mead" pratically means "spiced." Indeed, readers of the mead classic *The Closet of Sir Kenelm Digby: Opened* might find it difficult to believe that spices were not a part of every mead recipe. Virtually every recipe sees the meadmaker instructed to add cinnamon, nutmegs, marjoram, cloves, ginger root, or a combination of all of them. In the same way today's chefs use a particular spice blend to set their restaurant apart in the minds of their customers, meadmakers of old used specific spices to impart their signature to their meads. The history of spice in mead in northern Europe can be traced back to times before written history. As a result, spiced meads remain popular today.

Spice levels in mead range from just below the flavor threshold to massive expressions that define the mead and challenge honey for dominance in the nose and on the tongue. Whatever the spice level, the history of spiced mead or metheglin largely parallels that of spice and herb use from the Mediterranean to the north of Scandinavia. While many spices and herbs were sought as flavorings, others offered medicinal or tonic qualities. Carrying its own mythic qualities, mead provided the perfect medium for their delivery.

Much of global commerce developed to facilitate trade in spices. The earliest recorded use of cinnamon dates to approximately 5000 BC. Hebrews and Egyptians alike used it in religious ceremonies throughout the Indian subcontinent. Traders visited Zanzibar as far back as 3700 BC, presumably to obtain the precious cloves grown there. Biblical references to spices are multitude. Some of the most poetic arise from the Song of Solomon: "Awake, O north wind, and come, thou south; blow upon my garden, that the spices thereof may flow out."

The Romans spread spices throughout northern Europe, using many of the same varieties we know today. Both the Romans and the Greeks had a great taste for herbs, too. With few exceptions, the herbs that Westerners use today had their origins in the Mediterranean basin. Many were in household use in Egypt, Spain, or some part of the Greco-Roman world by about 1500 BC. In a world made small by supersonic air travel and the Internet, it seems positively remarkable that pepper and other spices were traded in mass quantities more than 1,500 years ago. In those days, trade routes went overland more that 7,500 miles without the aid of motorized travel.

In northern Europe in particular, the marriage of mead and spices was almost inevitable. The nobility preferred mead above all other beverages, both because of its quality and for the status it reflected on those who could afford it. Spices also represented power, wealth and stature. In the Middle Ages, spices—like honey—sometimes served as the medium of taxation and might be stipulated in ransoms. Countries and kingdoms fought over the major spice routes for many centuries, as control of spice routes ensured tremendous wealth. The need to chart an unassailable route to spices, not gold, drove Christopher Columbus to defy prevailing wisdom and risk sailing off the edge of the Earth.

Today, many think that medieval meadmakers used spices to cover major fermentation flaws or problems with ingredients and technique. I do not feel that the body of evidence bears this theory out. Initially, mead and its stature in the cultures of northern Europe were well ensconced in the realm of royalty and the nobility as far back as Pliny in the first century AD. Mead had been widely accepted as the beverage of the aristocracy by the time of *Beowulf* in AD 700. These references appear long before the common mead spices (those cited in Digby and earlier European literature from the ninth century to the Renaissance) were traded with regularity in the soon-to-be Norman or Anglo-Saxon realms. Not until the twelfth century did the spice trade routes into northern Europe develop fully.

In earlier times, meadmakers prepared musts using a wide variety of techniques that must have resulted in very drinkable products. In support of this conclusion, we find present-day meadmakers with a bent toward adventure regularly producing meads of outstanding quality with no must sanitation procedures whatsoever. Furthermore, most believe that meads made in this way will have superior aroma characteristics to mead made by any other method. Thus we have no reason to believe that medieval meads should have been routinely infected or rancid. Since mead without spices was prized ahead of wine or beer, the reason for adding spices to mead seems to have arisen more out of their flavors, aromas, and mystical cache than as a means to hide flaws.

Further, the recipes for highly spiced meads called for introduction of the spice or spices during the initial blending process—and not after the fermentation, where they would logically have been added if intended to cover flaws. Had spices been needed to mask the flaws apparent in mead, the perpetuation of unspiced recipes would seem incongruous, and yet they persist, right up through modern times.

Last, but not least, I find two reasons to believe that the honeys of old may have possessed aromas and flavors superior to the honey we have available today. First, the most highly prized European honeys come from deep forest blossoms, in particular the deep coniferous forests of Germany. Even today, it is among the most expensive and sought-after honey, a prize among honey enthusiasts. Unfortunately, the advance of human populations has decimated the habitats needed to support these flowers. As a result, these superior honeys would have been more abundant in earlier times.

The second, and perhaps more important point, relates to the type of honey used by those early European meadmakers. They used two very pure types: wild honey or honey from skep hives. Combs from either of these sources are used in a hive only one time. The purest honey, most of which would have been bound for the highest bidder (the nobility), would have been extracted first, and the comb set aside. This honey would have been used for meadmaking and for the table. The beekeeper or hive raider would then have made his or her own mead by placing the crushed combs in hot water and repeating the wash until all of the usable honey had been extracted; the meadmaking would follow with this sweet liquor. The combs of either source would have been melted down once they had been cleansed of honey, and the wax, prized for candlemaking, would have gone to market, to the church, or to the nobles as taxes.

This is quite different from modern beekeeping practices, in which the combs are uncapped, and the honey is then spin-extracted. The combs that make it through this procedure are then returned to the hive to be filled again, and are reused until they become so dark and discolored or impregnated with odor that they may in fact be affecting the honey they will store. They are then melted down to build new foundation or other beeswax products. While the resulting effect on the honey may not be substantial, it is certainly present, and it was never a factor in the age of skep hives and washed-comb meadmaking.

In light of the above, it seems logical the nobility added spice to mead for two simple reasons. First, spices offered the finest flavors for their "beverage of kings." As always, the rich want the best in all things. Since spices provided a fetching diversion from mundane diets, they were a natural addition for beverages as well as foods. Second, since spices were costly and rare, their use asserted wealth and position. European history confirms a heritage of status symbols among the upper class; the regular use of spices affirmed one's social standing.

Making metheglin today

Spiced mead has many uses. Drink it just as it comes from the bottle or feature it in mulled drink as a warm, soothing recuperative after outdoor adventures during the winter months. Some folks cook with metheglins, casting them as marinades and as bases for sauces. Here, dry metheglins created with surprising spices can lead to spectacular seafood and pasta sauces.

Be warned: Spices can be overdone! Unlike fruits, spices must be added in restrained and judicious doses to produce pleasant and inviting meads. Fruit, when added in bombastic quantities, simply gives the taste of fruit wine, and sometimes even like a fruit juice or liqueur. It does not become offensive or undrinkable; it's just fruitier. On the other hand, spices in excess can render a mead virtually unpalatable. In the worst cases, an overpowered metheglin will spoil your palate, leaving you unable to taste other flavors properly for an hour or longer. Cloves numb the tongue. Ginger root, cinnamon, cardamom, southernwood—pretty much any distinctive spice or herb—overpowers the palate when used without judicious care. I like the flavor of habanero pepper, but it packs so much heat that it has to be handled like high explosives in meadmaking. "Not very much" can quickly become "way too much," dooming the whole batch to use as brine for your next smoked turkey.

Still, good metheglin is a joy. The well-balanced spices of a fine metheglin bring delightful complexity and a balancing contrast to the honey. Such potions keep the drinker ever interested in the next sip, to unravel the organoleptic puzzle it presents. Like a perfectly balanced spring day, good metheglin offers warmth but not insufferable heat, sunlight but not intolerable brilliance, the perfect humidity for comfort and easy breathing and a breathtaking sunset to take one into a night of "perfect sleeping weather" with a head full of fine memories. You never knew you could do all that with some honey, some coriander, and some orange peel, but you can. And a nice hatch of *Ephemerella subvaria* and three respectable brown trout caught on #14 Hendrickson dry flies that you tied yourself, released unharmed, of course, and a beaver moving silently in the shallows, and a blue heron and several mallards, among them a mother and her ducklings, all in the river, unsuspecting as you come around the sandy spit of the bend, and ... wait, wrong hobby. But a fine metheglin fits right in there, too.

Many of the metheglins entered in the Mazer Cup have fallen into the "holiday spice" group, including some combination of nutmeg, ginger, cinnamon, and/or cloves. The match of these spices with honey seems quite natural, as they have long been associated with sweets and baked goods. In addition, some liqueurs include these spices, again pairing them with sweetness and alcohol.

Despite the popularity of these few spices, some of the most interesting and intriguing metheglins I have tasted came from meadmakers who broke away and worked with other flavors such as chamomile, orange zest, rosehips, lavender, and coriander. These and other spices complement the floral qualities and complex aromas of mead in an intriguing and most alluring fashion. Here the artistry of meadmaking prevails, much as the advanced and seemingly unbounded palette of a truly gifted painter pulls the viewer in and keeps the eye darting about. Thus, I believe that the metheglin frontiers remain unexplored. New spices and new combinations await.

Practical Advice on Metheglin

My guidelines for spices mirror those I gave for fruits, albeit with a few twists. In short, great metheglin requires great spices—the fresh, potent products that you won't find at your corner grocery. Mind you, I have made mead with supermarket spices and you can make some pretty good mead this way. But in these cases, real success comes mostly by accident or patience. For instance, the nutmeg metheglin I made five years ago this way (with freshly ground nutmeg, though) is really starting to come into its own. But the lush green valleys of excellence are reserved for those who would walk the miles away from the ease of the beaten path, and the same can be said for metheglin. Really fine spice is not going to be found at the corner store (unless you live on a really COOL corner), and some more serious attention will need to be paid to how you get the flavor balance correct if you seek to make really fine metheglin.

A good spice shop will present your imagination with attractive opportunities.

"Where, then," you ask, "do I find your so-called 'really fine spice,' oh You of the Great Hot Wind?" Well, in my case, at the same market where I am prone to go for fruit. In Detroit, the market of choice for culinary devotees is the Eastern Market, and one of the stores there is Rafal's Spices, one of the coolest places I know of. Between its brick walls are held some of the greatest tastes and aromas I have had the joy to behold. You can find a quality spice shop in most major metropolitan areas. Find a first-rate shop in your vicinity, and build a relationship with the management. From the first step you place in a good spice shop, you cannot help but be swept into appreciation of the efforts made by its proprietor to collect and offer the variety and caliber of spices they maintain.

Rafal's Spice Company has more than 500 jars of bulk spices, herbs, and medicinal herbs or herb teas on their shelves. The quality of all of the spices available there is superb. Donald Rafal, the owner, preaches the same dogma that you have heard before in this tome, "Get the highest-quality spice you can find, and make sure it is as fresh as possible." You need only open a bag of fresh Chinese cinnamon to comprehend the veracity of that statement. On the grocery store shelves, spices may attain wise old ages, and unless you go to a very progressive grocer, they will be in sealed containers, leaving their aroma and flavor characteristics to conjecture until opened. A trusted vendor of high-quality spices is in order, and is really the only assurance of quality and freshness.

That which differentiates a spice from an herb is really a matter of unfinished debate. Arbitrary classifications such as country or region of origin, or family or genus of plant species, are rife with contradictions and exceptions to the rule. Coriander, categorized by most as a spice, is the seed of the plant whose vegetation is known as cilantro, considered an herb. Spices and herbs can be the leaves, stems, seeds, bark, stamens, petals, fruits, and roots of plants from around the globe. Some hold that spices are the products of deciduous plants (tropical trees, for the most part) and that herbs are gathered from perennial or annual plants. Others have said

Spices and herbs, clockwise outside from center left: nylon tea bags for steeping small quantities of spices, bags of chamomile, cardamom, mace, star anise; star anise pods, chamomile blossoms, juniper berries, and vanilla bean. In the center: Whole cardamom, whole nutmeg, blades of mace.

that leaves and flowers are herbs, and seeds, roots, and usually stems are spices. Yet for each of these rules, you will find categorical exceptions. Mace is the flowery/leafy aril (coverlet) of the nutmeg seed, and yet is considered a spice. Saffron, considered by most to be a spice, is collected from the flower of its parent plant. Cinnamon is a bark. Call them what you will, herbs and spices are plant products we use to provide or enhance flavor in food and drink.

That said, it is a given that herbs and spices are vegetation. As such, they will maintain their peak quality for a short time and then begin to deteriorate. Most spices will retain their qualities best if purchased in whole or unground form. Allspice, cinnamon, cloves, nutmeg, and many other spices are available in whole or unprocessed forms, and will release their aromatic components most appealingly if freshly ground or cracked just before their use. Any number of grinders or mortar and pestle arrangements will do the trick, but there are a few points that will make the job less tedious. A good grinder will alleviate the frustration of chasing a coriander seed or juniper berry around the bowl of your mortar and pestle. Alternately, a larger pestle—just slightly smaller than the mortar—also will solve the problem. A coffee grinder, either manual or electric, will do the job adequately, but in any case, take care to coarsely grind rather than powder the spice, or hazes can result in your mead. If you do choose a mortar and pestle for the job, it is best to stick with a brass or porcelain model. Wooden and plastic versions are given to picking up and holding the smells of the spices ground therein; picking a grinder that can be effectively cleaned will help prevent the same problem.

What follows is a look at some of the spices and herbs that might be appropriate in mead. I'll examine the characteristics that make them so appealing, and the caveats you may want to observe when adding them to your mead. In some cases I have also included recommendations about appropriate amounts of these spices to use in 5-gallon batches. It is a dicey thing, this recommending of amounts of spices. Taste is a very subjective sense, and the perceived strength of flavor of any given spice will depend on many factors: age of the spice, location where it was grown and the growth conditions of that particular season, even variations from subspecies to subspecies. When I do not mention specific levels, I would recommend that you utilize small amounts of fresh spice or spice blend in a fiber "tea" bag.

The more meticulous among us may want to boil the bag for 5 minutes before using it in your mead. Place the spices in the bag, and push the bag into your secondary fermenter with a racking cane. Some people like to add a marble or two, or a clean stainless steel nut or bolt to persuade the bag to sink. Sample the mead regularly. Remember that spices tend to mellow over time. If you intend to age your mead for a considerable stretch (more than a year), you will want to overshoot the spice character by half again as much as you hope to have in your aged mead.

Spices Traditionally Associated With Mead

Allspice *Pimenta Officinalis*

One of the prizes of Columbus' travels, allspice hails from the West Indies. Allspice became an instant rage in the fifteenth century and has maintained its lofty position among the tropical spices. It is the green berry of a tropical evergreen, which is handpicked and dried. When dried, it becomes a dark reddish-brown, with flavors and aromas reminiscent of a blend of cloves, ginger, cinnamon, and nutmeg. The berries have a slight but pleasant astringency and also possess some of the tongue-numbing quality associated with cloves. Allspice produces heady fragrances in mead and is suited to any degree of dryness or sweetness.

Chili Peppers *Capsicum annuum, Capsicum frutescens*

The term chili (also chile, or chilli) is applied to a huge variety of hot, aromatic, and spicy peppers of the genus *Capsicum*. Though actually a fruit, the chili's role in culinary use and in meadmaking pushes it into the herb and spice portion of this book and in many competitions, as well. Spice authorities report more than 200 varieties in cultivation, with a vast range of flavors and intensities. Chilies, too, originate in the Western world (anyone familiar with cuisine from the British Isles knows they didn't originate there), and their arrival in Europe also shook things up considerably.

Chilies play beautifully in traditional meads and melomels. Their distinctive flavor and (hopefully) carefully controlled heat make for a delicious juxtaposition to the

Dried Chilis: front, chilie de arbol, chipotle; second row, pequin, habanero, birdseye; third row, New Mexico, ancho, jar of habanero, cascabel, pasilla.

sweetness and honey flavor of medium- to high-gravity meads, and can provide delightful counterbalance to the full-bodied fruitiness of strongly flavored melomels.

The "heat" of a chili has been quantified in a number of different ways. The most commonly used scale is the Scoville Unit rating, which enumerates the concentration of capsaicin, the heat-producing substance in peppers. The rating reflects the amount of a known medium that can be made to produce perceived "hotness" from a defined addition of pepper. Scoville counts can range from 0 to 10 for mild peppers on up to 200,000 units or more for the flaming, but also highly flavored, habanero. Other scales, such as Dremann's Pepper Hotness Scale, acknowledge habanero's heat but give hotter ratings to japones (Japanese), assam, and pequin, and grant the hottest rating to the tepin. None of these scales are based on scientific assays of capsaicin content; all of them are based on subjective judgments and should be viewed accordingly.

During handling or preparation of chilis, capsaicin can be transferred to your hands and subsequently to the face, eyes, etc. Accordingly, no matter which scale you are using, peppers require special attention in the kitchen in general, and in meadmaking in particular. Food-safe latex gloves are an option, but thorough cleaning—of hands, containers, and utensils—is mandatory.

It is my opinion that the ideal method of obtaining good balance in a chili mead is by calibrating the number of Scoville Units in the mead. This can be done by multiplying the Scoville rating by the number of grams utilized and dividing by the

table 10.1

Flavored Pepper Varieties and Their Heat Ratings

Variety Name Fresh	Dried	Scoville Units	Description
Anaheim		25,000	Green or red, somewhat sweet, used in rellenos
Ancho	Poblano	2,000	Orange red to mahogany, sweet, aromatic, smoky, fruit, spice flavors
Birdseye		130,000	Small, yellow-orange to red, no sweetness, intense persistent heat, flavorful
Cascabel	Chile bola	3,000	Round 1¼" fruit, brown mottled, complex earthy flavor, slight tannic tartness
Chile de Arbol		20,000	Long, thin red to brown, slightly sweet
Habanero		200,000	Intense heat, coupled with strong chili flavor and mild sweetness. Similar peppers include Scotch bonnet, Jamaica hot, and rocotillo
Jalapeño	Chipotle (smoked)	70,000	Green or red (may be known as huachinango), meaty, mild sweetness, vegetable pepper flavor. Chipotle: Smoked dried jalapeño, nutty, sweet, delicious
Japanese Chili	Japones	SU n/a (hot to very hot)	3-4 inches long, burnt orange, literally a Japanese hybrid
Mombassa		90,000	Highly touted, but I didn't get to taste this one
New Mexico		2,000	Red or green, large, fleshy, sweet, licorice notes
Pequin		185,000	Small, elongate, orange to red, corn, nutty tones, some smoke, hot hot hot
Serrano		SU n/a (hot to very hot)	Green or red, small, acid tartness and distinct heat
Tabasco		SU n/a (very hot)	Red, orange, and yellow, strong vegetable notes, lingering heat
Tepin		150,000	¼" to ⅓," round, thin-fleshed, sweet pepper flavor, followed by strong heat, filling the mouth to the back of the tongue
Thai		SU n/a (very hot)	Bright green or red, small, little to no sweetness

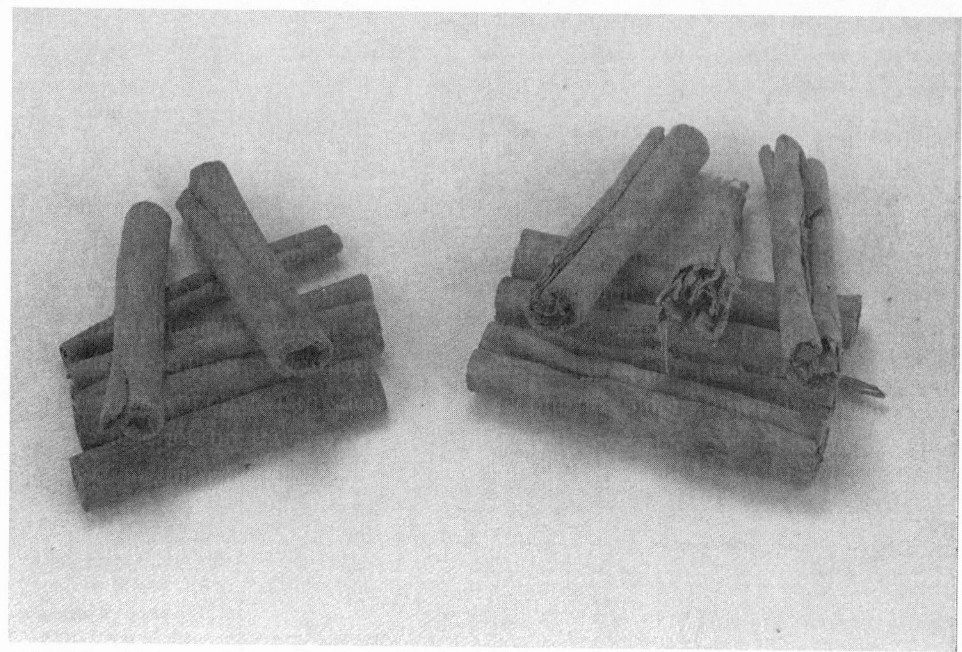

*Left: What most people know as "cinnamon sticks" are actually cassia (*Cinnamomum cassia blume*). They are stiffer, thicker and more solid. Right: True cinnamon (*Cinnamomum zeylanicum Lees*) quills, more delicate and yet distinctive in aroma and flavor.*

number of liters infused. Due to the subjective nature of the scale, this method is not foolproof or precisely replicable, but this will give you an approximate unit/liter rating that you will be able to standardize to meet your taste. Take a liter of traditional mead and add peppers of a known Scoville Unit gram by gram, tasting until you hit your threshold. It may be as low as 500 or as high as many thousand. Go slowly. Base your recipe on this reference number.

Cinnamon *Cinnamomun zeylanicum Lees,* Cassia *Cinnamomum cassia blume*

Cinnamon, as it is sold in the United States, is generally not true cinnamon—*Cinnamomun zeylanicum Lees*—but actually cassia, *Cinnamomum cassia blume*. True cinnamon is grown in Sri Lanka and portions of India. It is lighter in color and in flavor, more delicate in aroma, and somewhat sweeter than what we know as cinnamon. Cassia, on the other hand, is more reddish in cast and has a pungent and very warm, appealing aroma. Both cinnamon and cassia are the bark of a tropical *Lauracae* family evergreen, removed from cut branches and carefully dried into cinnamon sticks, known as quills. The rich aroma and bold flavor come from the volatile oils in the bark; the most flavorful have the highest volatile oil content.

There are several varieties of cinnamon available from spice merchants today. They are designated by their country or region of origin. Ceylon cinnamon, the true cinnamon, comes in thin, fragile, orange-gold quills. It has a softer, fruitier profile, with notes reminiscent of anise in the nose. Batavia cinnamon (*Cinnamomum burmanni*) from Indonesia, has a bigger flavor, a darker auburn color, and seems slightly woodier in its aroma and flavor. Saigon cinnamon (*Cinnamomum loureirii*), from Cambodia and Laos, is lighter in color than Batavia, and has a strong and sweet aroma and high volatile oil content. Chinese cinnamon also has high volatile oil content, with a darker brown orange cast and rich earthy aroma. Chinese cinnamon may not be available as quills, because it is generally ground before being exported. Sweetness is not needed to balance cinnamon, although it has been used that way in cuisine in much of the Western world. To keep from overpowering a dry mead, cinnamon does need a full mouthfeel from the base mead, though. Quills can be cracked into chips for use in muslin bags.

Cloves *Caryophyllus aromaticus, Eugenia Carophyllata*

The history of cloves is nearly as rich as that of cinnamon. Cloves were traded across parts of Europe as early as 700 BC, and were familiar to the Romans, Persians, Greeks, and Chinese. Cloves are the buds of the tropical *Myrtaceae* evergreen, which are picked, unopened, by hand and then dried. Their aroma is strong, earthy to almost musty, somewhat sweet and distinctively fragrant. The flavor is strong, biting, and will numb the tongue when ingested in quantity. Cloves from Madagascar are considered premium.

Due to their overpowering nature, cloves must be used sparingly in mead. For some reason, mead seems to provide the perfect medium for the transmission of clove's flavor and its numbing capacity. Perhaps this is due to mead's liquid nature and the extractive power of the alcohol. Too much clove character in a mead will produce a mead with limited application. One or two cloves in a 5-gallon batch will have an appreciable effect on flavor. Small amounts must be the rule; check the mead frequently to assess the level of flavor saturation.

Ginger *Zingiber officinale Roscoe*

Ginger is the rhizome of a tropical flowering plant native to Asia. It was a late comer to the European scene, having been brought to the New World by the Spanish in the 1600s. The spice is available in several forms: whole (unpeeled, peeled, and dried), dried ground, candied, and in syrup. It is used extensively around the world in medicines, cooking, and in alcoholic and nonalcoholic beverages. The fresh and dried versions have distinctly different profiles and can both be used in mead, but to my tastes the fresh version gets the nod. The finest fresh ginger comes from Jamaica.

Fresh ginger is a smooth-skinned, plump, tan to medium brown rhizome, with a larger central root and smaller buds. The skin and outer layers are fibrous, the inner core is firm and very juicy and fragrant. Its flavor is full, slightly astringent, and has a mild heat. The root can be crushed or slivered before being added to mead. Ginger's flavor and heat will mellow with time in a mead. Those seeking subtlety will find that 1 or 2 ounces of truly fresh, high-quality ginger will produce pronounced character in a 5-gallon batch. On the other hand, true ginger lovers may find dosings of 1 to 2 ounces per gallon more to their liking, and some use amounts up to a pound in a 5-gallon batch.

Mace and Nutmeg *Myristica Fragrans*

Both mace and nutmeg are produced from the fruit of the same evergreen tree, *Myristica fragrans*. Mace is the crimson-colored aril, or fleshy webbed skin, that envelopes the roughly 1-inch long, oval-to-nearly-round seed, which we know as nutmeg. When the fruit splits open, it is harvested, and the mace and nutmeg are separated and dried. Four hundred pounds of nutmeg will yield 1 pound of mace, which becomes a rusty orange brown and fragile when dried. Nutmeg and mace are available whole, as dried seeds and blades, respectively. The finest nutmeg is from the East Indies (Indonesia), while the finest mace is—debatably—either Indonesian or from the West Indian island of Grenada.

Nutmeg's soft, sweet flavor lacks astringency or any tongue-numbing quality; it is perfect for mead. Its flavor is mild and delicate, and its aroma can be fleeting. Nutmeg can be added in amounts from 1 to 4 ounces per 5 gallons.

Pepper *Piper nigrum*

This is the real thing, not the cousin of the bell pepper pizza topping. Peppercorns are the dried berries of a vine native to the East Indies and coastal India. It has the richest and most storied history of all the tropical spices, and exceeded gold in cost, ounce for ounce, at some points in Western history. Pepper may seem commonplace to us, but it is one of those elements of our lives that would be most conspicuous in its absence. Pepper is vibrantly pungent, fiercely aromatic (especially when fresh peppercorns are ground), and, like salt—with which it is inextricably wed—serves to accent the enjoyable flavors of the foods in which it is used, without disguising or overwhelming them.

Black and white pepper are derived from the same berry; the dark outer skin is removed before drying to make white pepper. Donald Rafal tells me that the perception that white pepper is stronger arises from the practice of grinding white pepper more finely, creating more surface area, and thus releasing more of its character. The peppercorns from the Tellicherry province of India and Malaysian Sarawak peppercorns are very highly regarded. Good but less expensive alternatives are available from Malabar, Singapore, and Allepey. Lampong black pepper has a distinctive herbal smoky character.

Pepper can be used in meads as a defining characteristic or to provide complexity and to "push out" or cause to bloom some of the other flavors you might seek to accent. In that role, a gram or two is all that is necessary. As the keystone of a metheglin, peppercorns bring out an earthy, very true-to-form aroma and flavor that would probably work well with darker, more aromatic and distinct honeys, such as buckwheat or tulip poplar. It is not for everyone; discretion might be the better part of valor here.

Saffron *Crocus sativus*

This too, is a granddaddy of a spice. It is still the most expensive spice in the world, coming in locally at fifty-five dollars an ounce for Spanish saffron, and even more for more uncommon varieties—prices of $4,500 a pound have been asked.

Saffron is made from the handpicked stigmas of a crocus flower grown in southern Europe and Asia. More than 75,000 of these stigmas are required to produce a pound of saffron. This process made saffron affordable in the past only to royalty and the extremely wealthy.

The dried stigmas, known as threads, are rich in aroma and in a deep yellow gold pigment, which make them very appealing to meadmakers. The aroma is not sweet, but is distinctive, exotic, and very inviting. In flavor and aroma, saffron will stand up to big honeys. In small quantities, the color saffron lends to mead is deep and elegant, a hue reminiscent of fine German auslese wines, and one that meadmakers find elusive. Too much will turn your mead bright yellow. Saffron begs to be added to mead. In every quality, saffron exudes extravagance; it is truly a symbol of luxury and indulgence.

Turmeric *Curcuma Longa L.*

Turmeric is a principal ingredient of curry blends, with a complex, mildly sweet profile. It is the dried and ground root of another member of the *Zingiberacae* family, making it a relative of ginger. Its flavor is reminiscent of ginger, with citrus and pepper notes, and it can possess some of the same bitter astringent character of ginger. Like ginger, it was native to Asia, but is now cultivated in the West Indies, especially Haiti. Turmeric, too, is lighter in color from countries in the East—light yellow to near orange—and darker when grown in the Americas, running to a darker sweet potato shade of orange. In recipes, especially liquids, the spice will generously lend its pigment to the medium, and it creates a striking hue in mead.

Herbs

Anise *Pimpinella anisum,* Star Anise *Illicium Verum*

Though originating in entirely different families, these two herbs produce the wonderful licorice notes of recipes and liqueurs. Star anise can be slightly sweeter in profile. The seeds of *P. anisum* and the pods of star anise should be ground/cracked immediately prior to use. Anise is a distinct and defining flavor that does not meet every palate with equal favor, but both have a marvelous floral aromatic quality that can add complexity and depth to both bouquet and flavor. The spices make for good components of spice blends when used in just-above-threshold levels: less than 1 ounce per 5 gallons.

Bergamot *Monarda fistulosa, M. didyma* (Oswego Tea)

Strikingly colorful, this herb, also known as beebalm, has been used in teas and other beverages for centuries. There are a dozen species in North America. It has a strong and strikingly appealing aroma from its high volatile oil content, described as citrus, lemon, or orange. It is familiar to many as the classic flavor of Earl Grey tea, its oil having been added to black tea. Bergamot is also used as a garnish or complement to fruits, making a good case for its inclusion in melomels, as well. Both the leaves (fresh or dried) and the fresh flowers (tart, highly flavored) can be used. The leaves will become more bitter after bloom and should be harvested beforehand. The flowers are popular with bees (hence the secondary name) and hummingbirds.

Cardamom *Elettaria cardamomum*

Perhaps more accurately described as a spice, the cardamom seed pod is harvested from a perennial plant of the *Zingiberacae* family native to India. The seed pods are dried whole in the sun, and are green or white (these have been bleached), slightly ribbed, and about ½" long and ¼" to 5⁄16" thick. The aroma of the crushed pods is citrus and bright, with lemon, sandalwood, and cinnamon notes. The taste profile of cardamom is unique, with the same flavors, along with a mild sweetness, very light numbing and astringency (both pleasant), and a lingering aftertaste that pervades the palate and the sinuses. Cardamom makes an excellent metheglin. Crush the whole seed pods thoroughly before using.

Chamomile *Chamaemelum nobile, Matricaria recutita*

While the majority of interest in chamomile has been in its use in teas, it deserves attention for its potential for meadmakers. Chamomile's aroma and flavor are a rich tapestry of apple, honey, berries, citrus, and rose. Its color, aroma and flavor plead to be bound to mead. In fact, the bouquet of chamomile may be the best match for the honey and alcohol notes of mead that I know of, especially when used with highly floral-scented honey varieties. The two Latin-named varieties cited above are known as Roman and German chamomile, respectively; the Roman is reputed to be stronger in nose. The dried flowers of the plant comprise this most versatile herb. I find it perfectly delighful in mead.

Coriander *Coriandrum Sativum*

Another incredible history surrounds coriander: The Indians mentioned it in Sanskrit writings some seven thousand years ago, and the Chinese also have been using it in candies, cakes, and drinks since 5000 BC. It is the dried seed of the plant, about 3 millimeters in diameter, slightly ribbed and not particularly dense. Coriander has a big aroma, sweet, estery, and appealing, reminiscent of oranges. It is the primary spice used in Belgian-style white (*wit*) beers and carries through beautifully with the esters produced by the yeast during fermentation. Unlike many other spices, coriander has a much larger range of acceptable "volume" in meads and will not destroy a mead at high concentrations. Coriander is a bit more ephemeral than the other spices listed here. You may wish to add it after your mead has sufficiently aged to be near its peak.

Fennel *Foeniculum vulgare*

Famous in Mediterranean foods, fennel seeds smell and taste very similar to anise and licorice. Like those two flavorings, a little can go a long way. Fennel's aroma and flavor are particularly susceptible to deterioration when heated, so a good case can be made for secondary or post-secondary addition. The stems and foliage are less commonly used.

Fenugreek *Trigonella foenum-graecum*

Fenugreek's uses throughout history have primarily been medicinal in nature, but it is still commonly used as a flavoring in preparation of chutneys, baked goods, ice cream, and a Middle Eastern candy known as halvah. The seeds and oils from the seeds are used; they have a maple and celerylike flavor and moderate to high aromatic content. In large quantity, the seeds become quite bitter. Fenugreek might be best used as part of a spice blend.

Grains of Paradise *Afromomum melegueta*

Grains of paradise have a long history of being used to spice beer, wine, and liqueurs. The West African spice is noted for a strong, camphorlike aroma and pungent, earthy, even woody flavor. The seeds are dried, and should be cracked or crushed before using.

Hops *Humulus lupus*

The flower cones of a rapidly growing vine, hops are a bitter, highly flavorful, and strongly aromatic herb. A key ingredient in beer, hops are also noted for many therapeutic uses, primarily as a sedative in hop pillows, but also as a tonic for ills ranging from rheumatism to flatulence (don't try to sell that one to the spouse of a beer drinker). The bitterness and hops' debatable powers derive from humulone and lupulone, two acidic compounds in the hop cones.

As in the history of beer, the use of hops in mead is not mentioned in recipes dating before the 1400s. The addition of hops to mead recipes may have arisen from the preservative qualities of the flowery cones. They are included regularly in recipes in modern brewing journals, primarily those associated with the home beermaking community.

Hops have been included in recipes for almost every type of mead, but their use seems most logical in pure metheglins, using hops as the primary flavoring ingredient, and in braggots, which include both malt and honey. As a rule, I am not a huge fan of hops in mead at all, but should you choose to utilize hops, there are a few varieties that possess notable flowery and perfumed, spicy aromas that would seem better suited to a marriage with honey. Saaz, a noble Czech hop, is very aromatic and easily distinguishable as a flowery, almost sweet hop variety. The East Kent Goldings variety is noted for citrusy, floral, and spicy notes. In ales, Kent Goldings offer a beautiful complement to the fruity, estery aromas created by the yeast fermentation. Both should provide an intriguing counterpoint to the aromatics of a mead. I'd suggest using American hybrid varieties like Cascade and Centennial with caution. Their bitterness and aroma characteristics can be overpowering.

The three components of hops' character are aroma, flavor, and bitterness. Each is extracted differently in brewing: bitterness through a prolonged boil, flavor through a shorter boil, and aroma through steeping at the end of the boil or in the cooled wort. Some aroma hops are added during or after the fermentation, in a process known as dry-hopping.

Juniper Berries *Juniperus communis*

The heart of the aroma and flavor of gin, juniper berries make a fine flavoring for mead but must be used with some care. Juniper berries are highly redolent, with a sprucy, clean, and very recognizable character. They have a mild astringency. They are available dried from finer spice merchants and can be added at any point in the meadmaking process. Crack but don't crush or grind juniper. Like all herbs and spices, juniper berries should be used soon, as their character can diminish markedly with age. They are a fine complement to mint.

Lavender *Lavandula augustifolia*

As with roses (see below), lavender and honey seem to be meant for each other like peanut butter and jelly, baseball and hot dogs, flyfishing and single-malt whisky. Dozens of varieties are cultivated throughout the West, with varying aromatic oil content and quality. With a soft, perfumed, and slightly sweet scent, lavender is still widely cultivated for a huge variety of uses.

For peak aromatic quality, lavender blossoms should be harvested immediately before opening or during the first half of the bloom of the crop. Pick your crop on a warm, dry day, as these are the ideal conditions for aromatic oil production. The blossoms have a range of colors that will not dye the mead, but rather create a soft, appealing blush. Two to 3 ounces at a time should be added during secondary fermentation.

Lavender can be easy to cultivate, but many varieties will not tolerate northern winter, and will require deep mulching. Lavender will fill your yard with a soothing, distinct aroma bound to remind you of someone or something pleasant in your past. For hardiness and character, Dick Dunn, janitor of the Mead Lover's Digest, recommends the English variety *Hidcote*, and noted that the leaves also can be used, if dried first.

Lemon Balm *Melissa officinalis*

The name creates an accurate mental picture. The leaves of this herb are highly perfumed and scented with lemon and a hint of mint (it is a member of the mint family). It is more aromatic than flavorful and could be combined with citrus fruit or honey to create layered complexity in a metheglin or melomel. The aroma is citrusy, but distinctly unique and memorable. Fresh leaves have a slightly more appealing nose than dried.

Lemon Grass *Cymbopogon citratus, C. flexuosus*

Used both fresh and dried, this West Indian grass is indeed reminiscent of lemon but also possesses a heady, earthy flavor with a modest astringency when used fresh in cooking. Used in small quantities, the stems provide complexity and a tart balance to sweet or fruity meads. Used in more prominent quantities, the nose becomes more woody, almost cedarlike, with other citrus, sandalwood, ginger, and jasmine notes.

Mint *Mentha X spicata, Mentha X villosa-nervata* (spearmint, English spearmint), *Mentha X piperita* (peppermint), *Mentha rotundifolia* (apple mint), *Mentha var. variegata* (pineapple mint), *M. aquatica var. crispa* (curly mint)

The many varieties of mint make for myriad and inviting options in metheglin. Mint contrasts very well with meads, and its character blends with dry, medium, and sweet meads with equal artistry. The varieties listed above are but a few of the possible choices. The differences between the varieties are quite striking, and your choice of mint for use in a mead should be made carefully.

Mint is available dried, in oils and extracts, and can be grown (perhaps too easily) in the garden in virtually any part of the globe. The dried and extracted oil options give the meadmaker some additional leeway in how and when they are added, but fresh mint is unsurpassed in presenting the delightful aroma and depth of flavor complexity that these plants can add to a mead. The addition of 2 ounces of fresh crushed mint leaves to a secondary fermenter is a highly recommended method. Should a sampling show that the mint character is below the desired threshold, 2 more ounces can be added, as many times as needed. Fresh mint can also be soaked in a small amount of neutral vodka or grain alcohol and added to the mead in secondary or at bottling. With the variety of mints that mirror the characters of fruits and other spices, mint blends well with other flavors, especially orange peel, lemon, chocolate (a Mazer Cup best-of-show winner), and strongly flavored honey varieties.

While it may seem heresy to some mead purists, a sweet mead served over ice, with a few bruised mint leaves and a splash of soda, makes a refreshing and very unique summer cooler.

Poppy Seed *Papaver rhoeas*

Cultivation of the poppy is the subject of controversy in some circles. Older sources cite the opium poppy, *Papaver somniferum*, as the source of poppy seeds, while newer texts refer to *P. rhoeas*, supposedly not an opium producer, as the preferred source. Still other sources claim the two cannot be differentiated. Both are cultivated widely by unknowing gardeners who love the large, deeply colored blooms, and by cooks seeking the seeds.

The seeds are removed from the dried base of the flower. Flavorful in a slightly spicy way, the seeds are somewhat oily; I haven't used them in mead for exactly that reason. Like nuts, they present a challenge in maintaining clarity and cleanliness of fermentation vessels, hoses, and racking canes.

Rose ***Rosacea (R. alba, R. centifolia, R. damascena, R. rugosa, R. rubiginosa, R. spinosissima, et al.)***

A hobby as full of variety and complexity and potentially as satisfying as fruit growing or meadmaking, the cultivating of roses holds infinite potential. The blossoms (and fruits, known as rosehips) are full of aroma and flavor and have been consumed in many forms for centuries. The petals are even mixed with honey as a confection in the Near East. Few combinations of flavors and aromas seem more obvious to me in theory, or are better wed in practice. And yes, rose petals definitely belong in mead, well enough for the mixture to merit a term of its own: *rhodomel*.

Roses come in countless varieties, each possessing its own characteristic scent. Certain varieties are more aromatic than others, and some in particular have been utilized in beverages and foods like salads. Long cherished for their bouquet are the tea and hybrid tea roses, so noted for their tealike scent. Other highly acclaimed aromatic types are the Rugosa roses (vigorous and disease resistant), the Fragrant Hybrid Perpetuals, Damasks, and some of the Bourbon and China roses. Differing from variety to variety, their characters may be lighter or more heady, resinous, honeylike, or reminiscent of other fruits, flowers, or perfumes. Some roses, like the Sweetbrier, exude their fragrance from their leaves as well as their blossoms. Burnet roses are considered a prime source of sweet rosehips.

Not all roses are truly appetizing in their aroma. A local arboretum or gardening club is a good way to become familiar with the varieties and their characteristics. Let your contacts know why you are interested in their varieties; they are far more likely to move you in the right direction if they know what you are planning to do.

Again, as with fruit, the home grower or connected individual will have access to more variety and much finer quality. Additionally, roses will present more or less of their character at differing points in the season, and even at different times of day. The ability to harvest the petals or rosehips (arguably more of a melomel ingredient) you intend to use at their peak will lead to commensurate contributions to the quality and character of your mead.

Meads can be racked directly onto the petals after primary fermentation, but again, the amount of roses used should be tempered and adjusted upward as necessary. Two ounces at a time is a good starting point. As with other herbs, rose petals can be frozen, and a vacuum-sealing device is well advised here.

Care must be taken when using garden roses in mead, as many commercially available rose pesticide and fungicide treatments should not be used in any food product. Take care, also, to be sure that any chemicals have not been applied inside of their safe use windows, which are described on the labels of all preparations intended for use on fruits and vegetables.

Vanilla ***Vanilla Planifolia***

Vanilla is the top commercially used flavor. The seed pods of a New World orchid are alternately dried and sweated during the curing process. The flavor is strong and soft at the same time, lacking bitterness, coupled with a sweet, full, and penetrating aroma.

The beans can be added directly to mead in the secondary. They can also be added to fruit during primary and secondary fermentations. The use of vanilla can be deceiving, in that it will build the flavor of that to which it is added, and is not obvious in its presence but notable in its absence. It is much like pushing up the middle frequencies of a sound system, creating fullness and "throat" for flavors it accents. Vanilla is used in just that context in chocolate and other confections, coffee liqueurs, dairy products, and baked goods. Its application in mead will work in the same way, especially in raspberry and cherry melomels and in metheglins with other spices. On its own, however, it can be a difficult flavor to capture in mead, mellowing and dissipating quickly, and becoming difficult to single out in the complexity of mead aroma and flavor.

Verbena, Lemon ***Aloysia triphylla***

This one is a prize, certainly. Although difficult to grow in cool climes, it is available dried commercially and can be container grown. It is lemony and minty but with a lingering, more vegetative leafy odor than lemon grass. The lemon and spicy character will become more pronounced with prolonged exposure in the fermenter. The leaves of this deciduous plant will impart some of their green color to your mead.

Way-out Stuff

With the possible exception of woodruff, none of these herbs have a readily apparent link with mead. On the other hand, some brave souls will want to stretch the boundaries of meadmaking, and these herbs may provide an interesting outlet for their energies. Small test batches are definitely in order.

Angelica ***Angelica archangelica officinalis***

A member of the carrot family, angelica is a large plant that bears some resemblance to celery. The stems and seeds also have licoricelike aroma and flavor. Angelica seed is used in liqueurs, but as an herb it is generally more often associated with fish dishes or used in baking. The leaves have a slightly sweet warmth and a bitter aftertaste, which some claim is more prominent in American angelica, *Angelica atropurpurea L.*

Basil ***Ocimum basilicum,*** **Lemon Basil** ***Ocimum citriodora***

A big flavor, and dearly loved in culinary circles, basil anchors pestos and Italian sauces. It is not traditionally paired with sweet flavors or wine, except in sauces. It does make an appearance in the Benedictine monks' liqueur Chartreuse. I have tasted one notably basil-flavored mead, from Chuck Wettergreen. It dominates the flavor profile and takes some getting used to. Chuck got big points for ingenuity, but basil must be used judiciously.

Borage ***Borago officinalis***

Known for two things—its distinctive cucumber aroma and flavor, and for its reputation for producing courage, (like makes like?)—borage is a fine candidate for a vinegar or marinade. Actually the third thing it's noted for is taking over anyplace it is planted, much like lemon balm. Use appropriate caution. It has been used in the past to flavor wine and beer, so the precedent is there. It is available fresh or dried, but some herbal authorities hold that only the fresh leaves or flowering tips of this herb will yield the finest culinary results.

Cumin ***Cuminum cyminum***

Cumin is known primarily for its role in Mexican and Spanish dishes. Its flavor is mildly acrid and very earthy, to the point of being unpleasant to some people. It takes a stretch to see how this would work its way into a mead, but if you try it, let me know how it works out.

Horehound ***Marrubium vulgare***

Horehound is best known to most Westerners by the hard candy so named. It is a member of the mint family native to lands surrounding the Mediterranean. Horehound is possessed of a distinct bitterness, which commands respect when horehound is to be used in food or drink.

Hyssop ***Hyssopus officinalis***

Definitively in the "way-out" category, hyssop is possessed of a strong medicinal and camphorlike odor. It is a mint, but is not sweet or mild in any sense of the word and is not often used in culinary applications. It is a first-rate honey plant and is prized by beekeepers for the distinct and pleasant honey borne of its blossoms. Used fresh in sparing quantities, the leaves would certainly add complexity to a metheglin.

Marjoram ***Origanum marjorana L.***

Most often associated with meats and main dishes, marjoram bears resemblance to oregano. It is used throughout Europe in poultry, fish, and vegetable dishes as well as cheese dishes, soups, and sauces.

Sweet Woodruff ***Galium odoratum, Asperula odorata***

The sprigs of this woodland herb have been used in alcoholic beverages since the thirteenth century. The German Mai Bowle of wine with woodruff and fruit may be the most well known, but woodruff is also used to flavor Berliner *weisse* beers and liqueurs. Its soft, mildly sweet flavor and very pleasant scent make woodruff a good candidate for use in mead. Coumarin gives woodruff an aroma reminiscent of vanilla. The Food and Drug Administration considers woodruff to be safe only when used in alcoholic beverages. Add a few sprigs of fresh or dried woodruff to a 5-gallon batch and taste a few weeks later; add additional sprigs to taste.

Making a Spice Blend

Spice blending, particularly when intended for use in metheglin, is a process that should be done diligently and with a definite plan in mind. Start small, mixing quarter teaspoons at a time, or using a gram scale to measure quantities, and always keep a pad of paper around for notes (especially if this activity is combined with mead consumption). Speaking of mead consumption, a bottle of cellar or room temperature show mead can be an excellent medium for evaluating the flavor of your spice blend. Pour a small amount, say 1 ounce or so, toss a tiny pinch of the blend into your glass, swirl, and then nose and taste the mead. Dramatic imbalances will be readily evident, and adjustments to the blend can be made additively or by preparing an entirely different composition.

While the practice doesn't fall into the truest sense of "metheglin," many meadmakers and chefs with an interest in mead have taken to adding various herbs and spices to mead to create marinades. Beyond that, some meadmakers have revived the art of making mead vinegars, which have been popular throughout the ages, if perhaps a bit pricey to produce. Mead vinegars and marinades are very flavorful and, especially when spiced, can add a whole new page to your Epicurean playbook.

chapter eleven
Grains and Braggot

The term "braggot" (a.k.a. "bragot" or "bracket") describes a mead made from malted barley or other malted grain in addition to honey. Often a beguiling and seductive beverage, it draws characteristics from both of its key ingredients to create a whole that is greater than the sum of its parts. The hybridization of these two fermented beverages—beer and mead—appears to have arisen out of resourcefulness.

The histories of beer brewing and meadmaking run back to earliest antiquity. It appears honey has been added to beer (or malt extract to mead, if you prefer) just as long. The *Hymn to Ninkasi* is an ode to Ninkasi, the Sumerian goddess of brewing, dating to about 1800 BC. A recipe in the *Hymn* mentions an ingredient alternately interpreted by brewing historians and other academics as liquefied dates or honey. The *Hymn's* brewer combines this proto-honey with water, barley, and bread made from barley before fermenting it into an alcoholic beverage.

More recent references to mixed honey/barley beverages appear throughout post-Renaissance Europe. To understand their preparation, we must first understand how brewers produce the sugars that they ferment.

Malted barley contains sugars tied up in long chains of starch. To harvest these sugars, brewers first conduct a mash by mixing hot water with the malt. This prompts the natural enzymes of the grain to break starch chains into fermentable sugars. Next, brewers harvest sugar-rich liquid through a process called lautering. Here, liquid escapes from the mash through a slotted platform that functions like a strainer. The husks and other grain solids remain above the sieve, while sugary liquid flows on to a collecting vessel. Once the mash liquid is collected, a substantial amount of sugar still remains trapped in the grain solids. To collect these, the brewer washes the grain bed with more hot water in a process called sparging. As the sparge water trickles through the grain, it transports additional sugar through the sieve, giving the brewer more fermentable liquid.

The highest concentration of sugars comes in the first runnings from the mash. During sparging, the sugar concentration drops steadily, eventually reaching an unproductive plateau. Today, some brewers continue the once-standard practice of taking the early runoff to make a strong beer and isolating the weaker second runnings for production of a "small" or "table" beer.

Sixteenth- and seventeenth-century recipes for braggot added honey to small beers before fermentation. This fortified the small beer, allowing production of a more robust product. Other recipes added honey to strong beers. Thus, while fortification of small beer may have prompted the initial combination of these two fermentables, the mixture proved tasty enough to employ in stronger products as well.

My attempts to re-create medieval and subsequent-era braggots—both with hops and without—produced products that I enjoy. These braggots started with quite high gravities, 1.090 or above, finishing as strong, treacle-sweet drinks, with complex bouquets.

I enjoy these delightful winter warmer braggots, and you may, too. But modern-day braggotmaking is a pursuit limited only by your imagination. Some will hold specifically to historic recipes, but I eschew such constraints. I have tasted wonderful braggots made after the styles of imperial stout, barley wine, and bock beer. I have had sumptuous elixirs made without hops, and hearty, aggressively hopped braggots that linger on the tongue for long minutes. Let your own personal preferences be your guide.

Although you need not become a homebrewer to make braggot, you'll need some knowledge of brewing techniques and ingredients to succeed. Before we get to the recipes, let me give a bit of this background.

Like meadmaking, brewing can be simple or complex. Indeed, brewing can become far more complicated than the most elaborate meadmaking procedures that I know. Purists make beer from scratch, using an involved process known as "all-grain brewing." Alternately, beer can be made from packaged dry or liquid malt extracts. These malt extracts are commercially produced concentrated beer wort, containing either a small amount of water or none at all. Malt extracts make creating a braggot a much simpler process. Of course, as with any creative process, you will have a greater degree of control and perhaps better flavors if you start with the raw grains, but that can be a pretty demanding pursuit.

For those interested in working with raw grains, I have included a sidebar describing the common brewing grains and their characteristics. If you don't already brew beer, you might want to read the basic bible of homebrewing, Charlie Papazian's *The New Complete Joy of Homebrewing.*

As I have mentioned, malt extracts come in both dried and liquid forms, and each is offered in a host of styles. Maltsters brew up worts to match just about any beer style and then concentrate them into liquid malt extracts suitable for mixing with honey. You'll find less diversity in dry malt extracts, yet they come in a range of body and color gradations that make them suitable for braggot as well.

While not all braggots use hops, you'll need a bit of background on this raw material as well. Hops possess hundreds of flavor-active compounds that can contribute bitterness, as well as a range of other flavors and aromas. Like roses or apples, hops come in many different varieties, and each has distinct characteristics.

Hops are used to provide bitterness to balance the sweetness and body of a braggot. Variety shown here: Centennial

When boiled for up to 90 minutes, hops add bitterness to any brew. The extent of bitterness depends upon the length of the boil (longer equals more bitter), the amount of hops added, and the concentration of something called "alpha acids" in the hop itself. Since alpha acids convert to bittering compounds during boiling, the higher alpha acid levels produce greater bitterness.

Hops also yield flavor and aroma compounds ranging from floral and perfumy through spicy, herbal, and citrus, then on to earthy and even pungent or skunky. Hops impart these flavors and aromas when boiled for a short time (less than 15 minutes) or simply incubated with warm must or even cool fermented mead for various periods. The exact flavor produced depends upon the variety chosen and the method of addition.

Every hop variety has a characteristic level of bitter-producing alpha acids as well as its own particular aroma and flavor traits. Personally, I'm fond of Cascades, Fuggles, Bullion, and East Kent Goldings in braggot. As with grain, you'll want to do further reading if you want to really explore this aspect of braggot. One rule you will need to observe is to keep fermenting or finished hopped braggots away from sunlight or fluorescent lights, which can cause the reaction that gives light-struck beer a characteristic "skunky" smell.

If you are already an all-grain brewer, you have considerable experience, and I will not bore you with details. I will include an all-grain recipe in the recipes chapter for you to use or modify to create a braggot.

If you are not an all-grain brewer, you can still get the benefit of using grain in your braggot without the huge investment of time and expense needed to get into all-grain brewing as a hobby. You'll want to find a homebrew shop or on-line supplier that will sell you pre-ground malt by the pound. You may or may not want to add hops, which provide the bitterness in beer as well as some natural preservative qualities. With malt, hops, and honey, and a few common cooking utensils, you can perform a basic mash and sparge out the beginnings of a dynamite braggot. If you'd prefer to dispense with the challenges of using grain, I have provided directions for using malt extract (also available at shops or on-line) below.

The one utensil you may not have in your kitchen is a thermometer with a range from about 60° F to 220° F (26° C to 104° C).They can be found at most culinary stores, or dairy thermometers can be purchased at homebrew shops. In addition, you'll need two good-sized stockpots (8 quarts or more), a large spoon, a large colander-sized strainer, a smaller pot, and a teapot. Here we go.

Don't Cry for Me Spargentina Barley Wine-Style Braggot

This braggot will be amber to tawny brown in color with a dense, cream-to-tan-colored head. It will have a noticeably caramel sweet nose entwined with honey and malt. The hops should not be evident in the aroma but should provide a pleasant, mildly bitter counterpoint to the full and distinctly sweet body. If you do not elect to add hops, this braggot will have a much sweeter profile on the tongue and may be suited to small, after-dinner dosages.

Makes 5 Gallons (18.92 L)

Whole grain option:

4	**lbs. (1.82 kg) crushed pale malt**
0.5	**lb. (227 g) crushed crystal malt**

Alternative extract option:

3.3	**lbs. (1.5 kg) pale malt extract syrup or 3 lbs. (1.36 kg) pale dry malt extract**

Ingredients for both methods:

2	**oz. (56.7 g) Cascade hop pellets, ~5.5 alpha acid units (optional)**
10	**lbs. (4.55 kg) medium amber honey. I recommend tulip poplar or tupelo, if available. Berry-blossom crop honeys are also very appealing.**
2	**tsp. (19.8 g) yeast nutrient**
2	**tsp. (19.8 g) yeast energizer**
10	**g Lalvin D-47 yeast**

Whole Grain Procedure

Step One: Sanitize a 7-gallon (25 L or larger) plastic fermenter or 6-gallon (22.5 L) or larger carboy. Fill partially with 2.5 gallons (9.5 L) of water, and chill to 55° F (13° C) or cooler, if possible.

Step Two: In large stockpot, heat 4.5 quarts (17 L) of water to 170° F (77° C). Stir in the crushed grains.The resulting mash should be the consistency of thin cooked cereal and should stabilize between 145° F and 155° F (63° C and

68° C). Stir well, and hold the mash in that range for about 30 minutes. If the mash dips below 142° F (61° C), add heat slowly, stirring constantly, to bring it up above 145° F (63° C). Stir occasionally. Fill the smaller pot and the teapot with water, and heat to 185° F (85° C).

Step Three: After 30 minutes, you are ready to sparge. Place the strainer over the second stockpot, and carefully spoon/pour the mash into the strainer. Some liquid will strain into the pot below. With the teapot, rinse the grains by slowly pouring the hot water over the grain bed. Try to rinse the entire grain bed by pouring some liquid over the entire surface of the grain. Using the teapot makes this simpler. Fill it from the other pot when it is empty. Repeat until you have poured about 1 gallon (3.8 L) of water over the grains.

The resulting liquid should total about 6 to 7 quarts (5.7 to 6.6 L). It should taste malty and sweet, with a slight caramelized flavor.

Step Four: At this point, you can add the optional hops if you wish. Bring the liquid to a boil for 1 hour.

Alternative Malt Extract Procedures:

Step One: Sanitize a 5-gallon (18.92 L) plastic fermenter or 6-gallon (22.5 L) or larger carboy. Fill partially with 2.5 gallons (9.5 L) of water, and chill to 55° F (13° C) or cooler, if possible.

Step Two: In a large stockpot, bring 5 quarts (4.7 L) of water to a boil, then shut off the flame and add the malt extract you have selected, and hops, if you wish. After mixing thoroughly, turn on the heat again and boil the liquid and hops for 1 hour.

Recipe Completion:

Step Five: Remove the boiled extract or whole-grain malt mixture from the heat and add the honey. Stir well, and allow to cool. The wort/must should be no hotter than 100° F (38° C) if you are using a glass carboy. Transfer the wort/must to the fermenter containing cool water. The resulting mixture should be about 65° F to 75° F (18.5° C to 24° C).

Step Six: Add yeast nutrient and yeast energizer, stir well, then add the yeast, which has previously been rehydrated according to package instructions.

Affix a fermentation lock and wait for the fun to begin. You'll want to rack this to a secondary fermenter once the primary fermentation has slowed, and bottle after all signs of fermentation have ceased.

I like to carbonate this by adding a half-cup of honey at bottling. You can substitute ¾ cup (177.5 ml) of corn sugar, or ½ cup (118.3 ml) of corn sugar plus ½ cup (118.3 ml) dry malt extract. It will carbonate fully in the bottles after two to four weeks.

You can modify this recipe to create a whole panoply of different braggots with unique colors, aromas, and flavors. By using more or less malt or honey, or by utilizing

Malted Barley: The Brewers Honey

The barley used for malting comes in two types, two-row and six-row, based on the way it grows on the stalk. Both types are used commonly, with two-row being used more often in ales, and six-row being used more commonly in American-style lagers. Both of these types can be crafted into more individualized malted barley products through differences in the malting process.

Barley is "malted" by a precise set of steps, which permit the grain to partially germinate and then arrest the germination process by heating or "kilning."The amount of germination—and the duration and amount of heat used in the kilning process—will determine the type of malt produced, and thus the effect that type of malt will have on the flavor and aroma of a beer in which it is used. Kilning malts at higher temperatures will effectively kill off their enzymes.

Some of the more common types of malt are:

Pale malt: A two-row malt, which is high in enzymes and converts starches to sugars very effectively. Light in color, with mouth-filling malty flavor.

Lager malt: Can be either two- or six-row. Many American lager malts are bred for high enzymatic content. Also light in color. European lager malt may have lower enzymatic power than pale malt.

Chocolate malt: A roasted malt with a color and bitter/sweet flavor characteristic of chocolate. No enzymatic power.

Black patent malt: Dark, highly roasted malt used in very dark beers such as porter and stout. No enzymatic power.

Vienna malt: A lager malt kilned at temperatures higher than pale or lager malt, but low enough to preserve enzymatic activity, yielding a delightfully toasted but not roasted or burnt character. Lower enzymatic power.

Munich malt: Similar to Vienna malt but kilned at slightly higher temps for a more toasted aroma and flavor. Both Vienna and Munich malts produce a distinctly rich, lingering malty character and slightly darker color in beers and braggots.

Crystal malt: Two-row malt toasted at higher temperatures to a darker hue than Vienna, but still lighter than chocolate malt. So called because the endosperm (meat) of the grain is kilned to the point of becoming clear and glassy. Crystal malt adds sweetness and body. Available in a variety of roasts. No enzymatic power.

Caramel malt: Similar to crystal malt but germinated and kilned less thoroughly so as to caramelize, but not completely clarify, the endosperm. Produces more throaty, robust flavor than crystal malt, with more toastiness and less pronounced sweetness.

Wheat malt: Not barley at all, but wheat. Produces softer, cereal-like character and some spiciness. Lower enzymatic power.

Roasted barley: Made from unmalted barley, this is a very dark and roasty grain used in stouts. No enzymatic power.

lighter or darker honey, you can create a lighter- or fuller-bodied braggot. More distinct will be the changes you can make by using other types of malted barley or extract.

If you are not a homebrewer, it will serve you well to become familiar with different styles of beer before choosing one to pair with honey. There are many good books on beer and beer styles available; I recommend Michael Jackson's *World Guide to Beer* and *Beer Companion*, or alternately, Fred Eckhardt's *The Essentials of Beer Style*.

When crafting a recipe for braggot, take care not to exceed the sugar tolerance of the yeast you are using. A good rule of thumb is that like honey, 1 pound of malt extract will raise the gravity of your must about 0.008 points in a 5-gallon batch. The must gravity should not exceed 1.120 for a yeast with low sugar tolerance, and 1.150 for a yeast with high sugar tolerance.

If you are not already a brewer, but would like to gain more knowledge about hops, beer, beer styles, and how to match malt with honey, you should consider joining the American Homebrewers Association (AHA) or contacting a local homebrewing club. The AHA's magazine, *Zymurgy,* regularly features articles on malt, hops, and brewing that will be very useful to a fledgling braggotmaker.

Homebrewing clubs have sprung up virtually across the globe. You can find locations and contact information on clubs in the United States at the American Homebrewers Association Web site, www.beertown.org. You'll find the members of brew clubs to be a jovial and gregarious lot, eager to share their knowledge and experience. To paraphrase Will Rogers, you have many friends there you haven't met.

Just as brewers have combined malt with a vast array of fruits and spices, so too can you in your braggot. Cherry braggot, hot pepper braggot, coriander-and-orange peel braggot—any combination that strikes a chord in your imagination is worth exploring.

part four

Recipes

chapter twelve

Putting the Process and Ingredients Together

Top-quality mead ingredients and a poor recipe beat poor ingredients and a top-quality recipe nine times out of ten. That's why 90% of this book deals with ingredients and only 10% with specific recipes.

The recipes I give you in this chapter should serve as starting points for your own creative flair. No recipe could ever satisfy every mead lover's tastes. First, a tested recipe simply serves as a sound basis for the preparation of some dynamite mead. Second, many variables affect meadmaking. No one single recipe, no single technique will catapult your efforts from frightful to fantastic. What defines a great mead is all in the taste of the drinker, so you are the final judge of whether or not these recipes meet your expectations or desires.

The ingredients I recommend for each recipe reflect practical experience. I (and some of my trusted friends) have used them and been satisfied with the results. That said, the precise ingredients in each recipe don't always represent my ideal choices. They were what I had at hand, or what I could get when I went to make a mead. They produced good mead, and I feel comfortable passing them on to you. When you try these recipes you should be prepared to exercise the same flexibility in your preparation that I did in mine. You may choose to substitute other honey varieties or yeast strains, either because you don't have what is listed here, or just because you want to try something different. Please don't think you can't make delicious mead if you can't find "2 pounds of fresh, unpitted North Star tart cherries" or don't have any Earl Grey tea on hand. You can make great mead, and you will. Locating and obtaining high-quality ingredients can be a source of pleasure in and of itself. Find and use the best substitutes you can, and try to avoid adding any anxiety to your recipe. Life is just too short for that.

Vacations and meadmaking share common traits. Both start with expectations—a set of ideas about how things will turn out. But once the adventure begins, things may follow an unexpected course. When this happens, go with the flow. You are

successful if you like what you get, not if you get what you expected. So many variables affect the flavor of mead that you should never be disappointed simply because the finished product isn't exactly what you envisioned. Your friends and relatives won't know what you were shooting for; they will only know that they like what you made.

I don't really recommend making mead with untried honeys that you don't find appealing in the jar. The chances are, if you don't like the way it smells fresh, you aren't going to like the way it tastes as a mead. Similarly, if you go off the deep end and try a carrot, onion, and habanero pepper metheglin, you should probably take a gallon of a base mead then add small amounts of the additional ingredients to the secondary fermentation in a controlled fashion. Alternately, you can make an elixir, as mentioned in the chapter on fruit. As one who has experimented widely, I'll tell you that it can be very tough to come up with a use for 5 gallons of Cajun-dill-pumpkin mead—even if you are a liberal user of marinades. Go slow at first, then stoke it up if you like what you've made.

Balance and Innovation

Flavor, like beauty, depends largely on the beholder. Thus, I would never profess to offer anyone the perfect recipe—or one ideal mead. Some people believe that melomels or metheglins must have an "even" balance between honey character and other flavors such as fruit or herbs. I think that's balderdash. Great wines, great Scotch whiskies, even many great foods hang their hats on being way out of "balance"—highlighting one of rather than equalizing all of their respective components.

Sure, some great meads strike a hair-splitting balance between all their components, each taking an equal share of the spotlight. But life offers more than perfectly mitered corners. If you want to make yourself a raspberry melomel with 20 pounds of fruit in five gallons, go right ahead (tasting it over the years as it softens will be a fascinating experience). Cherry and rosehips melo-metheglin? Vanilla-peach-ginger-pineapple-almost-ice-cream-topping-whatsitz? Let 'er rip. The message here is, if you want to take a crack at it, go ahead. Virtually all human progress has resulted from someone changing, amplifying or, omitting some part of the conventional mix. Most real progress isn't accomplished in great leaps; it is a slow encroachment on ignorance achieved by people who are willing to take a chance.

Of course you need to employ sanitation procedures for every batch in all the usual places—even if I don't explicitly mention it. Feel free to choose the sanitation techniques that suit your own inclinations, even if I mention a specific approach in a particular recipe. You'll always need to sanitize every piece of equipment that will come in contact with your must every time you prepare a batch, rack, or bottle.

Let's begin with a few base recipes for show and traditional meads, and build from there.

Dry Show Mead

Dry meads like this one can be made almost Champagnelike when carbonated in the bottle for a sparkling effervescence. They are wonderful accompaniments to appetizers, fish, and pasta dishes, or can be enjoyed alone. A little oak in the aging process will give a dry mead complexity and boost its mouthfeel.

Makes 5 gallons (18.93 L)

10	**lbs. (2.27 kg) high-quality varietal honey**
4	**gal. (15.14 L) water, approximately; enough to make to 5 gallons**
2	**tsp. (9.9 mL) yeast energizer**
2	**tsp. (9.9 mL) yeast nutrient**
1	**liter starter of Steinberger yeast**
•	**OG: 1.080 (19.33° P)**
•	**FG: 0.998 (-0.45° P)**

Sanitize must, then pitch the yeast starter at 60-70° F (16-21° C). Stir vigorously to oxygenate. Ferment completely, then rack to secondary, and age until clear. Add 1 ounce of oak chips for four to seven days before bottling, if desired. Bottle when you are ready.

Medium Show Mead

This mead will retain more of the character of the honey in the nose. It also will taste slightly sweeter, linger a bit longer on the tongue, and be more viscous in its mouthfeel. Medium meads are a great choice when preparing mead for a wider audience, like weddings or other celebrations.

Makes 5 gallons (18.93 L)

12.5-14	**lbs. (5.7-6.4 kg) high-quality varietal honey**
4	**gal. (15.14 L) water, approximately; enough to make 5 gallons (15.14 L)**
2	**tsp. (9.9 mL) yeast energizer**

2 **tsp. (9.9 mL) yeast nutrient**
1 **liter starter of Lalvin D-47 yeast**
• **OG: 1.094-1.112 (22.4-26.4° P)**
• **FG: 1.010 (2.56° P)**

Sanitize must, then pitch the yeast starter at 60-70° F (16-21° C). Stir vigorously to oxygenate. Ferment completely, watching for signs of slowing fermentation, and use calcium carbonate to keep the pH above 3.7 or so to keep the yeast happy. Rack to secondary and age until clear. Bottle when you are ready.

Sweet Show Mead

Sweet meads are generally still, as the yeast will knock itself out trying to deal with all that sugar. Bottle carbonation is difficult, if not impossible, to achieve. This recipe will yield a very sweet dessert mead, with distinct honey character and profound legs. Its color will be a pretty reflection on the original honey, and the aroma will cling to the glass even after it is empty. Excellent served with a fruit and cheese platter.

Makes 5 gallons (18.93 L)

15-18 **lbs. (6.8-8.2 kg) high-quality varietal honey**
4 **gal. (15.14 L) water, approximately; enough to make to 5 gallons**
2 **tsp. (9.9 mL) yeast energizer**
2 **tsp. (9.9 mL) yeast nutrient**
1 **liter starter of Lalvin D-47 yeast**
• **OG: 1.120-1.135 (28-31.4° P)**
• **FG: 1.025 (6.33° P)**

Sanitize must, then pitch the yeast starter at 60-70° F (16-21° C). Stir vigorously to oxygenate. Ferment completely, watching for signs of slowing fermentation, and use calcium carbonate to keep the pH above 3.7 or so to keep the yeast happy. Rack to secondary and age until clear. Bottle when you are ready.

Dry Nutmeg Metheglin

This mead took two years to settle down, but it is now a delight to accompany meals of fish, pasta, or chicken. It is dry, but the Epernay yeast brings out the aromas of both the honey and the nutmeg. It is also one of the more pleasant meads to look at. It is light and delicate, making a pretty picture in a crystal glass.

Makes 5 gallons (18.93 L)

15	**lbs. (6.82 kg) white clover honey**
4	**gal. (15.14 L) water, approximately; enough to make to 5 gallons**
1	**oz. (scant) (I used 27.5 g) freshly ground nutmeg**
2	**3-inch (76 mm) cinnamon sticks**
2	**tsp. (9.9 mL) yeast energizer**
1	**tsp. (4.9 mL) yeast nutrient**
500	**ml Epernay yeast starter**
500	**ml starter of Pasteur Champagne yeast**
•	**OG: 1.104 (24.6° P)**
•	**FG: 1.000 (0° P)**

Flash heat all ingredients except the yeast in 1 gallon boiling water. When mixed, the blend will stabilize at 160° F (71° C) for 15 minutes; chill to 75° F (24° C). Pour into fermenter (I adjusted pH with calcium carbonate to 4.0), add water to 5 gallons (18.93 L), aerate well, and pitch yeast. At bottling, adjust acidity with 2-4 teaspoons (9.9-19.8 mL) acid blend, if desired.

Cherry Melomel

This mead is very sweet and very tart at the same time. The unpitted cherries add a woody, sherrylike note. The color is rich red, the mouthfeel is big, and the aftertaste is lingering, fruity, honeylike, but with a solid bite from the tart cherry acidity. This mead is quite sweet—nearly a liqueur—and makes for a nice after-dinner glass, going well with cheesecake or other desserts.

Makes 5 gallons (18.93 L)

13	**lbs. (5.9 kg) star thistle honey**
4	**lbs. (1.8 kg) wildflower honey**
1.5	**tsp. (7.4 mL) yeast energizer**
2	**tsp. (9.9 mL) yeast nutrient**
1	**gal. (3.78 L) water**
3	**gal. (11.35 L) pasteurized tart cherry juice, refrigerated to 34 °F (1 °C). (I used Swanson's Juice.)**
2	**lbs. (907 g) fresh, unpitted North Star or other tart cherries**
1	**liter starter of Wyeast dry mead yeast**
•	**OG: 1.142 (33.6° P)**
•	**FG: 1.032 (8.05° P)**

Bring water to a boil, remove from heat, add honey, yeast energizer, and yeast nutrient, then pasteurize at 160° F (71° C) for 10 minutes. Force chill to 90° F

(32° C), add 1 gallon of the cherry juice, then transfer to fermenter and add remaining cherry juice. The resulting mixture should be about 75-80° F (24-27° C). Aerate well, pitch yeast. Ferment in primary for 3 to 4 weeks, or until fermentation slows. Rack to secondary fermenter and add the cherries.

These cherries replace the lost volume from the yeast in the primary fermenter and fill the secondary right to the neck of the carboy. Let age 3 to 6 months or longer in secondary, bottle when you feel like it.

Multi-berry Melomel

Both Dan McConnell and I arrived at this concoction separately, although not in identical incarnations. Dan calls his "Purple Haze," and I dubbed mine "Mambo in Your Mouth." Both of the names accurately portray the depth and complexity of this creation. The blend of many berries in a full-bodied but dry mead makes for a tongue-dancing spectacle of flavors that darts quickly from being like a fine Bordeaux, to a fruity, almost sangria-like beverage, to being a stellar mead. Each of the fruit ingredients will present itself at different times during the drinking, influenced by the warming of the mead, oxidation in the glass, and the evolution of your palate. It ages as well as any wine I know of and has not failed to impress people even as the number of bottles in the cellar dwindles. This mead will benefit from some form of oak aging.

"Mambo In Your Mouth"

Makes 5 gallons (18.93 L)

12	**lbs. (5.45 kg) white clover honey**
3	**gal. (11.35 L) water**
2	**tsp. (9.9 mL) yeast energizer**
2	**tsp. (9.9 mL) yeast nutrient**
3	**lbs. (1.36 kg) strawberries**
3.5	**lbs. (1.59 kg) wild black raspberries**
1.5	**lbs. (682 g) red raspberries**
2	**lbs. (907 g) blueberries**
2.5	**lbs. (1.14 kg) dark sweet cherries**
	Your choice of yeast (see below)
•	**OG: 1.092 (22.1° P)**

Ferment the base must consisting of honey, energizer, nutrient, water, and, of course, the yeast for 2 to 4 weeks (until primary activity slows), then transfer to widemouthed fermenter, and add the fruits. I have used a variety of yeast strains with this mead, and have had good luck with Epernay, Montrachet, and Prise de Mousse. Use as large a starter as you can.

Due to the variety of fruits, and to their different seasonal availability, I have used frozen fruit in this recipe. The (wild) black raspberries are the key. You can pick them in season and augment them with other hand-picked or store-bought frozen fruits. The trick is using a variety of deeply colored berries. I really enjoy the throaty complexity of black currants in Lindeman's Cassis lambic beer. The next time I get a good harvest, I plan to add some to a new version of this recipe.

If you are very particular about sanitation, you may choose to short the water and the honey slightly in the initial fermentation. Then heat all of the fruit, some water, and the remainder of the honey to about 155° F (68° C) for 15 minutes to kill off any wild yeasts or particularly virulent bacteria before adding this mixture to the secondary fermentation.

Leave this mead on the fruit for at least a couple of weeks. You will want to rack this a couple of times before bottling. It will be a deep, rich, purple color, with a huge nose and a solid dose of tannin when it is young, which will round out and become pleasant over the years.

Peach Ginger Melomel

The enticing aroma of ripe peaches and crushed ginger emanating from the fermentation lock will confirm for you the inviting nature of this mead. It is just as intriguing in the glass.

You can make this mead drier or sweeter to taste. This mead is very appealing at higher gravity, retaining much of the sweet and spicy character of a fresh, juicy peach. As with so many other recipes, I have also made this mead with as many as 20 pounds (9 kg) of fruit in a 5-gallon (18.93 L) batch, and it sure didn't hurt. For those in the northern climes, it can be a sip of summer when you need it most.

Makes 5 gallons (18.93 L)

12 **lbs. (5.45 kg) white clover or other high-quality varietal honey**
3 **gal. (11.36 L) water, approximately; enough to make 5 gallons**
2 **tsp. (9.9 mL) yeast energizer**
2 **tsp. (9.9 mL) yeast nutrient**
2.5 **tsp. (12.32 mL) pectinase—pectic enzyme, optional but highly recommended**
10-12 **lbs. (4.54-5.45 kg) fresh peaches, blanched, peeled, and halved**
1.5-2 **oz. (42.5-56.7 g) peeled and mashed ginger root, optional, but recommended**
1 **liter starter of Lalvin D-47 yeast**

The OG is kind of superfluous here, as the peaches will make the reading unreliable and even deceptive. Due to the nature of the peaches during fermentation (they are unwieldy, at best), I have used the fruit-in-the-primary method on this mead, with good results. The use of nutrients may be redundant, since the fruit contributes both nitrogen and trace nutrients. In that case, the primary ferment will be quite vigorous.

Peaches and ginger smell terrific together, but without the pectinase, they'll make a mead that will be a cloudy mess for several months at a minimum. As with many melomels, two or more rackings will be helpful in achieving clarity. As a side note, it won't hurt you to bottle some of the less clear residue from that last half-gallon at the bottom of the fermenter after you have siphoned off the clearest portion. These may not be the bottles you will serve to your guests during your Christmas bash, but the sediment will settle out nicely in the bottle, and the fruit character will be decidedly more pronounced. Waste not, want not. Decant carefully and enjoy.

Fall's Bounty Cyser

I make cyser very regularly. My apple trees yield dozens of gallons of cider in even bad years, and a good year has produced more than a hundred gallons. I have to do something with it.

Good cysers are a cornucopia of smells: a complex blend of apple aromas from a mix of different varieties, combined with spices, honey, and fermentation notes. Cysers can be slate dry to sopping sweet. They can be hugely fruity, or can lean strongly toward the honey, and can incorporate many other ingredients (brown sugar, molasses, dates, raisins, currants), each contributing a voice to the chorus, as well.

This cyser ferments out with a distinct apple nose, supported with lots of honey and just a hint of spiciness from the dates and raisins. I like it with Thanksgiving dinner. The apple aromas, full flavor, and tart finish stand up to turkey, stuffing, and salty gravy just nicely. It is quite alcoholic.

Makes 5 gallons (18.93 L)

4 gal. (15.14 L) fresh pressed apple cider: Jonathan, Northern Spy, and Red and Golden Delicious provide the bulk of my blend
8 lbs. (3.64 kg) medium- to full-bodied honey
2 tsp. (9.9 mL) yeast energizer
1 tsp. (4.9 mL) yeast nutrient
1 lb. (453.6 g) dark brown sugar
0.5 lb. (226.8 g) chopped dates
0.5 lb. (226.8 g) raisins
10 g Lalvin D-47 yeast (rehydrated)
Water to 5 gallons (18.93 L)

I do not sanitize this must at all and have never measured the gravity. I simply mix all of the ingredients, and pitch the yeast. If you are more concerned with possible contamination, you could sanitize this with sulfites, and pitch the yeast 24 hours later.

I have also made this cyser by allowing the yeast from the apples to ferment the must. It is a risky proposition, but it worked well for me and compared favorably to the same recipe fermented with commercial yeast.

For those who like spices with their apples, you can mix 1 teaspoon each of cinnamon and nutmeg and three cloves (*not* three teaspoons) in a muslin tea bag, and suspend that in your secondary fermenter until you reach your desired spice level.

Hefty Braggot

This is an all-grain recipe for those familiar with all-grain brewing techniques. This is a big ale-mead, meant for cool fall nights. The head is rich, dense, and creamy, and the aroma is so profound it will push its way into your nose after each swallow. The flavor is caramelly sweet, with the honey and malt hanging on your tongue alongside the hop bitterness in a long-lived aftertaste. It goes beautifully with hearty meat dishes like steak pie or pot roast, but will also complement spicy dishes, particularly Mexican food.

If you are a hop lover, you can virtually double the amount of hops in this recipe. The body will stand up to it, and though the sweetness/bitterness balance will be aggressive when young (6 to 9 months!), it will mellow to a low roar over the course of a year. This braggot-de-garde is definitely one that can be cellared for two years or more without any appreciable loss of appeal.

Makes 5 gallons (18.93 L)

8 lbs. (3.64 kg) pale ale malt, crushed
2 lbs. (907 g) Vienna malt, crushed
1 lb. (454 g) dextrin malt, crushed
3 oz. (85 g) Cascade hops (25 IBU) 60 min.
1 oz. (28.35 g) Cascade hops (8 IBU) 30 min.
1 oz. (28.35 g) Cascade hops, 2 min.
9 lbs. (4.09 kg) honey—one with a big aroma, or a blend of several varieties
2 tsp. (9.9 mL) yeast energizer
2 tsp. (9.9 mL) yeast nutrient
10 g Lalvin D-47 yeast, rehydrated

- **OG: 1.120 (28.1° P)**
- **FG: 1.018 (4.6° P)**

I use an infusion mash. Mash in grains with 11 quarts (10.41 L) water at 180° F (82° C), hold at about 146° F (63° C), rest 30 minutes, test for starch conversion. Heat to 165° F (about 74° C) to mash-out. Sparge with 3.5 gallons (13.25 L) at 185° F (85° C). Sparge directly onto bittering hops in boil kettle. Boil 60 minutes, adding hops as scheduled. After 60 minutes, cut heat, add yeast energizer and nutrient, honey, and stir. Chill to 70° F (21° C), transfer to fermenter, aerate vigorously, pitch yeast.

Extract Alternative Method

Those seeking to use extract can substitute 6 pounds (2.72 kg) of amber dry malt extract, add water to 5 gallons (18.93 L), and proceed with the boil. If it is not practical to boil 5 gallons of liquid with the equipment you have, you can also boil the extract with a smaller quantity of water, adding the hops and honey as indicated, and add water to make up the 5-gallon batch size before pitching.

Make sure you use a fermenter with plenty of headspace. This ferment will be vigorous, and will generate LOTS of krausen. Bottle with ¾ cup (178 mL) of corn sugar, or keg and carbonate by your chosen method.

Dan McConnell's Riesling Pyment

In Michigan, many grape varieties are picked before they reach their ideal sugar content. Under perfect growing conditions, Riesling grapes can reach a Brix reading of 23 or above. The juice in this recipe was well below that. This pyment takes advantage of the balance of tart grape juice with the throaty dose of honey. It is among the best meads I have ever tasted, simultaneously distinctly grapey and yet redolent and smacking of honey. It finishes with a powerful acidic sharpness followed by a lasting honey sweetness.

Dan keeps records like many winemakers, with sugar readings in Brix and titratable acidity (TA).

Makes 5 gallons (18.93 L)

- 5 **gal. (18.93 L) Ann Arbor Riesling grape juice (1992), sulfited at the vineyard**
- 7 **lbs. (3.18 kg) honey**
- 1 **gal. (3.785 L) water**
- 14 **g Lalvin K1-V1116**
- 1 **lb. (453.6 g) honey**
- 1 **qt. (946.3 mL) water**

- **Original TA: 1.1%**
- **Brix: 19**
- **pH: 2.99**
- **Final TA: 1.1%**

- **Brix: 5**
- **pH: 3.12**
- **Fermented at 64° F (18° C)**

Remove 1 gallon (3.785 L) of the juice, sulfite (one Campden tablet), and freeze. Mix 7 lbs. (3.18 kg) honey and 1 gallon (3.785 L) water, add to the 4 gallons (15.14 L) of juice to raise Brix to 29.

After 1 week, mix additional 1 pound of honey and quart of water and add to must. After 2 months, allow frozen juice to thaw approximately 50%, discard the ice, and add this concentrated juice and 1 Campden tablet. After 1 year, rack off of the primary lees, sulfite (2.5 Campden tablets), potassium sorbate (2 teaspoons/9.9 mL) and bottle (cork finished).

Oblacinska Cherry Riesling Pyment

This is another of Dan McConnell's delicious pyments. It uses Riesling concentrate and tart Oblacinska cherries. It is wonderfully crisp, semi-dry, and full of fruit, with a typical Riesling "twang" in the finish. The flavors of the grapes, cherries, and honey play off each other delightfully; the balance is right on. The color is a rich Rosé, and the bouquet is fresh, inviting, and confidently floral and fruity.

I know you won't be able to find Oblacinska cherries, but it would be a better world if you could. Dr. Amy Iezzoni was kind enough to let us harvest some from the MSU Agricultural Experiment Station. Amy has released another variety called Ballaton, which is also very flavorful and will impart a wonderful color to your mead. You can use any variety of fresh or frozen tart cherries.

Dan used a 1-gallon (3.785 L) D-47 starter. You might find it easier to rehydrate 10 grams of yeast, and add water to 5 gallons (18.93 L) in the primary. As with "Mambo in Your Mouth," the post-primary fermentation addition of the fruit renders the idea of gravity readings pretty much pointless.

Makes 5 gallons (18.93 L)

3	**(46 fl.-oz.) cans (4.08 L) Alexander's Riesling Concentrate**
0.5	**gal. (1.89 L) Hathaway fruit blossom honey: approximately 6 lbs.**
	Water to 4 gallons (15.14 L) in primary
D-47	**yeast culture from 1 gal. (3.785 L) honey-based starter**
5	**lbs. (2.27 kg) Oblacinska cherries, added to the secondary fermenter**

Ferment at 70° F (21° C). After 1 month, rack off of the primary lees onto the Oblacinska cherries (previously frozen). After 6 months, rack the mead off the cherries into a clean carboy. Bottle when clear.

chapter thirteen

Appreciating Your Mead

Once you have gone to the time and expense of preparing a mead, you will be well served to take some measures to give it its due as you drink it.

Glassware

The right glassware is critical to allowing your mead the chance to make a great showing for all of your senses.

First, I recommend using only clear glassware to serve meads, and crystal whenever possible. Tints and patterns detract from your ability to appreciate clarity and color. Cut glass is nice to look at, but blown glass will make a truer presentation.

The shape of your glasses also will have an impact on your impression of the mead. Stemmed red- and white-wine tasting glasses do a nice job of presenting a visual while helping to concentrate the aromas for nosing. The wider bowl of a red-wine glass enhances the experience by presenting a larger surface area and more airspace for evaporation, and then concentrating the aroma and bouquet at the smaller opening. The same is true of a brandy snifter. Either of those shapes is a good choice for an all-around mead sampling glass.

Temperature

The best temperature for drinking meads is a matter of personal preference. That said, I find the bouquet and flavor of most of the meads I consume to be at their peak at cellar to room temperature (52° F to 70° F) (11° C to 21° C). I do enjoy some light and dry traditional meads and cysers chilled (38° F to 45° F, (3° C to 7° C), much as one might serve a white wine.

Don't chill your glasses. Chilled foods or beverages actually reduce the ability of your taste buds to perceive flavor. Since dissolved gasses are more stable in cold liquids, cooler beverages also will evaporate fewer of the aromatic compounds that contribute so much to your impression of both scent and taste.

With proper care, a dark fruit melomel may just be hitting its stride at ten years.

Evaluation

Start by looking at your mead. Is it clear? Does it have "legs," the viscous rivulets of mead that cling to the sides of the glass?

Now move on to smelling your mead. Swirling the glass will liberate as much aroma as the air will hold. Another good trick to maximize the concentration of the aromas and bouquet is to swirl gently while covering the opening of the glass with the palm of your hand, removing it as you begin to inhale. Put your nose deep into the glass, and inhale slowly and smoothly.

As you smell, try to sort out your thoughts of the aroma. Do you enjoy it? Does it leave you with reminiscences of other smells with which you are familiar? If you can, try to pick out the various fruits and spices that you smell. They may or may not be in the recipe; the compounds that make you think of a given spice or fruit may be in there, even if the spice or fruit is not.

Now taste the mead. Sip slowly and deliberately. It can be helpful to draw a small amount of air into your mouth as you sip. Some people even prefer to aerate the mead into a mist by inhaling through pursed lips and pulling the vaporized mead onto the tongue.

Try to perform the same mental task of isolating the different flavors you perceive. You can break the taste sensation down into phases. Make note of the first flavors to hit your tongue as you draw the mead into your mouth. This is known as the "fore" or the attack. Roll the mead around in your mouth, making sure it touches all the regions of your tongue and the taste buds in the other areas of your mouth. The flavors you note as the mead passes through your mouth and as you swallow are known as "the mid." Those you taste afterwards, the ones that linger on your tongue and that you smell again as you exhale, are the "aftertaste." Each will be distinct and different.

Smell the glass repeatedly as you drink and again after you have emptied it. Try to note the changes in the flavor, aroma, and bouquet with the passage of time. The first smells and sips from a fresh glass of mead will be markedly different from the last.

It is a good practice to make some notes in your journal about each mead, tasting more than once and describing your impressions at different ages: six months, a year, two years. Try to be concise in describing what you find lacking or overdone in your mead, and by what amounts. Could it use twice as much fruit? Twenty percent less ginger root? Such notes can be invaluable in adjusting your recipes to perfect future batches.

Hosting a Mead Tasting

If you choose to do a tasting event with some friends or relatives, try to use uniform glassware, if you can. Serve the meads from lightest to darkest and driest to sweetest, but allow for intensity of flavor. For example, it is better to serve a lighter-flavored dry or medium melomel—even if it is darker in color—before a robust, dessert-sweet metheglin made with a heavy dose of spice.

A white tablecloth is a nice touch at a tasting, as it lets the colors of the mead really show. Some mildly flavored food, such as fruit, crackers, bread, and mild cheese, will make a nice counterpoint to the mead. If you would like to serve more hearty fare, such as fish, smoked meats, or richer hors d'oeuvres, it is not a bad idea to hold them back until your tasters have had a chance to form their initial impressions. Then bring out the heavy stuff, and let folks decide which meads they feel pair up well with the different foods.

Four or five meads will make for a nice array of colors and flavors. Serve no more than an ounce or so of each mead to your guests. Let them decide which of the meads they would like to explore more fully. Never let guests drive after too much indulgence.

Letting Your Mead Breathe

Like red wines, dark melomels and even some robust traditional meads may benefit from a brief "airing." Airing is the practice of opening a beverage and allowing it to breathe, or push off some of its more volatile and sometimes rough aromas. The effect also will occur if the mead is poured and allowed to set in the glass. Five or ten minutes is usually sufficient. Among wine enthusiasts, the benefit of this practice is a matter of some debate, but I can attest to its value with mead. If you have several bottles in your collection, you may wish to experiment by drinking one bottle immediately after opening, and letting another air, and noting your preference.

Mead Drinks

I am not above making a mead spritzer now and again. In a tall glass, mix mead and soda water in equal parts. You can add mint leaves, fruit slices, or a wedge of lemon or lime. I find this works best with sweeter meads, especially melomels.

You can also make mulled mead. Heat the mead slowly in a saucepan, making sure to keep the temperature below 170° F (77° C). Add spices to taste: cinnamon, a clove or two, ginger, and allspice are nice. It may sound odd, but these can be served with a candy stick.

Above all, understand that there is no rule of mead appreciation more important than that you should drink your mead in the fashion you most enjoy. If foie gras, salmon with a *beurre blanc,* and some sautéed morel mushrooms are the bee's knees for you, great. But if you prefer your mead from a paper cup with tube steaks, more power to you. You *made* the stuff. Don't let anybody tell you how *not* to drink it.

appendix one

Honey and Other Suppliers

The names of most of the honey suppliers listed here were provided to me by the National Honey Board. Some were gathered via the Internet. Not all of the suppliers here will sell all of the varieties listed in every size they pack. Some may also be willing to pack custom sizes of specific honeys—if you are willing to wait until they are packaging that honey to have your order filled. Prices may vary considerably; call around and make sure you are getting a deal with which you will be happy. This appendix is subdivided into separate lists for suppliers of honey, spices, and mead only suppliers. A list of relevent websites appears at the end of this appendix.

Sources of spices and other meadmaking items are included at the bottom of the list, as well as a list of web sites of interest to meadmakers.

Honey Suppliers

Bee Natural Honey Co.
Gary Avins
P.O. Box 4085
14240 S.W. 256th St.
Princeton, FL 33031
Ph: (305) 258-1110
Fax: (305) 258-5580
E-mail: bnatural@bellsouth.net
Varietals: avocado, clover, orange blossom, tupelo, wildflower
Quantities: 3 lb., 5 lb., 60 lb. (5 gal.), 55 gal.
Payment: check, money order
Shipping: UPS

Bee's Knees Honey Factory
Charles Lilley, Robert Murphy, K. Smith
520 S.W. Yamhill, Suite Roof Garden #2
Portland, OR 97204
Ph: (503) 225-0755, (503) 640-5757
Fax: (503) 225-0216, (503) 640-0895
E-mail: gkhf_i@aol.com
Web site: www.beeskneeshoney.com
Varietals: alfalfa, blackberry, blueberry, clover, fireweed, orange blossom, raspberry, sage, snowberry, thistle
Imported varietals:
Canada: clover, fireweed
Quantities: 1 lb., 12 lb., 3.5 gal., 60 lb. (5 gal.), 30 gal., 55 gal.

Bosque Honey Farm
Jerry Cole
600 N. Bosque Loop
Bosque Farms, NM 87068
Ph: (505) 869-2841
Varietals: alfalfa, cotton, mesquite, sage
Quantities: 1lb., 2 lb., 3 lb., 6 lb., 12 lb. (gal.), 40 lb., 50 lb., 60 lb. (5 gal.)
Payment: check, money order
Shipping: UPS, mail

China Products North America
Ronald P. Phillips
100 Jericho Quadrangle, Suite 308
Jericho, NY 11753
Ph: (516) 935-3880
Fax: (516) 935-3959
China Products is an importer suited to sales to commercial meaderies. Contact them to get the names of distributors of their honeys in your area.
Varietals: alfalfa, avocado, blackberry, blueberry, buckwheat, clover, fireweed, orange blossom, raspberry, sage, snowberry, thistle, tupelo, wildflower
Imported varietals:
Argentina: alfalfa, clover, eucalyptus, sunflower.
Canada: alfalfa, canola, clover.
China: acacia, buckwheat, orange blossom, rapeseed, sunflower.
India: eucalyptus, rapeseed.
Mexico: mesquite, sunflower.
Vietnam: rubber, coffee.
Quantities: 55 gal.

Dawes Hill Honey
Doug Colombo
12 S. State St.
P.O. Box 429
Nunda, NY 14517
Ph: (716) 468-2535
Fax: (716) 468-5995
E-mail: oanb@servtech.com
Mail order and on-site sales by case or 5 gal. bucket only. Call for catalog.
Additional distributors:
Stow Mills, Chesterfield, NH: (800) 451-4520
Cornucopia Natural Foods, Dayville, CT: (203) 779-2800
Northeast Cooperative, Brattleboro, VT: (802) 257-5856
Varietals: alfalfa, blueberry, buckwheat, clover, orange blossom, raspberry, tupelo
Quantities: 1 lb., 2 lb., 5 lb., 60 lb. (5 gal.), 55 gal.
Payment: cash, check, money order
Shipping: UPS

Draper's Super Bee Apiaries
William E. Draper
Rural Route 1, Box 97
Millerton, PA 16936
Ph: (800) 233-4273, (717) 537-2381
Fax: (717) 537-2727
E-mail: draperb@ptd.net
Web site: www.draperbee.com
Tours and on-site sales available at above address
Varietals: alfalfa, basswood, buckwheat, clover, goldenrod, orange blossom, sourwood, tulip poplar, tupelo, wildflower
Quantities: 1 lb., 2 lb., 5 lb., 12 lb. (gal.), 60 lb. (5 gal.), 30 gal., 55 gal.
Payment: Visa, MC, Discover, check, money order
Shipping: UPS

Dutch Gold Honey
Jill M. Clark
2220 Dutch Gold Drive
Lancaster, PA 17601
Ph: (717) 393-1716
Fax: (717) 393-8687
Web site: www.dutchgoldhoney.com
On-site sales at above address

Varietals: alfalfa, avocado, blueberry, buckwheat, clover, orange blossom, safflower, sage, tupelo, wildflower
Quantities: 1 lb., 3 lb., 5 lb., 6 lb., 60 lb. (5 gal.), 55 gal.
Payment: check, money order
Shipping: UPS, mail, FedEx

Fischer Honey Co.
Joe Callaway
2001 Poplar St.
North Little Rock, AR 72114
Ph: (501) 758-1123
Fax: (501) 758-8601
Varietals: clover, cotton, orange blossom, soybean
Quantities: 1 lb., 2 lb., 4 lb., plastic half-gallons, 12 lb. (gal.), 60 lb. (5 gal.), 55 gal.
Payment: cash, check, money order
Shipping: UPS

Fisher Honey Co.
Dianne Yoder
1 Belle Ave., Bldg. 21
Lewiston, PA 17044
Ph: (717) 242-4373
Fax: (717) 242-3978
Web site: www.fisherhoney.com
E-mail: fisherhoney@lcworkshop.com
Varietals: basswood, clover, orange blossom, wildflower
Quantities: 1 lb., 2 lb., 60 lb. (5 gal.), 55 gal.
Payment: Visa, MC, Discover, check, money order
Shipping: UPS, FedEx, mail

Fruitwood Orchards
Everett Wright
419 Elk Road
Monroeville, NJ 08343
Ph: (609) 881-7748
Fax: (609) 863-8104
Varietals: alfalfa, blueberry, clover, orange blossom, tupelo, wildflower
Quantities: 1 lb., 2 lb., 5 lb., plastic gallon, 60 lb. (5 gal.), 55 gal.
Payment: cash, money order
Shipping: UPS

Glorybee Foods
Elke Crafts
120 N. Seneca
P.O. Box 2744
Eugene, OR 97402
Ph: (800) 456-7923, (541) 689-0913
Fax: (541) 689-9692
E-mail: sales@glorybee.com
Web site: www.glorybee.com
Varietals: alfalfa, blackberry, clover, coastal blossom blend, fireweed, orange blossom, raspberry, star thistle, wildflower
Quantities: 1 lb., 40 lb. (3.5 gal.), 60 lb. (5 gal.), 55 gal.
Payment: Visa, MC, Discover, check, money order
Shipping: UPS

Groeb Farms
Ernest L. Groeb
10464 Bryan Highway
Onsted, MI 49265
Ph: (517) 467-2065
Fax: (517) 467-2840

Florida office:
3220 S.E. Highway 484
P.O. Box 398
Belleview, FL 34421
Ph: (352) 245-2995
Fax: (352) 245-6490
Web site: www.groebfarms.com
Varietals: buckwheat, clover, orange blossom, wildflower
Quantities: 2 lb., 5 lb., 6 lb., 60 lb. (5 gal.), 55 gal.

Hawaiian Honey House
Walter Patton
27-703 Kaieie Road
Papaikou, HI 96781
Ph: (808) 964-5401
Fax: (808) 964-5401
E-mail: hihoney@ilhawaii.net
Web site: www.hawaiihoney.com
Varietals: citrus, Christmas berry, Lehua, macadamia
Quantities: 1 lb., 2.5 lb., (5 gal.), 55 gal.

Honey Acres
Eugene Bruegemann
N1557 Highway 67
P.O. Box 346
Shippun, WI 53003
Ph: (800) 558-7745, (414) 474-4411
Fax: (414) 474-018
Varietals: basswood, buckwheat, clover, orange blossom, wildflower (catalog available on request)
Quantities: 1 lb., 2 lb., 3 lb., 5 lb., 12 lb. (gal.), 60 lb. (5 gal.), 55 gal.
Payment: MC, Visa
Shipping: UPS, mail, FedEx by request

Island of the Moon Apiaries
Jerry Kaplan
17560 County Road 85B
Esparto, CA 95627
Ph: (916) 787-3993
Fax: (916) 787-3993
E-mail: oi2dle@aol.com
Varietals: clover, eucalyptus, orange blossom, star thistle, tupelo, wildflower
Quantities: 1 lb., 2 lb., 3 lb., 6 lb., 30 lb. (2.5 gal.), 60 lb. (5 gal.), 55 gal.
Payment: Visa, MC, Discover, check, money order
Shipping: UPS, FedEx, mail

Joann's Honey
Joann Olmstrom
3164 Maple Court
Reedsport, OR 97467
Ph: (541) 271-4726
Fax: (541) 271-4726
On-site sales. Varieties may change from season to season.
Varietals: alfalfa, blackberry, Western buckwheat, cabbage, several varieties of clover, fireweed, foxglove, meadowfoam, pumpkin, raspberry, Oregon wildflower
Quantities: 1 lb., 2 lb., 6 lb. (half-gallon), 24 lb. (2 gal.), 36 lb. (3 gal.), 48 lb. (4 gal.), 60 lb. (5 gal.), 55 gal.
Payment: cash, check, money order
Shipping: UPS

Kallas Honey Farm
Perry Kallas
6270 N. Sunny Point Road
Milwaukee, WI 53217
Ph: (414) 964-3810
Fax: (414) 964-3809
On-site sales, many other honey-related products, pure maple syrup
Varietals: alfalfa, buckwheat, clover, cranberry, orange blossom, sunflower, wildflower
Quantities: 1 lb., 2 lb., 5 lb. plastic, 12 lb. (gal.), 4 gal., 60 lb. (5 gal.), 55 gal.
Payment: Visa, MC, cash, check, money order
Shipping: UPS

Kost Family Apiary
John A. Kost
1408 Bunce Road
Frewsburg, NY 14738
Ph: (716) 569-3148
E-mail: buzzme@madbbs.com
Varietals: aster/goldenrod blend, basswood, black locust
Quantities: 1 lb., 3 lb., 5 lb., 12 lb. (plastic gal.), 60 lb. (5 gal.), 55 gal.
Payment: cash, check, money order
Shipping: UPS, Parcel Post

Laney Honey Co.
Tom Laney
25725 New Road
North Liberty, IN 46554
Ph: (219) 656-8701
Varietals: apple*, autumn wildflower blend, blueberry, buckwheat, clover, cranberry*, orange blossom, Michigan star thistle, wildflower
** Some varietals may only be packed in smaller quantities. Will custom-pack some orders when varieties are available. Will mix half-gallons in cases of six.*
Quantities: 19 oz., 22 oz., 5 lb., 6 lb. half-gallon plastic, 60 lb. (5 gal.)
Payment: Visa, MC, cash, check, money order
Shipping: UPS

McClure's Honey and Maple Products
Steve Palmer
46 North Littleton Road
Littleton, NH 03561
Ph: (603) 444-6246
Fax: (603) 444-6659

On-site sales. Varietals are sold in cases of 1 lb. jars only.

Varietals: alfalfa, blueberry, buckwheat, clover, cranberry, orange blossom, raspberry, tupelo, wildflower

Imported varietals:

Argentina: floral blend

Quantities: 1 lb., 2 lb., 5 lb., 6 lb., 60 lb. (5 gal.), 55 gal. (see above)

Payment: Visa, MC, cash, check, money order

Shipping: UPS

Miller's American Honey Co.

Merrill Paxman

P.O. Box 500

Colton, CA 92324

Ph: (909) 825-1722

Fax: (909) 825-5932

Note: California and Western buckwheat are lighter in color and flavor than Eastern or Midwestern varieties. Varietals shipped in 5 lb. jug or case lot only.

On-site sales

Web site: www.millershoney.com

Varietals: California buckwheat, clover, eucalyptus, mesquite, orange blossom, sage

Imported varietals:

China: acacia

Quantities: 1 lb., 3 lb., 5 lb., 30 lb., 60 lb. (5 gal.), 55 gal.

Payment: Visa, MC, Discover, cash, check, money order

Shipping: UPS, FedEx, mail

Moonshine Trading Co.

Ishai Zeldner

P.O. Box 896

Winters, CA 95694

Ph: (530) 753-0601, (800) 678-1226

Fax: (530) 753-5301

Prices may be above average, but they are very particular about quality. Call ahead to arrange on-site sales. Other varietals may be available.

Varietals: black button sage, Christmas berry, clover, eucalyptus, fireweed, High Plains sweet clover, Lehua, orange blossom, Southwestern desert blend, tupelo, wildflower, yellow star thistle

Quantities: 1 lb., 12 lb. (gal.), 60 lb. (5 gal.), 55 gal.

Payment: Visa, MC, cash, check, money order

Shipping: UPS, common carrier

Rulison Honey Farms
Mark or Gary Rulison
237 Shellstone Road
Amsterdam, NY 12010
Ph: (518) 843-1619
E-mail: rulison@telenet.net
On-site sales, limited but growing mail order sales
Varietals: buckwheat, clover, orange blossom, wildflower
Quantities: 1 lb., 2 lb., 2.5 lb., 5 lb. plastic, 60 lb. (5 gal.), 55 gal.
Payment: cash, check, money order
Shipping: UPS, mail

Sandt's Honey Co.
Lee Sandt
714 Wagener Lane
Easton, PA 18040
Ph: (610) 252-6511
Fax: (610) 252-9069
Varietals: alfalfa, blueberry, buckwheat, clover, desert flower blend, orange blossom, sage, tupelo, wildflower
Quantities: 1 lb., 2 lb., 3 lb., 5 lb., 12 lb. (gal.), 60 lb. (5 gal.), 55 gal.
Payment: Visa, MC, Discover, check, money order
Shipping: UPS, FedEx, mail

Silver Meadow Honey/Robson's Old West Honey
Celia Robinson
Hwy 60, P.O. Box 428
Aquila, AZ 85230
Ph: (520) 685-2439
Fax: (520) 685-2343
On-site sales
Varietals: cat's claw, clover, mesquite, orange blossom
Quantities: 1 lb., 2 lb., 3 lb., 5 lb. plastic, 1 gal. pail, 60 lb. (5 gal.), 55 gal.
Payment: cash, check, money order
Shipping: UPS

Silverbow Honey Co.
Jody Arbuckle
1120 E. Wheeler Road
Moses Lake, WA 98837
Ph: (509) 765-6616
Fax: (509) 765-6549

Credit for commercial accounts available. On-site sales. Varietals shipped in 1-gal. or larger sizes only. Baking honey available.
Varietals: blackberry, blueberry, clover, fireweed, orange blossom
Imported varietals:
China: acacia
Quantities: 1 lb., 3 lb., 5 lb., 6 lb., 60 lb. (5 gal.), 55 gal.
Payment: Visa, MC, cash, check, money order
Shipping: UPS, common carrier

Stiles Apiaries
Grant Stiles
859 King George Road
Fords, NJ 08863
Ph: (732) 661-0700
Varietals: blueberry, clover, gallberry, holly, tulip poplar, wildflower
Quantities: 1 lb., 2 lb., 3 lb., 5 lb. (plastic), 1 gal. plastic, 60 lb. (5 gal.), 55 gal.
Payment: cash, check, money order, credit cards may be accepted shortly
Shipping: UPS, mail

Tropical Blossom Honey Co.
J. Douglas McGinnis or Patricia McGinnis
106 N. Ridgewood Ave.
P.O. Box 8
Edgewater, FL 32132
Ph: (904) 428-9027
Fax: (904) 423-8469
Some on-site sales. Ship by case lot only.
Varietals: Florida wildflower (saw palmetto, gallberry), orange blossom, tupelo (in season)
Quantities: 1 lb., 22 oz., 2 lb., 40 oz., 3 lb., 5 lb., 6 lb. (half-gallon plastic), 12 lb. (gal.), 60 lb. (5 gal.), 55 gal.
Payment: cash, check, money order
Shipping: UPS

Virginia Honey Co.
Art Palmer
Route 7 West
P.O. Box 246
Berryville, VA 22611
Ph: (540) 955-1304
Fax: (540) 955-4868
Varietals: buckwheat, clover, orange blossom, tupelo, wildflower

Imported varietals:
China: acacia, buckwheat
Quantities: 5 lb. plastic, plastic gallon, 60 lb. (5 gal.), 55 gal. Call for complete info.
Payment: cash, check, money order
Shipping: UPS, common carrier

Wixson Honey
Roscoe S. Wixson
4937 Lakemont Road
Dundee, NY 14837
Ph: (607) 243-7301
Fax: (607) 243-7143
On-site sales
Varietals: alfalfa, buckwheat, clover, orange blossom, tupelo (in season), wildflower
Quantities: 5 lb. plastic pail, 60 lb. (5 gal.), 55 gal.
Payment: cash, check, money order
Shipping: UPS

Spice Suppliers

Rafal Spice Co. (pronounced "raffle")
Donald Rafal
2521 Russell St.
Detroit, MI 48207
Ph: (313) 259-6373
Web site: www.rafalspicecompany.com
Spices, spice grinders, teas, natural fiber reusable tea bags, tea balls
Payment: Visa, MC, check, money order (Discover and American Express accepted at the store only)
Shipping: UPS
Free catalog

Penzeys Spices
19300 W. Janacek Court
Brookfield, WI 53045
Ph: (262) 785-7637, (800) 741-7787
Web site: www.penzeys.com
Payment: Visa, MC, Discover
Shipping: UPS
Free catalog
Other locations in central and eastern United States.

Fruit and Herb Growing

North American Fruit Explorers (NAFEX)
1716 Apples Road
Chapin, IL 62628
Web site: www.nafex.org
This is an organization of fruit hobbyists who share information and resources through web-based resources and a quarterly newsletter. A rich source of deep fruit-growing knowledge held by those with firsthand experience.

Seed Savers Exchange
3076 North Winn Road
Decorah, IA 52101
Web site: www.seedsavers.com
Repository of old and threatened vegetable and garden plants. Antique roses, herb seeds, historic orchard.

Classical Fruits
Hoyt and Franny Adair
8831 AL Hwy 157
Moulton, AL 35650
Web site: http://biz.hiwaay.net/~fruit/about/index.shtml
Ph: (256) 974-8813
Apple and pear fruit trees in a large number of varieties.

Applesource
Tom & Jill Vorbeck
1716 Apples Road
Chapin, IL 62628
Ph: (800) 588-3854
Fax: (217) 245-7844
Web site: www.applesource.com
E-mail: vorbeck@csj.net
More than 75 varieties of apples (fruit, not trees) sold via mail order. An excellent opportunity to sample the tremendous variety of flavors and textures that abound in the apple universe.

Wine and Meadmaking Supplies

These are two vendors with whom I have had positive personal experience.

The Wine Barrel Plus
30303 Plymouth Road
Livonia, MI 48150
Ph: (734) 522-WINE (9463)
Fax: (734) 522-3764
Web site: www.winebarrel.com
E-mail: mark@winebarrel.com
Payment: Visa, MC, debit card, cash
Shipping: UPS
Complete line of homebrewing and winemaking supplies: ingredients, nutrients, equipment of all sorts (including barrels), literature, and honey. Full line of grape juice products, from pure juice to canned concentrates and everything in between.

The Beverage People
Byron Burch/Nancy Vineyard
840 Piner Road #14
Santa Rosa, CA 95403
Ph: (707) 544-2520, (800) 544-1867
Fax: (707) 544-5729
Web site: www.thebeveragepeople.com
E-mail: thebeveragepeople@hotmail.com (Nancy Vineyard)
Payment: Visa, MC, American Express, check, money order
Shipping: UPS
Comprehensive line of beer, mead, and winemaking supplies, free catalog, newsletter, club discount, gift certificates. Notable for their mead nutrient, the only product of its kind I know of.

Web Sites of Interest

www.farmworld.com/a/fw6603.html

Listing of several honey producers and beekeeping product suppliers across the country.

www.nhb.org

The National Honey Board's site. Abundant information and resources about honey and beekeepers in the United States.

www.honeylocator.com

Listings of hundreds of honey producers and distributors from around the country, organized by state and by honey variety.

www.gotmead.com

Among the oldest and certainly one of the most comprehensive web sites for finding meadmaking ingredients, equipment, and info. Self-described "Meadwench" Vicky Rowe serves up an abundance of resources that support amateurs and professionals. The best place to start on the web for mead info.

www.talisman.com/mead

This is the page that gets you into the trove of mead resources marshaled by Dick Dunn, including the Mead Lover's Digest, an e-mail digest for those interested in sharing info on meadmaking.

www.meadhq.com

A new but potentially valuable on-line magazine put together by Gregg Stearns.

www.aboutmead.com

Chris Hadden's well-thought-out site, with pages for both amateur meadmakers and fans of commercial offerings. Advice on meadmaking, lists of U.S. and international meaderies, and a growing collection of tasting notes on commercial meads.

www.lallemandwine.com

Entry point to info about Lallemand's strains and other products. Very informative.

www.winepros.org/wine101/grape_profiles/varietals.htm

Helpful information on grape varieties and their characteristics. Good reading for pyment aficionados.

www.honeywine.com

Detailed information on commercial meads from across the U.S., as well as resources and friendly discussion about mead.

appendix two
CONVERSION CHARTS

table A2.1

UNITED STATES/METRIC EQUIVALENTS FOR COMMON VOLUME AND WEIGHT MEASURES

US	Metric
1 Gallon	3.785 L
0.2642 gal.	1 L
5 gal.	18.9266 L
5.284 gal.	20 L
1 fl. oz.	29.5735 mL
1 cup	236.6 mL
0.0338 fl. oz.	1 mL
4.227 cups	1 L
1 pound	0.4536 kg
1 ounce	28.35 g
2.204 lb.	1 kg
0.0353 oz.	1 g
1 tbsp.	14.787 mL

table A2.2

Celsius/Fahrenheit Equivalents

Degrees Celsius	Degrees Fahrenheit	Degrees Celsius	Degrees Fahrenheit
0 C	32 F	-17.8 C	0 F
5 C	41 F	-15 C	5 F
10 C	50 F	-12.2 C	10 F
15 C	59 F	-9.4 C	15 F
20 C	68 F	-6.7 C	20 F
25 C	77 F	-3.9 C	25 F
30 C	86 F	-1.1 C	30 F
35 C	95 F	1.7 C	35 F
40 C	104 F	4.4 C	40 F
45 C	113 F	7.2 C	45 F
50 C	122 F	10 C	50 F
55 C	131 F	12.8 C	55 F
60 C	140 F	15.6 C	60 F
65 C	149 F	18.9 C	65 F
70 C	158 F	21.1 C	70 F
75 C	167 F	23.9 C	75 F
80 C	176 F	26.7 C	80 F
85 C	185 F	29.4 C	85 F
90 C	194 F	32.2 C	90 F
95 C	203 F	37.8 C	100 F
100 C	212 F	43.3 C	110 F
		48.9 C	120 F
		54.4 C	130 F
		60 C	140 F
		62.8 C	145 F
		65.6 C	150 F
		71.1 C	160 F
		76.7 C	170 F
		82.2 C	180 F
		87.8 C	190 F
		93.3 C	200 F
		98.9 C	210 F

The equation for converting Fahrenheit to Celsius is:

(Degrees F - 32) x (5/9) = Degrees C

Aerate: To force air or oxygen into a solution, either by agitation or bubbling of gas through the solution.

Aerobic: Occurring in the presence of oxygen. Used to describe fermentation phase responsible for high rates of yeast reproduction.

Aftertaste: The set of perceptions left on the palate during the minutes after a mead is swallowed. The aftertaste also is influenced by the aromas and bouquet of the mead evoked as air passes through the mouth and nasal passages.

Aging: The process of keeping a mead in storage, either in bottle or in the carboy (bulk), while it changes and matures. Also referred to as cellaring.

Aldehyde: Key component of the fermentation, precursor to alcohol. One of the aldehydes results from exposure of a mead to air or oxygen, yielding a sherrylike or paper/cardboard odor and taste.

Alpha acid: Constituent of hops that contributes bitterness. Alpha acid levels in hops can range from 3-15%.

Amino acids: Nitrogenous compounds that contribute free amino acid to the yeast during the early phases of fermentation. Not abundant in most honey varieties.

Anaerobic: Occurring in the absence of oxygen. The phase of fermentation during which most of the alcohol production takes place.

Apiarist: A beekeeper.

Aroma: The smell emanating from a mead.

Attenuation: Degree to which yeast has fermented available sugar into alcohol. Highly attenuating yeasts produce the most alcohol and leave little sugar in the finished mead.

Autolysis: Death of the yeast cells, sometimes resulting in off aromas and flavors.

Balance: The use of contrasting tastes to provide counterpoint. Can be contrast of sugar to acid, body/mouthfeel to acid, or body to bitterness (as in some beers and braggots).

Balling (degrees): Gravity measurement system representing percentage of solids in a solution, based on cane sugar.

Big: Term used to describe meads or wines with pronounced aroma and bouquet and intense mouthfeel: dense flavors, high alcohol levels (sometimes, but not always), and prolonged aftertaste. Also: bombastic, extreme. Usually a compliment.

Blanc: French for white, common in grape varietal names.

Blowoff: Practice of attaching a hose to the opening (hole or drilled stopper) of a fermenter, to permit rapid venting of gas or fermentation-produced foam (krausen).

Body: The perceived amount of heft or fullness presented by a mead when held in the mouth and/or swallowed.

Bouquet: The combined olfactory impression of a mead or wine created by the combination of the ingredients, the fermentation process, and conditioning or aging.

Brix: Measurement of the sugar content as a percentage of a fruit, fruit juice, or must.

Buffer: Substance that ameliorates changes in pH.

Carbonation: Process of dissolving carbon dioxide into a solution, in our case a finished mead. Also describes the condition of having dissolved CO_2 in a beverage. Bottle or natural carbonation is accomplished by allowing the yeast to ferment a small amount of sugar in the bottle. To create artificial carbonation, CO_2 is added and forced into the solution by pressure.

Carboy: A glass or plastic bottle often used for bottled water.

glossary

Colloids: Gelatinous substance in honey. Colloids are attributed with binding some of the aromatic compounds that give honey its rich, floral aromas.

Colony: A functioning population unit of approximately 30,000–60,000 bees, consisting of a queen, male drones, and female worker bees. The colony lives in a hive.

Diacetyl: Chemical compound responsible for buttery or butterscotch flavors and aromas.

Dry (also dryness): Having little or no residual sugar content.

Ester: Aromatic compound composed of an acid and an alcohol, responsible for fruity aroma(s) in meads. Esters can account for a wide range of aromas, including banana, papaya, apple, plum, rose and tulip floral, pineapple, grape, pear, coconut, berry, citrus, and many others.

Extraction: The process of removing honey from the combs. There are generally two extractions per year for most (non-commercial pollinator) beekeepers.

Fermentation: Conversion of sugar and oxygen to alcohol and carbon dioxide, performed through metabolic activity by yeast.

Fermenter: A vessel in which fermentations occur. Can be plastic, glass, or stainless steel.

Fermentation lock (also airlock): One-way barrier devices used to allow gasses to escape but not enter a fermenter.

Final gravity (FG): Gravity of a mead, beer, or wine after the yeast has attenuated the sugar, either completely or to its point of ethanol tolerance.

Flocculation: The settling of yeast to the bottom of a fermenter or vessel on the completion of the fermentation. Yeasts are said to flocculate well if they clear completely and form a well-packed sediment.

Floral: Adjective used to describe aromas and scents in honey, mead, and beer.

Floral source: Term used to describe the nectar source frequented by bees during foraging, especially when delineated in the type of honey, i.e.: orange blossom honey.

Flow: Also "honey flow." A period of peak honey production by bees, the result of an abundance of nectar. In most northern climates, the first major flow begins in May.

Frames: The removable wooden structures inside of a Langstroth-type beehive, on which bees build comb for brood and honey.

Free Amino Nitrogen: Nitrogen available to yeast in the form of amino compounds in a must. FAN is critical to the ability of yeast to populate a must rapidly and begin a healthy fermentation.

Gravity: Numerical representation of the amount of solid (in our case sugar from honey) dissolved in a liquid. Can be expressed in degrees Balling (Brix), points of specific gravity, or Plato.

Harvest: The process of removing combs and honey from the hive(s); there is a lighter early harvest from the spring "flow," and a darker, more densely flavored fall harvest.

Higher alcohols: Term used to describe alcohols other than ethanol that are present in mead or other fermented beverages. Often present in small amounts, which can be exacerbated by stressed yeast and/or prolonged fermentation. They include amyl alcohol, pentanol, hexanol, octanol, nonanol. Their aromas can be appealing but also can be the source of unpleasant solventlike and grassy odors.

Hive: A structure used to house a colony of bees. Can be constructed in a number of shapes from wood, pottery, straw, or other materials.

Indicator: Substance (phenolphthalein) used to indicate the end point of titration. It retains its color at pH 7.0 (acid neutralization point).

Hydrometer: Instrument used for measuring gravity.

Hygroscopic: Given to absorbing moisture from the atmosphere. Honey is hygroscopic.

Langstroth hive: Modern wooden hive system consisting of stackable supers, in which removable vertical frames are hung.

Mouthfeel: The impression of a mead as it is taken into the mouth and swallowed. Can be broken down into fore (early, as the mead hits the tongue), mid (as the mead is held in the mouth prior to swallowing), and aft (as and just after the mead is swallowed). The mouthfeel of a mead can be influenced by residual sugar, alcohol, body, acid levels, and other flavor components.

glossary

Must: The unfermented or fermenting blend of honey, water, and other ingredients. Also commonly used to describe fruit or grape mixtures before or during fermentation.

Nectar: The sugary, slightly viscous solution produced by flower and collected by bees. Also an ancient Greek term for mead.

Original gravity (OG): Gravity of a must prior to attenuation.

Oxidation: The process of oxygen combining with other flavor compounds in mead, wine or beer. The term "oxidized" applies to the condition that results. Oxidation is the cause of the flavor that characterizes sherry and port wines. Considered a fault in most instances, especially when occurring inadvertently or at high levels.

Pectin: Carbohydrate substance (acids and esters forming linear polysaccharide chains) found in fruit and plants, which is responsible for gelatinization of solutions if heated above 180° F (82° C).

Pentosans: Gum-like complex carbohydrates that constitute some of the non-sugar solids present in honey.

pH: Numerical representation of the ratio of the amount of acid and base in a solution. Ranges from 0 to 14; lower values are more acidic, 7 is neutral, higher values are more alkaline, or basic. Mead fermentations will occur most rapidly at around 3.7.

Phenols: Aromatic hydroxyl compounds, such as lignin and tannin. Described as pleasantly tart to astringent or medicinal in aroma and taste. Descriptors include bitter, burnt, green, dusty, silky, smoky, antiseptic, and creosote. There are many different phenolic compounds, desirable and undesirable. Phenolic influences can soften during aging.

Pitching: Adding yeast to a must.

ppm: Parts per million.

Plato: Gravity measurement that expresses in degrees the amount of sucrose dissolved per 100 grams of solution. Very accurate system often used by commercial wineries and breweries (see "Gravity").

Primary fermentation: The fermentation ensuing immediately after pitching, generally vigorous if proper yeast nutrition guidelines and pitching procedures were followed. Lasts from three to seven days, depending on the strain of yeast employed.

Racking: The process of transferring must or fermented mead from one container to another. Done to separate mead from yeast, fruit, or other sediment, and to aid in clarification. Accomplished most often by siphoning.

Reagent: Compound involved in a chemical reaction. In titration, a compound of a known strength that can be used to determine properties of substance being measured.

Residual sugar: Sugar remaining in a mead after fermentation is complete. Residual sugar levels can range from less than 0.5% in dry meads to 2 or 3% or more in sweet or dessert meads.

Secondary fermentation: The completion of the attenuation of the sugars in a wort, occurring after the vigorous primary fermentation has subsided, and often after the racking of the mead to a second vessel.

Skep: The conical, woven straw type of hive, still used in some areas of the world.

Starter: A culture of yeast. Starters are created to boost the number of yeast cells added to the must at the beginning of the fermentation.

Sulfite: Most often potassium metabisulfite, an antibacterial and antioxidant compound used to prepare or stabilize must or finished mead.

Super: Boxlike structure in which frames (generally 10) are hung in a Langstroth-style beehive. Several supers can be stacked atop one another. A larger, brood super is topped with supers for collecting honey.

Sweetness: Perception resulting from the presence of residual or additional honey (sugar) in a finished mead. Compared with those for grape wines, the consensus parameters for finished sweetness in meads are higher (sweeter): below 1.007 for dry, below 1.015 for medium, and above 1.015 for sweet.

Tannin: Phenolic compound(s) derived from oak, grape skins/stems, and some cider apple and crabapple varieties. Contributes to the body and "backbone" of a wine, mead, or cider; it is pleasantly astringent in appropriate quantities.

Tartness: Flavor and condition resulting from acidity. Can be mouth puckering.

Titratable acidity: The total amount of acid in a juice or must, determined as a percentage tartaric acid by titration with sodium hydroxide and a phenolphthalein indicator.

Vanillin: Aromatic and flavor compound extracted from oak during the aging process. Very desirable component of bouquet and aftertaste.

Varietal: From a single variety. Used to describe honey (delineating the primary source of floral forage for the bees during nectar collection) and wines (containing grapes of primarily or solely one variety).

Wort: Unfermented beer, obtained by mashing and/or use of malt extract.

Yeast: A single-celled organism, Kingdom: Fungi. Responsible for the conversion of sugar in must into alcohol and carbon dioxide.

Acton, Bryan, and Peter Duncan. *Making Mead.* London: Amateur Winemaker, 1984.

Allen, H. Warner. *A History of Wine.* New York: Horizon Press, 1961.

American Wine Society. *The Complete Handbook of Winemaking.* Ann Arbor, Mich.: G.W. Kent, 1993.

Brickell, Christopher, ed. *The American Horticultural Society Encyclopedia of Gardening*. New York: Dorling Kindersley, 1993.

Correnty, Paul. *The Art of Cidermaking.* Boulder, Colo.: Brewers Publications, 1995.

Cox, Jeff. *From Vines to Wines.* Pownal, Vt.: Garden Way Publishing, 1985.

Crane, Eva. *The Archaeology of Beekeeping.* Ithaca, N.Y.: Cornell University Press, 1983.

Crane, Eva, ed. *Honey, A Comprehensive Survey.* London: William Heinemann, 1975.

Crockett, James Underwood. *Roses*. New York: Time-Life Books, 1971.

De Roche, Max. *The Foods of Love.* New York: Arcade Publishing, 1991.

Downing, Andrew J. *Fruits and Fruit Trees of America* (originally 1846). Temecula, Calif.: Reprint Services, 1993.

Duncan, Peter, and Bryan Acton. *Progressive Winemaking.* Ann Arbor, Mich: G.W. Kent, 1996.

Foster, Steven. *Herbal Renaissance.* Salt Lake City: Gibbs Smith, 1993.

Gayre, Robert, and Charlie Papazian. *Brewing Mead: Wassail! In Mazers of Mead.* Boulder, Colo.: Brewers Publications, 1986.

Graham, Joe M., ed. *The Hive and the Honey Bee*, Hamilton, Ill.: Dadant & Sons, 1992.

Grootendorst, Theodore. *Southmeadow Fruit Gardens: Choice and Unusual Fruit Varieties for the Connoisseur and Home Gardener.* Self-published, 1976.

Grubb, Norman. *Cherries.* London: Crosby Lockwood and Son, 1949.

Gump, Barry H., and David J. Pruett, eds. *Beer and Wine Production.* Washington, D.C.: American Chemical Society, 1993.

Harris, James F., and Mark H. Waymack. *Single Malt Whiskies of Scotland.* LaSalle, Ill.: Open Court, 1992.

Hessayon, D. G. *The Fruit Expert.* New York: Expert Books, 1993.

Jackson, Michael. *The World Guide to Beer.* Philadelphia: Running Press, 1977.

Johnson, Hugh. *Vintage: The Story of Wine.* New York: Simon and Schuster, 1989.

Katz, Solomon H., and Fritz Maytag. "Brewing an Ancient Beer." *Archaeology* 44 (July-August 1991): 24-33.

Kowalchik, Claire, and William H. Hylton, eds. *Rodale's Illustrated Encyclopedia of Herbs.* Emmaus, Pa.: Rodale Press, 1987.

Leonard, William Ellery. *Beowulf, A New Verse Translation for Fireside and Class Room.* New York: Heritage Press, 1923.

Lucas, A., and J. R. Harris. *Ancient Egyptian Materials and Industries.* London: Edward Arnold, 1962.

McNair, James K. *The World of Herbs and Spices.* San Francisco: Ortho Books, 1978.

bibliography

Miller, Dave. *The Complete Handbook of Home Brewing.* Pownal, Vt.: Garden Way Publishing, 1988.

Miller, Mark. *The Great Chile Book.* Berkeley, Calif.: Ten Speed Press, 1991.

Miloradovich, Milo. *Growing and Using Herbs and Spices.* New York: Dover Publications, 1986.

Morse, Roger A. *Making Mead (Honey Wine): History, Recipes, Methods, and Equipment.* Cheshire, Conn.: Wicwas Press, 1980.

Morse, Roger, and Steinkraus, Keith. "Wines From the Fermentation of Honey." In Crane, Eva, ed. Honey, A Comprehensive Survey. London: William Heinemann, 1975.

Morton, Julia Francis. *Herbs and Spices.* Racine, Wis.: Golden Press, 1976.

National Honey Board. *Honey Suppliers Directory.* Boulder, Colo.: National Honey Board, 1993.

Noonan, Gregory J. *New Brewing Lager Beer.* Boulder, Colo.: Brewers Publications, 1996.

Norman, Jill. *The Complete Book of Spices.* New York: Viking Studio Books, 1991.

Organic Gardening Magazine staff, eds. *The Encyclopedia of Organic Gardening.* Emmaus, Pa.: Rodale Press, 1978.

Otto, Stella. *The Backyard Orchardist.* Maple City, Mich.: Ottographics, 1993.

Parrinder, Geoffrey. *Religions of the World From Primitive Beliefs to Modern Faiths.* New York: Grosset & Dunlap, 1971.

Reed, Gerald, & Tilak W. Nagodawithana. *Yeast Technology.* New York: Van Nostrand Rheinhold, 1991.

Renfrow, Cindy. *A Sip Through Time: A Collection of Old Brewing Recipes.* Self-published, 1995.

Ross, John F. "Suiting Up for the Honey Wars." *Smithsonian* 32 (August 2001): 78-85.

Sahni, Julie. *Savoring Spices and Herbs.* New York: William Morrow, 1996.

Tannahill, Reay. *Food in History.* New York: Three Rivers Press, 1988.

Wagner, Philip M. *Grapes Into Wine: A Guide to Winemaking in America.* New York: Alfred A. Knopf, 1976.

White, Jonathan W., Jr. "Composition of Honey." In Crane, Eva, ed. Honey, A Comprehensive Survey. London: William Heinemann, 1975.

White, Jonathan W., Jr., M. L. Riethof, M. H. Subers, and I. Kushnif. *Composition of American Honeys.* Technical Bulletin 1261. Philadelphia: Eastern Utilization Research and Development Division, Agricultural Research Service, 1962.

Whynott, Douglas. *Following the Bloom.* Harrisville, Pa.: Stackpole Books, 1991.

Wilder, Louise Beebe. *The Fragrant Garden.* 1934. Reprint. New York: Dover Publications, 1974.

Yepsen, Roger. *Apples.* New York: W. W. Norton, 1994.